DYNAMICS
OF
THEOLOGY

by
Roger Haight, S.J.

ORBIS BOOKS

Maryknoll, New York 10545

Founded in 1970, Orbis Books endeavors to publish works that enlighten the mind, nourish the spirit, and challenge the conscience. The publishing arm of the Maryknoll Fathers & Brothers, Orbis seeks to explore the global dimensions of the Christian faith and mission, to invite dialogue with diverse cultures and religious traditions, and to serve the cause of reconciliation and peace. The books published reflect the views of their authors and do not represent the official position of the Society. To learn more about Maryknoll and Orbis Books, please visit our webstite at www.maryknoll.com.

Library of Congress Cataloging-in-Publication Data

Haight, Roger.
    Dynamics of theology / by Roger Haight.
        p. cm.
    Includes bibliographical references and indexes.
    Originally published: New York : Paulist Press, c1990.
    ISBN 1-57075-387-3 (pbk.)
        1. Theology.   I. Title.

BR118.H34   2001
230´.01—dc21   2001032898

CONTENTS

V. METHOD

CONCLUSION

In Memory of

Marjorie Tuite, O.P.

PREFACE TO THE SECOND EDITION

Dynamics of Theology was written in 1989 and the substance of the work remains unchanged in this new edition. It presents an analysis of the sources, nature, structure, method, and goals of theology as a discipline. As a work of fundamental theology, one that is apt for use as an introduction to the discipline, it represents theology at a foundational level. It considers the key elements of theology: faith and revelation, scripture as a source for theology, the nature of talk about God, and the interpretive character of the discipline. While it does not explore the range of different approaches to the discipline of theology, the book presents a view of theology that is synthetic and coherent, without pretending that this view of things could possibly control the whole field to the exclusion of other views. By and large, this work is not polemic, but seeks to integrate into itself elements of tacks in theology that diverge from the one presented here. In most of the basic positions represented here I have not changed my mind. But at the same time a number of the topics developed in this book have been developed further with the publication of *Jesus Symbol of God.** This latter work is essentially an application of the theoretical conception of the discipline of theology found here to the subject matter Jesus Christ. It thus develops further the manner in which Christian faith is directed to its object, God, through the mediation of its focusing symbol, Jesus of Nazareth. It investigates revelation more concretely in terms of the revealer who is central to Christian faith, Jesus of Nazareth. Scripture, especially the New Testament, contains the classic witness to the revelation mediated by Jesus Christ, and the manner in which Jesus Christ appears in the New Testament, as an historical figure and interpreted as the Christ, receives

---

* Roger Haight, *Jesus Symbol of God* (Maryknoll, N.Y.: Orbis Books, 1999).

more concrete analysis in that work than it does here. *Jesus Symbol of God* also develops in a far more concrete way the notion of symbol, Jesus himself as concrete symbol, and the interpretive symbolic conceptions of him. And, finally, the method that is outlined in this work is brought to bear on Jesus Christ in the later work. In short, the conception of theology constructed here is further developed by being employed in the area of christology.

I have added an Afterword to this edition of *Dynamics* to indicate at some greater length the relationship between the conception of theology developed here and the work in christology that came after it and how I see it applying further to an understanding of the church. I am grateful to Orbis Books for bringing out this new edition of *Dynamics of Theology*.

Weston Jesuit School of Theology
March 27, 2001

PREFACE

This work grew out of a perception of a specific problem in theological education today. A brief statement of this concern and how this work seeks to address it will help to introduce the intentionality of the book.

More than at any time in the previous history of the human race current intellectual culture is conscious of historicity. Along with this historical consciousness comes a sense of contingency, pluralism, and change. Few people today would deny the basic elements of historical consciousness; everyone shares the experience that generates it in some measure. But there are many different degrees of historical consciousness and of the perceptions that accompany it. They can range from a general positive and open attitude to change to a deep sense of scandal and disorientation. If everything is historically relative, so that no stable formulation of truth is available to us, does this lead inevitably to the undermining of all values and finally to some kind of nihilism?

At the very least historical consciousness can engender a feeling of insecurity. This feeling has its own manifestation in theological schools, especially in the education of people for ministry in the church. Some students cannot accept the radical openness of history, and they lapse into some form of fundamentalism or traditionalism that simply clings to theological formulas of the past. Others are generally open to the possibility of a reinterpretation of Christian doctrine that is faithful to tradition yet relevant to our new situation. But they do not know how to enter into this process of interpretation, and in the end they merely repeat what their church has said in the past. These reactions show up, for example, in those schools or churches that require, either for closure of their program of study or for ordination, a comprehensive knowledge of basic Christian doctrines. A good number of students completing such a review, after three or four years of intense theological study, often can do no better than repeat the phrases of the catechism of their youth.

The reasons for this particular lack of theological sophistication extend far beyond an insecurity engendered by historical consciousness. It may well be that individual professors, faculties, or programs either foster this reaction or fail to communicate the tools for theological reflection appropriate to the task of reinterpretation. But at the same time our cultural situation, insofar as it is characterized by historical consciousness, calls for a constant systematic examination of the premises of theology. At the very least, students should be exposed to the fact that mere repetition of theological formulas does no service to the people of God, and may be a form of infidelity and lack of responsibility to the Christian message.

This work is an essay in fundamental or foundational theology. It consists in a reflection on the foundations upon which theological statements rest. It will try to lay out in as straightforward a manner as possible an interpretation of the bases for theological statements, and hence the discipline itself, as well as the underlying logic of their intelligibility and credibility.

In this book I make no distinction between scriptural, theological, doctrinal, and dogmatic statements. Rather I describe all of these theological statements in terms that they share in common. Thus, for example, all theological statements have their anthropological basis in faith. They imply or directly refer to something revealed within an experience of transcendence. They are all historically conditioned. Distinctions among theological assertions can be made on the basis of the internal logic of the content they express and their place and function in the Christian churches. I shall implicitly deal with the grounds of such distinctions. But for the most part my concern is for what all theological affirmations share in common.

From one point of view, this work may be considered as a prolegomenon to theology, or as an introduction to the discipline. It does not deal directly with the content of the Christian message, but rather with the sources through or by which that content is delivered to us. It does not argue from scripture or church authority, for it asks the question of how one can conceive that a scripture of the past or a church tradition can be a religious or theological authority in an historically conscious culture. The response to many of these questions can only be an appeal to common experience of people within the community of faith.

From another point of view, however, this work is itself a constructive theological interpretation. It unfolds from within the discipline of theology, so that, like most introductions to theology, its argument can be appreciated only after a study of the content of the Christian message. In this sense it is designed as a work of theological reflection, a bending back of the theological imagination upon itself in a critical questioning of such issues as these: From where do theological assertions come? What is the logic that distinguishes theological affirmations from other kinds of human knowing? What premises and unspoken assumptions undergird the construction of theological positions?

I have chosen five main areas in which to locate the fundamental principles or foundations of theological assertion. That there are five is somewhat arbitrary because they both overlap and could be expanded by subdivision. In any case they represent key areas for determining the nature of theology as a discipline and provide the loci for crucial insight. These five topics are faith, revelation, scripture, religious symbol, and methodology. Each of these five areas has been divided into two short chapters. The first consists in a general consideration or theory of the topic in question; the second brings this theoretical conception to bear directly on the nature of theological statements.

The accounts of these five topics are extremely limited; each section is not meant to be adequate to the subject matter in itself, so to speak, and does not treat it in an integral fashion. A full account of faith, revelation, and so on could very well begin at a different starting point and stress aspects that are neglected here. Therefore in no case can any one of these treatments be considered as a full account of the particular subject matter. Rather these chapters represent particular interpretations the elements of which are governed by a principle of selectivity. I have chosen and dwelt upon those aspects of each of these phenomena that I believe come to bear most pointedly upon the subject matter of this book, namely, the inner logic of theological statement.

The underlying theme of this essay is critical or questioning. My conception of the particular problem of theological education in the church today accounts for this distinctive approach. My goal is to provide grounds for the creative interpretation or reinterpretation of traditional doctrines. Historical consciousness today is a given. The intention here is to show that the reaction to historical consciousness should not be reactionary, in such a way that it withdraws from culture to find an enclave of security in the repetition of what appear to many in our world as the archaic formulas of a past world. In a way, one must ask the searching questions that undermine every fundamentalistic reliance on tradition in order to open up a new security of insight and illuminating meaning which allows that same tradition to come alive again within an historical consciousness.

From where I stand in the educational system of the church, it seems that more critical and imaginative interpretation is required on the part of the church in the way it presents its message to the world today. We are genuinely moving into dramatically new frontiers in our common humanity and as a church. Unless the church in its ministers and ministries can find the freedom which is engendered by historical consciousness to dramatically reinterpret its message, it will not preserve that message but surely compromise and even contradict it by default. What is required then is a conscious release from traditionalism in order to keep the tradition alive and meaningful. And this requires a critical understanding of the very foundations of theology.

Thus the goal of this book is to provide the fundamental grounds for the retrieval of traditional doctrine in new creative interpretations that come to bear upon life in our world as it is today.

Many debts are acquired in the course of preparing a work such as this over and above those owed to the many authors with whom one is in dialogue in shaping one's own position. I would like to single out two groups of people to whom I am especially grateful. The first consists of those students, both in class and in consultation, with whom I have shared these ideas, discussed them formally in groups, and from whom I have learned a great deal. I also owe to their reception of these lines of thought the encouragement that they may be useful to a wider audience.

Secondly, I wish to express my thanks to the community of Jesuits of the Ateneo de Manila University in the Philippines with whom I lived as a guest while composing the first draft of this book. Their reception of me among them as an old friend and brother created an easy atmosphere conducive to hard work. My special thanks goes to the rector of the community who made this possible, Asandas Balchand, S.J.

INTRODUCTION

This is an essay in fundamental theology. Its aim is to explore systematically the foundations of theology. What is theological knowledge? On what basis does one speak theologically? How does one arrive at a theological position?

These fundamental questions have elicited a variety of responses. In this introduction I want to lay out some of the presuppositions that lie behind this particular attempt to answer them. In some measure these presuppositions help to explain the method and conclusions of this work. They operate as first principles, not in the sense of axioms from which conclusions may be deduced, but as elements of experience that constantly qualify the theological imagination at work. Some measure of sympathetic appreciation of these principles is needed for a positive entering into the overall argument.

At least four such convictions are at work in this way. They concern the nature of theology and three aspects of human existence, its historicity, its transcendentality, and its dynamic freedom in action.

THEOLOGY AS APOLOGETIC

We begin with a merely general conception of the discipline of theology, because the task of this book is to define it further. Theology today may be understood as a discipline which seeks to understand and determine the underlying truth of all reality. Christian theology does not merely talk about God. Rather theology attempts to construe all things, the world, human existence, human history and society, as well as God from within the vision that is mediated to the Christian community by its religious symbols. As will be shown later, the faith and revelation mediated by Christian symbols add no new knowledge, in a strict sense of knowledge, about the world. But Christian symbols mediate an en-

1

counter with transcendence that transforms all our ordinary or scientific knowledge about finite reality. This broad and completely open view of theology as dealing with the whole of reality is not merely a priori but describes, I think, the way Christian theology has operated through the centuries.

All theology today must be apologetic. The term "apologetic" here does not refer to an effort to prove or demonstrate the truth of the Christian vision against other conceptions of reality. Because of the historicity of revelation, indeed of all truth, Christian theology will always be confessional.[1] "Apologetic" therefore carries the burden of self-explanation before "the other" and "the world," and its goal is to establish meaning and its universal relevance in terms of common human experience.

A comparison and contrast of this view of theology as dealing with all of reality with Thomas Aquinas' conception of it will illustrate the apologetic dimension of the discipline that is required today. Aquinas too conceived of theology as dealing with the whole of reality. The Sacred Doctrine of his *Summa Theologiae* treated every imaginable question and subject matter from the perspective of Christian revelation. According to M.-D. Chenu, Aquinas' project rested upon what Chenu calls a theory or principle of subalternation.[2] According to this principle, one discipline or science can be established by its subject matter and mode of knowledge being drawn up into another and unfolding within its principles. In other words, one science, discipline, or set of principles may become intrinsic to another by being drawn up into a "higher" or "deeper" set of principles known in another science. Current examples might be found in many scientific projects today, such as physics, which unfolds within the principles and axioms of mathematics. In the case of Aquinas, knowledge of the world, of Aristotle's physics and metaphysics, is drawn up into and "subalternated by" the principles of revelation. Although this project unfolded for the most part in an objective way in Aquinas, the principle can also operate today subjectively or heuristically. In either case the principle joins together faith and reason, while allowing for their distinction. In the case of both Aquinas and Chenu the principle justified the intrinsic role of reason in theology and the universal scope of its questioning and being questioned.

The contrast of our situation today with that of both Aquinas in his Christian culture and Chenu in his polemics with post-modernist neo-scholasticism highlights the apologetic quality that theology must bear today. In both these men the intention of the principle of subalternation was to draw critical reason into the discipline of theology which remained regulated by the accepted truths of revelation. Today the task of theology is to explain the principles of faith and revelation and to "justify" their place in the reasonable discourse of human beings with each other. This shift in our situation and our new recognition of it defines theology's apologetic structure. Theology is a discipline that involves critical reason. But this reason is drawn up into the framework of the experience mediated by Christian symbols. The apologetic task of theology is to explain or make intelligible how these foundations of faith, revelation, and the symbolic language of transcendence make sense and are universally relevant to human life.

A fuller account of the internal need that theology be apologetic will be contained implicitly in the anthropological reflections which follow. But an account of the shift that requires this apologetic structure can be seen in three reflections. First, the apologetic nature of theology, according to Paul Tillich, means that theology must respond to the situation in which it unfolds.[3] By a simple and expanded psychological law, theology can only be understood if it bears some relation to contemporary human experience and language. Contemporary experience, more pointedly religious experience, is that to which theology must appeal in order to make sense. Second, the Christian message has always claimed to be universally relevant. Christian faith and revelation deal with a salvation that has a bearing on all humankind. But, third, both the religious dimensions of human experience and the universality of the relevance of Christian revelation have been seriously called into question in our times. Secularization in the west, the traditional home of Christianity, and the rising to prominence of the other great religions outside the west but with global impact, mean that the Christian theologian cannot any longer simply "presuppose" or "take for granted" the premises upon which fundamental theology built in the past. Both within the church, in its address to Christians who also live in the world, and in its missionary address to the world and society, Christian theology must explain itself.[4]

In sum, Christian theology must assume an apologetic character. In this book this apologetic character is reflected in two ways. Each of the five topics will begin with a broad, generalized, and anthropological consideration which is meant to be apologetic. Then the themes established from this anthropological point of view will be brought to bear on the particular issues of the foundations for theological reasoning and assertion.

SOCIAL HISTORICITY

A second premise guiding these reflections may be called the social historicity of human existence and the historical consciousness that insight into this historicity generates. When one tries to imagine human existence concretely and as a whole, one cannot escape the realization of its historicity. The human phenomenon stretches over a vast period of time, and this temporality has involved development and regression, rises and falls along a variety of axes, and along each axis constant change and novelty. The historical nature of human existence implies the constant inevitable changes that are wrought by time itself.

Ernst Troeltsch's definition of this historical dimension of human existence locates its distinctive quality in individuality or particularity.[5] All human phenomena, that is, from societies, to unfolding events and their narratives, to individuals themselves, are particular; they are defined in themselves by the particular time, place, and circumstances by which they are constituted and circumscribed. This web of related particularities that make up each segment of human existence entails contingency. The recognition of this contingency in human existence carries with it the threatening and disorienting aspect of historical consciousness.

The idea of the social constitution of human existence is intimately connected with historicity. It stems from the same concrete and historical imagination. Paradoxically, when one tries to define the concrete human person within an historically conscious framework, the idea of a discretely autonomous individual self all but disappears. No unique individual person is merely that, because each comes to be and develops in a network of relations that operate to define the self. Thus not only is human existence as a whole a social phenomenon, but also each human person has been socially constituted.

H. Richard Niebuhr has captured the social constitution of human existence neatly with his conception of the responding self.[6] Niebuhr locates the ethical dimension of personal responsibility within the larger anthropological framework of each person as a responding self. From the first moment of existence and at every moment in it the human person is acted upon. The person is as it were a center of relationships through which a whole host of influences and actions are operative at every imaginable level. Each person then is constituted by a network of dynamic relationships. Every self-initiated action is at the same time responsive to the impact of the world, others, and society. Thus human beings never simply interact directly as bare individuals. We are always bound together socially by an external world which we share in common, by objectified patterns of understanding mediated by language, and by common behavioral expectations mediated by social ethos. Thus the very nature of the individual person is itself social.

With the realization of the historicity and social constitution of human existence, it becomes impossible to design a definitive anthropology. Characterizations of the human as such become either too abstract to be useful or are simply contradicted by actual historical existence. From an historical point of view, if one wants to understand human existence, one must study its history, for history represents the actuality of the human. History does not yield to a-prioristic understanding; as far as history is concerned, "what you see is what you get." At best anthropology can be retrieved as a social and comparative discipline. But the history of societies too is always in a flux of dynamic interrelationships and remains open-ended into a future of development and change.

Finally, historical, social, human existence is not characterized primarily by order but by disorder. This foundational insight has been the deepest contribution of liberation theology to Christian theology. Social existence for the far greater portion of the human race today can only be characterized as primarily negative in terms of the criteria of human suffering. The point of departure for a theology attuned to the social, historical condition of human existence cannot be positive; it must be a negative experience that reacts against the outrages to the *humanum* which history itself presents before us.[7]

In this book the ambiguities of social historical consciousness, its negativities and positivities, come to bear on the topics considered on a variety of levels. This dimension is explicitly highlighted in the question of method where a method of correlation between Christian symbols and anthropology is proposed. Also an adequate understanding of faith, revelation, scripture, and symbol must incorporate into itself this social dimension. Moreover, the negative aspect of our common social historical situation in the world today highlights the apologetic character that theology must assume. Theological understanding cannot prescind from the actual situation of so many human beings who are victims of social suffering. And, more positively, only historical consciousness can open up the Christian imagination in freedom to the task of reinterpretation. Historical consciousness is the condition for the possibility of creative theology.

TRANSCENDENTAL ANALYSIS

Some theologians who have gained an historicist perspective on human existence turn against transcendental analysis. This is an error. The grounds for and the possibility of some form of transcendental analysis are implicitly affirmed in the very act of denying this method.

By transcendental analysis I mean a reflection on human existence that is able to uncover the universal in the particular. Transcendence in its primary sense simply means "going beyond." As a method of investigating the human, therefore, transcendental analysis entails the conviction that a critical examination of the concrete human subject can yield genuine insight into elements that go beyond particular experience, that are common to human existence as such, and thus are dimensions of human nature.[8] Transcendental analysis itself goes beyond or beneath merely psychologically conscious experiences to the conditions which make them possible at all. Thus transcendental analysis can make general statements about the human condition that may be valid, as potentialities and virtualities, whether or not a particular culture, society, or set of persons is explicitly aware of such experiences.

The grounds for the validity of some form of transcendental analysis appear both simple and to some extent unverifiable. One has a sense of and a "faith" in the unity of the species or the race across its diverse manifestations. This experience correlates with and is ratified by monotheism, a revelation of one God who is the God of all. The inner imperative for and logic of truth in important matters transcends any idea of "truth for me." The strongest argument for the validity of some form of transcendentality lies in the phenomenon of communication. If the historicist premise of individuality were pushed to its ultimate extreme, there could be no human communication: each individual would be locked in his or her own private system of meaning. The very possibility, which is not in every case actualized, of human communication with others implies a common dimension to human existence. Thus some implicit form of transcendental understanding lies at the heart of every system of knowledge, every theology, even historically conscious theology.

It is crucial at this point to affirm categorically that transcendental analysis cannot overcome historicity but only the most radical form of anarchic relativism and solipsism. Apart from these desperate extremes, historical consciousness loses none of its force. Moreover the critics of transcendental analysis are correct insofar as it now appears to have been abused in the past. Transcendental analysis has been reductionistic, providing a merely abstract, or individualistic, or privatistic interpretation of human existence that did not take into account the concrete historical data that make up the actual reality of human existence. Therefore transcendental analysis does not provide the possibility for developing a full anthropology. At best it may provide a framework within which one can determine "anthropological constants" that universally characterize historical existence.[9]

Transcendental analysis, as a method of inquiring about human existence, should not be separated from a social historical method. When it is not tied to an historical imagination, transcendental analysis becomes inadequate to the phenomenon studied. But both of these methods find their grounds in real but distinct dimensions of human existence. Every human experience is singular, unique, and individual. Even human reasoning itself, in all its functions, is historically conditioned and thus is characterized by a dimension of unique particularity. Yet within every human experience there are deep dimensions which are characteristic of the human as such. All human beings, for example, are reasonable and possess languages that enable them to reason. Karl Rahner has made a distinction, but not a separation, between these two dimensions of human experience which preserves their unity and difference and thus provides a theoretical framework for holding these two methods of analysis together. All human experience, according to Rahner, has both a categorical and a transcendental dimension. Every human experience is a response of an individual to this or that; it is an historical experience that is specified by a determined object. It is historically conditioned. Yet within this categorical dimension of experience one can discover factors that go beyond "my" experience and are shared in common with all human beings.[10]

Transcendental analysis will play a major role in this book. It is virtually impossible to approach apologetically such topics as faith, revelation, and religious symbol, all of which are related to epistemology, without the use of transcendental analysis. But in each case this will be balanced by an analysis from an historicist viewpoint. The very structure of faith and revelation, and the functioning of religious symbols, must embody the distinction and tension between the transcendental and categorical dimensions of experience.

ACTION

In *An Alternative Vision* I characterized human existence as freedom in a substantive sense synonymous with spirit.[11] In this book I wish to expand that characterization with the category of action. This does not negate what is entailed by the idea of freedom; human action includes freedom and at some points is synonymous with it. What the category of action adds to freedom is direct reference to its dynamic quality. Freedom is most truly itself when it is freedom in action.

The meaning of the term action is borrowed from the philosophy of Maurice Blondel, although my intention here is not to present an historical account of his thought.[12] Action in its most general sense refers to existence, in this case human existence. Human existence is action. But action denotes a human existence always in act; it is a dynamic existing. Like the term existence itself, action is analogous; existence takes many forms, and the action that is human existence unfolds at a variety of levels. Beyond the sheer act of existing, the human person acts biologically and psychologically; knowing is action; willing is action; doing this or that is action. When action is fully human, when it is mediated by conscious intelligence, action is scarcely distinct from freedom in act.

Assuming the perspective on human existence provided by the category of action steers one in the direction of a dynamic philosophy of life. Blondel called his philosophy of action a pragmatism, and it shared some similarities with the philosophy of William James, even though Blondel's premises were quite different. But it is difficult to assume the label pragmatism today because of the many distorted interpretations of the term.[13] Yet conceiving human existence as action gives one's thinking a vitalistic or energistic cast. Human life is action; it is for action; its purpose is to discover and create. Human existence is a project.[14] This stress on the active purposeful dimension of human existence sets an orientation for this book. But it should not be understood in an excluding sense. Obviously enough, human existence is also constituted by passivities, by being acted upon, and one must try to hold these polarities in balance. Blondel's intricate transcendental analysis of human action in no way engenders what has come to be called pejoratively "activism."

In fact, the opposite is the case. Action integrates within itself the many dimensions of human existence, and the open and analogous meaning of the category allows one to analyze this wholeness. The many polarities of human existence can be held together in tension with or in relation to each other within the deeper substratum of action. Knowing, willing, and doing are all forms of action which further constitute the human person in being this way or that way. Intellect and will are not unrelated; knowing is for willing, and willing for action in the sense of doing. The action that is sheer existence is constantly and dynamically erupting through consciousness, reflection, knowing, and willing into further positing of itself in concrete behaviors.[15]

Theory and practice are not antithetical but held together in a relationship of action. Theory is for practice, and praxis refers to the practice borne through reflective consciousness. Praxis signifies knowing, reflective, critically determined, and directed action.

A theory of action can be used to sort out how the individual and social dimensions of human existence flow into and interact with each other. From one point of view the human person is a quasi-autonomous bundle of action. The person is action; one cannot not act, so that we are what we do. The human person constitutes his or her self in being by action. Yet the person is also acted upon from within by forces outside the perimeter of conscious self-possession. The person is also constituted by agencies outside the self, and to which one must respond, from the world, from other persons, from society as a whole. The *actio* of one is the *passio* of another. Action, then, can be conceived of as the cement of society. The objective structures of institutions consist of the dynamic patterns of actions that often appear static but are actually always in motion.

This dynamic concept of action is operative throughout this essay. It will help define the very nature of faith, the purpose of revelation, the dynamics of religious symbol, the communication of scripture, and the logic of theological method. Finally, it provides the foundational concept for an integral conception of spirituality. Since spirituality is the Christian life in action, and the purpose of theology is to nurture spirituality, the perspective defined by a philosophy of action may be seen as a principle that coordinates the whole work.

This hasty sketch of these four themes undoubtedly leaves many questions unanswered. But they are not the subject matter of this book. They have not been critically established or explained at length but simply stated in order to define the perspective, the premises, the bias, the principles that govern this essay. Other principles too are surely at work.[16] But these four govern the orientation, sometimes explicitly, always implicitly, of the development which follows.

THE LOGIC OF THIS WORK

Finally, something more should be said about the structure and division of this work. It is both similar to and different from other essays in fundamental theology in the Roman Catholic tradition.[17] The questions the book seeks to answer in its most direct form are: What is a theological assertion and how does one interpret its meaning? Other more general questions are implied in these two and thus are also directly addressed. For example, what is theology? How does one form a theological position? These questions define what is meant by fundamental theology as it is used here. The issues addressed are fundamental in relation to the whole discipline of theology.

The responses to these questions are generated by investigating what are commonly considered the foundations of theology. They are those areas or topics upon which the whole discipline of theology rests.

A simple enumeration of the areas treated and why they are considered as fundamental will reveal the simple logic of the book as a whole.

Faith

It is commonly agreed that theology deals with faith and the object of faith. Theological statements are statements of faith. It follows that, if one wants to know what a theological statement is, one should know something of the nature, structure, and dynamics of the faith which is the very ground of theology. Thus we shall begin by asking about the nature of faith, the epistemology of faith, and how it is related to other forms of knowing. This part will also inquire into faith from a social historical point of view, since theological statements are shared by communities as part of their institutional structure. This consideration of faith will yield some general first conclusions about the nature of theology as a discipline and the formal or generic meaning of theological statements as such.

Revelation

The object of faith, what faith is a human response to, is transcendent and beyond knowledge of this world. What is transcendent must be "given" to faith, "from above," so to speak. No empirical evidence can be marshaled to demonstrate an object of faith. The object of faith must be revealed; faith is faith in revelation or in what is revealed. Thus the source of Christian theological affirmations is said to be revelation. It follows that one must have some conception of revelation, its structure and dynamics, in order to understand theological statements. In fact all theology includes some implicit concept of revelation in its performance. The first of the two chapters on revelation will propose a general theory, and the second will analyze the epistemological structure of revelation: What is communicated and how? The second of the two chapters will conclude with reflections on the relation between revelation and theology.

Scripture

Christian revelation is very closely tied to Christian scripture; in the past the two have been identified. Thus Christian theology is dependent on scripture; scripture is the main source, for some the exclusive source, for theological affirmations, and all Christian theological assertions must somehow relate back to scripture. But some very serious problems arise when one looks carefully at the classical doctrines that support this structure. The first is the doctrine of inspiration which held that God is the author of this book. It is interesting to compare that doctrine with the supposition of all modern exegetes and biblical scholars. The very premises which have allowed for a biblical renewal, namely that these are human books, written by human authors, for definite audiences, with definite human presuppositions in mind and so on, seem to subvert the classical notion of inspiration. Practically all of the insights of contemporary biblical scholarship rest on a naturalist and historicist premise and presumption of the human and historical nature of these writings. The second is the doctrine of inerrancy. But where is the inerrancy? The presuppositions of biblical scholarship explain better why, as historically conditioned pieces of writing, the scriptures are filled with errors and inconsistencies. Can the doctrines of inspiration and inerrancy be salvaged? Need they be? If not, how are contemporary doctrines to be seen to be based on scripture? The first of two chapters on scripture will attempt to define the status of this book in the church. In the light of that general theory, the second chapter will explore how scripture can be used in theology; it examines the relation of theology to its source in scripture.

Religious Symbols

Although the category of symbol is not introduced into the argument until this point, the sections on faith and revelation will implicitly take the position that statements of faith are symbolic statements, and that revelation consists in symbolic communication with what is transcendent. In the section on scripture, I will propose that scripture is a book that is symbolic or one that contains a whole host of religious symbols. Therefore scripture should be used symbolically. This section on symbol thus flows from these constructive ideas. In the first of two chapters I deal with a general theory of religious symbols taken from Paul Tillich, Karl Rahner, and others. The question concerns the nature of religious symbols: What is a religious symbol? The second chapter will deal with how symbols function, how they disclose dimensions of reality that allow for religious and theological statements. It will also consider how they function in Christian life personally and socially. Since theological statements are symbolic and theology a symbolic discipline, this section on religious symbols will disclose from a different viewpoint more about the discipline itself.

Method in Theology

For many theologians today theology is hermeneutical. In this view hermeneutics is the discipline that defines the logic and rules for interpreting the meaning of human expressions of meaning and value. And method in theology is programmatic putting into practice a system for interpreting the tradition. Given what has been said about revelation as the source for theology and the normative place of scripture in the discipline, this way of viewing things has merit. Theological method is hermeneutical; it seeks to interpret tradition into meaningful statements for today's world. The first chapter on hermeneutical theory will be extremely general and simply defend the necessity and possibility of theological reinterpretation. It will also give a general account of the structure and goal of theological interpretation. The second chapter will explain the logic of a method of correlation as corresponding to these general principles. The point in all of this will be to illustrate how method is crucial in theology. By defining the logic of the way one interprets and understands theological affirmations, method goes a long way in determining how this or that doctrine is actually being understood.

All of these five topic areas reveal something about the nature of theological assertion and the dynamics of theology as a discipline. No one area is treated here in such a way that it tells the whole story. Thus it is important when reading any given section to realize that limits have been imposed on the subject matter. For example, in the section on faith I have tried to reach conclusions from a merely anthropological point of view. I have tried as much as possible not to consider the content of faith. Such a merely formal consideration does not answer questions that may be better treated under the topic of revelation, or religious experience, or the dynamics of symbolic communication. Yet each topic provides a different viewpoint and thus adds a new perspective on the complex discipline called theology. The hope is that in the final chapter or conclusion the various aspects of theology will fall into place and fit together in a coherent, practical and useful way.

I

FAITH

Chapter One

FAITH AS A DIMENSION OF THE HUMAN

Faith is a universal human phenomenon. All people live by some faith. An approach to faith as a common dimension of human existence itself enables one to characterize its most fundamental structure and most salient qualities.

The reflections and conclusions which follow are generated by a transcendental analysis. This consists in an appeal to a reflection on common human experience,[1] to a descriptive and critical analysis of the phenomenon of faith in the human subject. Many of the advances in the theology of faith in the modern period have come from a turn to the human subject and a description of faith in its first moment as a human act, response, and attitude. The point here is not to reproduce this phenomenological analysis, but to draw on the work of theologians who have investigated faith and helped in clarifying its nature. The goal is not to break new ground, but to lay down in an organized fashion basic principles that will help in the understanding of the nature of theological assertion.

The logic of this initial chapter in relation to the whole work may be stated in the following way. The question underlying the investigation is generic: What is theology? What is the meaning of a theological affirmation? It is commonly agreed that theological assertions are statements of faith. But what is the nature of the faith of which they are the expression? Since it is the case that theological statements and Christian doctrines are expressions of faith, an understanding of them at their deepest level entails a reflective appreciation of the nature of the faith they express. An understanding of faith opens up the deeper logic of theological language. The reciprocity between faith and theological statement means too that an understanding of the nature of faith also provides principles for the interpretation of the meaning of the statements that flow from faith. At least the structure of meaning, the frame-

15

work within which it should be appreciated, flows from the kind of experience that generates the particular language.

This concise treatment of faith begins with an apologetic and anthropological consideration of faith as a universal dimension of human existence. From this perspective I will consider the following aspects of faith that have a direct bearing on the understanding of Christian theology and doctrine: the nature of faith, its object, its relation to knowing and to beliefs, and, finally, the relation between faith and action.

FAITH AS A UNIVERSAL HUMAN PHENOMENON

We begin with the conception of human existence that provides the framework for these reflections and from there move to the anthropological grounds for universal faith.

Human existence consists in freedom. Human beings are spiritual. They stand out from other forms of life by the powers of the human spirit. The term "freedom," used in a substantive sense, can be substituted for spirit. Human existence is constituted at the juncture of freedom and nature.[2] Freedom here does not mean merely the power to choose. Beneath this power lies the dynamism of freedom itself to think, to commit the self with determination, to act in a stable and consistent manner. The human spirit manifests itself as freedom foundationally: the freedom of the mind from concrete sensible data to form abstract and general ideas constituted by language; the freedom not only to know but the reflective ability to know the self as knowing; the freedom to think, weigh alternatives, decide, dedicate the self, and act purposefully. This deep level of freedom, this substantive freedom, is synonymous with the human spirit and characterizes the human as distinct from other kinds of beings.

But freedom is not really freedom unless it passes into act. A mere potency for freedom remains a possibility. The full reality of freedom consists in action. Thus the concrete reality and full manifestations of human existence always reside in freedom-in-action. The actualization of freedom defines the actuality of human existence. And this actualization carries within itself the necessity of faith. Faith accompanies action as a necessary constitutive element of the human. This can be shown from the dynamics of human action itself.[3]

A transcendental analysis of human action reveals various intentionalities that make up its structure and deeper logic. At its most profound level action is a quest that seeks to achieve new being. Action is not aimed at nothingness, but precisely the establishment of the self in new being. No being and no action of human being seeks non-being.[4] In the end each human person is implicitly both impelled and drawn toward absolute being.[5] For example, the human action of knowing participates in a drive or a quest simply to know the truth. Beneath the actions of inquiry and research lies a binding impulse that demands a unity of intelligibility that is one, whole, and comprehensive.[6] On the level of human desire for the good, Maurice Blondel describes at length the deeper will that animates every choice of this or that object. This "willing itself" necessarily reaches out for the absolute good in itself.[7]

In our time these positive impulses appear most clearly against the background of mortal threats to meaning and existence. It may be that this positive direction of human existence can only be recognized by a negative contrast experience.[8] For example each person must live in the face of mortality and the fact of worldly extinction. This threat to coherence becomes intensified by the history of innocent suffering all around us. We live in a world of wild pluralism which calls into question every tradition and the notion of truth itself. Confronted with an anarchy of possible values that attract human commitment, it seems impossible to discover any basis for some order in human society. The sheer fact that these experiences constitute threats to human existence indicates a human dynamism to overcome them. The quest for salvation, then, has been inscribed into the very structure and dynamics of human freedom in action.

Yet when one searches the horizon of finite existence for that which will bestow salvation, it cannot be found. Nothing presents itself, nothing is available, that can encompass the inner desire that animates human action. The very recognition of the ultimate finitude of the totality of this-worldly truth and value becomes itself a contrast experience revealing the infinity toward which human action tends. In the end, no finite object, no coherent set of inner-worldly values, can supply what is demanded by the logic of human action, for this can only be infinite and absolute being.

It is this non-availability which determines faith as a constitutive dimension of human life. For even in the absence of an object that corresponds to the demands of action human beings still must choose. People accept some center of gravity that balances the weights of the various values in their lives. They adopt a system of meaning that establishes certain truths as fundamental. Societies inculcate a variety of objects of faith that provide a unity, comprehensive order, and intelligibility to life. These are objects of faith, because faith is the clinging commitment to those objects, truths, and values which give meaning to human existence at its most fundamental level. When the members of any society or culture internalize these basic values into their lives, they may not be recognized as objects of faith. They may appear as self-evident truths. But historical consciousness has instructed us on the extent to which faith pervades human life. The sheer pluralism of such fundamental values shows that they are transcendent objects of faith.

This approach from a concrete, existential, and historical point of view shows that all human beings live according to some form of faith. Faith is a common human phenomenon, an essential dimension of human action that constitutes integral human existence. All people have faith. Such a view may seem contradicted by certain data. For example, Søren Kierkegaard has described at length the life of the aesthete whose action is determined by successive pleasures.[9] Like butterflies, some people cannot commit themselves to anything stable, or even in a stable way to a class of things. North American culture has engendered passionate consumers, a whole society of people who need, buy, and use things up, ever new things, and whose life of work seems geared to this end.

Although H. Richard Niebuhr describes faith in one central and commanding transcendent value as an ideal, the fact is that people are usually polytheists or henotheists who either have many different faiths or whose god is always compromised by lesser gods.[10] Yet beneath seemingly erratic behavior, insofar as it is responsible at all, one can find by reductive analysis a dedication, a faith commitment, a direction, a path upon which the heart has been set. The object of faith may rank fairly low on any scale of values. It may be concealed from reflective evaluation. It can lie embedded in the implicit logic of a person's or a people's behavior. But some object of faith is always operative insofar as it is constituted by the sum total of all one's actual decisions.

The proposition that all live by faith has enormous apologetic value. It also carries a liberating power for a Christian self-understanding which labors under the threat of doubt. The ultimate issue in the question of faith does not deal with yes or no, faith or unfaith. Rather the point at issue is always which faith to choose: Which faith makes most sense? This is one of the positive and constructive themes of historical consciousness that has considerable practical value. The pluralism of the objects of faith shows that faith is faith and not demonstrable knowing, and that it is universal and inescapable.

This apologetic and anthropological approach to faith also releases faith in a transcendent object from the charge of a heteronomy that negates human freedom. The question of faith is the question of salvation. But it also asks what object, which value, what supreme reality is most worthy of the dedication and commitment of human freedom. The value of human freedom may be measured by the object of its faith. This is illustrated by a line from the movie *Becket* placed in the mouth of Thomas Becket by screen writer Robert Bolt. Thomas Becket, who has lived the life of a Kierkegaardian aesthete, is suddenly appointed archbishop of Canterbury and thus guardian of the interests of God's church. In the dramatic moment of acceptance, in a moment of prayer before the altar of a side chapel in the cathedral, he says these astonishing words: "I thank you, Lord, for giving me an object worthy of my freedom." The presumptuous and exalted view of human freedom implied in these words seems to be a reversal of values that borders on blasphemy. Yet the paradox of faith is that the height of the object of commitment exalts freedom itself. Coupled with this is the Christian conviction that God has established human freedom as a capacity for infinity. But before examining the transcendent character of the object of faith, something should be said of the nature of faith.

THE NATURE OF FAITH

In this work the term "faith" always refers to a human response. Thus faith is subjective, and "subjective" should never be understood as "merely subjective" as though it had no object outside the self. Faith can also be understood in an objective sense as in the phrase "the Christian faith." But I shall reserve the term "belief" to refer to the object of faith insofar as it is captured in language and concept.[11]

Attempts to crystallize the nature of the human response that is faith in concise terms abound in modern theology. Friedrich Schleiermacher analyzed the ground of religious faith in what he called the experience of absolute dependence. Schleiermacher did not mean by this a psychological feeling nor an experience mediated through a distinct religious faculty. Arrived at by a form of transcendental analysis, it refers to an underlying experienced condition of being dependent in one's being.[12] For Kierkegaard, the preeminent theologian of faith of the nineteenth century, faith is a more intentional "infinite passion," where both terms underscore the intensity of commitment to its object that constitutes faith.[13]

Paul Tillich, in his classic *Dynamics of Faith*, has taken these two themes and woven them together in his definition of faith as "ultimate concern."[14] The phrase is filled with subtle potentialities of meaning. For example, ultimate concern can be understood in both a subjective and objective sense. It also includes simultaneous active and passive dimensions. Subjectively and actively ultimate concern corresponds to Kierkegaard's infinite passionate commitment. To express the passive dimension of faith, Tillich often uses the passive voice: faith is being grasped by an ultimate concern.[15] When the objective concern is really ultimate, transcendent, and infinite, it is experienced as that upon which one stakes one's being.

The essential point of this characterization of faith lies in the recognition that faith consists in a dynamic commitment of the whole of human freedom in action. Faith as an existential reality means that faith is real only insofar as it is an actual human reaction and response to reality.[16] This response cannot be reduced to any specific "faculty." It is not simply intellectual assent; not a pure decision of the will; not merely an emotional feeling.[17] None of these aspects should be excluded from faith. But the idea of a commitment of freedom, because it is a more diffuse description of faith, is able to accommodate the richness and diversity of its many aspects. Faith reaches out from the depth of human freedom. Whether it be defined as ultimate concern or as "setting one's heart upon,"[18] it takes the form of an engagement of all of a human being's energies and powers. It can in turn be mediated by a variety of different kinds of experiences: a response to beauty, a negative response to human suffering, an attraction to a supreme value or good, a decision to direct one's whole life in a certain way.

Faith is central and centering: central because it emerges out of the center of one's free being; centering because it unifies, integrates, and holds together all aspects of the personality. Of course, such a characterization of faith describes it in an almost ideal form. Faith takes on different psychological forms according to different stages in its development.[19] The principal or confessed object of faith may actually have rivals that may or may not be conscious. Faith most distinctively is an adult phenomenon, although it can still exist in less developed forms. Even though they are human, new-borns do not have faith in the sense described here, any more than they possess language in a developed way. Yet one should see continuities; basic human trust can be nurtured from the very beginning of human life.[20]

It is important to underscore the two distinct but inseparable themes within authentic faith alluded to earlier, the passive and the active. Faith consists in a being acted upon and a submission to values that transcend the self. The commitment of faith entails a kind of dependence and being filled with the value of that to which one surrenders the self. But along this axis of receiving, and as active response to being acted upon, faith also entails fidelity and loyalty to the object of faith. The commitment of faith is a kind of loyalty to a cause and the dedication of one's freedom to the values it entails.[21] This essentially active dimension of faith, often neglected in theologies of faith, is crucial for an understanding of the actuality of faith.

Finally, as the theology of faith is adjusted to the framework of historical consciousness, it becomes more and more difficult really to distinguish faith and hope. Indeed, hope can be considered as faith within an historical context.[22] What I am suggesting here is not a substitution of hope for faith, but a view of faith that fuses it with hope on the deeper level at which they cannot be distinguished. Karl Rahner has described hope as a deeper and more fundamental human response to reality than faith, one that consists in a sheer openness to and basic trust in being itself.[23] Surely faith or hope in any developed form must be more object-specific than this; Rahner characterizes only the human potentiality for faith in this view of hope. Yet since faith too constitutes the deepest and most central response of human beings to reality, one should realize that on a deep level faith and hope are indistinguishably one.[24] This view of faith will allow a theology of faith to do full justice to human historicity and the negativities of actual historical consciousness. Faith entails trust in and loyalty to historical existence in the past and present and into the future simultaneously.

This brief characterization of the nature of faith will be all-important for understanding the kind of statements that are made in theology.

THE OBJECT OF FAITH

Another theme crucial for understanding the nature of theological assertion is the object of faith. The object of faith is, or at least should be, absolutely transcendent. The premise for this position consists in the phenomenology of human existence that displays it as reaching out or striving for the infinite. Human beings want to be; they want to be absolutely. The only way to be absolutely is to reach for an infinite and absolute object and, once it is given, to cling to it by faith. Thus the transcendence of the object of faith is arrived at by measuring the nature of faith against the inner stimulus or drive that gives rise to it.

This logic is seen in Tillich's theology of faith. Subjectively faith is an ultimate concern. To be such coherently faith must attach itself to an object that is itself unlimited, absolute, infinite, transcendent, ultimate, beyond everything in this world which is by contrast limited, relative, finite, and not ultimate. The correspondence between faith and its object, between value-response and value, within the dynamics of faith itself provides a criterion for its own authenticity.[25] Faith reaches out for and clings to something that is transcendent, beyond the finitude of this world and everything in it taken together.

This intrinsic criterion of faith calls for some adjustment of terminology. It seems clear that people may place their whole confidence and loyalty in objects that are less than absolutely transcendent. The phenomenology of trust and commitment to nation, power, and wealth displays the manner in which these can easily take on religious dimensions; they can function as God-like substitutes for a genuine object of faith. Should such commitment be called faith? And are these phenomena religious? These questions can be begged at this point. One may simply assume theologically that the transcendence of the object of faith is a criterion for the genuineness of religious faith. If the object of faith is not transcendent, the faith in question is not genuinely religious, because the object of authentic religious faith should be strictly transcendent. Finite reality, in itself, should not be an object of religious faith, even though it will be shown that faith always entails some connection with the reality of this world.

With this understanding of the dynamics of the faith which underlies theology, one also has a fairly clear although very general criterion for appreciating what a theological statement is. Strictly speaking theological language must involve transcendent mystery. If it does not, it is not a statement of faith and not a theological assertion. In the tradition of Christian theology the proper object of faith has, generally speaking, been limited to God. The reason for this arises out of the phenomenological analyses that have been outlined. It follows from this that language or affirmations that do not entail an experience of transcendence, but are warranted by empirical evidence, are not strictly speaking theological affirmations. For example, that Jesus was a human being is not a statement of faith. That the church is a community of disciples of Jesus needs no faith to be appreciated at face value, although human infidelity may make it appear as a matter for faith. These are empirical judgments; a theological statement involves transcendence; of themselves these are not theological propositions. This view leads us to the issue of the relation between faith and knowledge.

FAITH AND KNOWING

The transcendent nature of the object of authentic religious faith raises the question of whether or not such an object can be known. What is the relation of faith to human knowing? The issue is subtle and we shall return to it in the next chapter under the heading of critical reason.

But as an initial essay into this complex area, we can lay down this tensive proposition: since the object of faith is transcendent, it cannot be known in the ordinary sense of human knowing; yet faith does have a cognitive dimension.

Faith is not knowledge. The knowledge referred to here is the knowledge human beings have of things in and of this world. Ordinarily people speak of what they know to be the case when there is some kind of directly available evidence that determines the knowing. This evidence should be public in the sense that in principle it is available to all. Assent to what is knowable and actually known would be expected of all if the evidence were made available to all. Knowing in the ordinary sense of the term thus deals with finite reality. In one way or another it always depends on empirical evidence, even when it requires inference beyond empirical data. Knowing means that people grasp something, comprehend it, understand it, control it in the measure that they have achieved an adequate mastery of the data. Thus what human beings really know is in some way verifiable. Knowing may be based on logical premises and suppositions, but what is known would be commonly accepted if anyone considered the evidence and reasoned in a similar manner. Knowing therefore ordinarily refers to the process of understanding objects of this world which are finite and able to be comprehended on the basis of public and verifiable evidence.[26]

Faith is not knowing, does not constitute knowledge, at least not the kind of knowing that has been described. What people commit themselves to in authentic religious faith, with infinite passion, they do not know because the object is transcendent. Faith would not be religious faith, not the dynamism of basic hope and trust toward a transcendent object, if it were an object of knowledge. This becomes clear in the consideration of some examples of objects of faith that are foundational: the benign nature of ultimate reality as a whole; the ultimate value of being as opposed to non-being; the permanent significance of existing; the worth of human life and even one's own life, the two of which are inseparable; that God is, or is personal, or is benevolent; that life in general and one's own life include a goal and purpose; that there is a permanent and essentially consistent human way to live and that it can be determined.

Human beings do not know these things; they are objects of faith. All of these issues are surrounded by controversy. They can be decided by no appeal to empirical evidence, for there is as much data in support of one side of these issues as the other. Each of these propositions has its deniers as well as its affirmers. In each case, of denial or affirmation, one is dealing with faith because one does not *know* the answer. Faith is assent or denial by means of a commitment to something that transcends this-worldly evidence. Verification of the object of religious faith in a strict sense can only be eschatological. The truth of faith will become fully manifest at the end of life through death.

Because the object of faith is transcendent, and not a datum for human knowing, it must be *given* to a person; it must be revealed. This appears in the phenomenology of faith itself as a human response. The object of faith is not arrived at by human achievement, nor by investigation, nor by conclusive inference. It is experienced as "given to the subject," from "above."[27] Here one finds the deeper reason why the Christian theology of faith has always spoken of faith as the effect of grace, as caused by revelation, as a gift of God as Spirit. Even in the giving, however, what is given cannot be controlled, but stands revealed as absolute mystery in its transcendence. Faith, then, is as qualitatively different from knowing as mystery is from a problem.[28] Mystery remains incomprehensible in its being revealed, and the mind even within faith cannot unravel it; a problem is theoretically solvable, and the quest goes on for more evidence to penetrate and control it. Faith deals with transcendence, knowledge deals with the finite reality of this world.

At this point one could develop the theme of the cognitive dimension of faith in dialectical tension with the affirmation that faith is not knowing in the ordinary sense. Against the view that one knows nothing in faith, one can speak of another kind of knowing, the knowledge of religious experience, that is itself a qualitatively different kind of knowing from knowledge of finite reality. A religious experience is religious insofar as its object is experienced and recognized as transcendent. This necessary discussion will complement what has been said thus far about faith and knowing, but we shall take up this question under the topics of revelation and religious symbols.

Although faith and ordinary human knowing are different kinds of human response to reality, they should not and cannot be separated from each other. One needs distinctions here and not separations, for faith and knowing are inseparable. The two forms of human response interpenetrate. Human being is one, and human consciousness is unified. Although the differences between faith and knowledge can be clearly shown on the basis of their objects, the distinction between them does not mean the isolation of one from another. Three examples will illustrate how faith interacts with ordinary knowing.[29]

First, faith interacts with the human power of imagination. It is notoriously difficult to define exactly what imagination is, but one can describe how it functions. Let us assume that imagination consists in the human mind forming and projecting images of reality, culled from experience of this world, in a creative way to illumine further data of experience. Not to be equated with fancy or fantasy in any pejorative sense, imagination functions constructively to creatively react to the data of experience by interpretation of it. One cannot know the transcendent object of faith, but one necessarily forms images of it. There is no "pure" faith experience, for all experience is at the same time interpreting and an interpreted experience. One cannot have faith in God without imagining or constructing images of God.[30] We shall say much more about the genesis of faith further on, but at this point it appears to be inseparable from human imagination. Through imagination all human knowledge about this world enters into the process of forming concepts of transcendence within consciousness, of construing, imagining, and interpreting what the object of faith is.

Second, faith's interpretation of its object bends back to interpret the world. Although the object of faith transcends the world, still, being in relation to this transcendent object floods light on one's understanding of the world. Faith has implications not only for how one lives in the world, but also for a qualitative appreciation of the whole realm of finite reality that can be strictly speaking known. For example, from one point of view faith in God as personal does not change the content of one's understanding of the workings of nature. But from another point of view the interpenetration of this faith with knowing can yield an entirely new context for appraising the same understanding. It is construed differently because of a new expanded horizon and content of consciousness.

Third, it follows that faith always coexists with ideologies, when ideologies in the terms of Juan Luis Segundo are taken as distinct from faith but intermingled with faith and correlative to it.[31] In Segundo an ideology refers to any system of understanding of this-worldly reality. All understandings of the world that are ultimately based on empirical data make up ideologies. This extremely general category, which takes on significance in distinction from faith, includes all scientific knowing that derives from a wide variety of empirical sources. Ideologies are oriented toward efficacy, that is, toward the way finite reality works in relation to the human subject as an agent of action. Faith is precisely distinct from this knowledge as an acceptance of and commitment to transcendent ideas, values, data, reality. But faith and some ideology are inseparable; faith cannot exist without such an understanding of the world, nor can human beings maintain ideologies about the world without some underlying interpretation by faith. Faith thus necessarily coexists with some set of ideologies. Moreover faith and ideologies, although distinct, mutually influence each other. There should be a reciprocal relationship of correspondence between faith and an ideology. Ideally faith and ideologies when held together should be consistent.

Much more will have to be said concerning the distinction and dynamic interrelationship between faith and knowing. But this much has been established: faith and knowing about this world are qualitatively distinct human responses, yet they are inseparable and mutually interpenetrate and influence each other. This formulation leads us to the question of the relation between faith and believing which is also crucial for Christian theology.

FAITH AND BELIEFS

The question of the distinction and relation of faith and belief flows from what has been outlined with regard to faith and knowledge. Faith is not reducible to belief; faith is more than believing; rather beliefs may be considered expressions of faith that are distinct from faith itself.[32]

It will be helpful at the start of this discussion simply to sort out the meaning of the terms. The word "believing" runs parallel in meaning with "faith" as it is used here to designate a subjective human response. Believing suggests acceptance of something as true on the basis of testimony, or the word of another, perhaps because of the authority of the witness. It seems clear that faith as a surrender and loyalty of the whole person in the form of a commitment far transcends although it inevitably includes believing. The substantive "belief," by contrast, tends toward having an objective meaning. It is understood here as referring to an expression of that which is believed. A belief thus consists in an objective characterization in language and concept of the object of believing and the object of faith. The thesis here maintains that faith in the transcendent object of faith and the characterization, interpretation, and definition of that object of faith as a belief are distinct or different. Further questions concerning the dynamic interaction between faith and beliefs, the genesis of beliefs as expressions of faith, will be taken up later with the topic of revelation.

The relevance of this issue also deserves preliminary comments. Its importance is not merely theoretical, because what is at stake here comes to bear concretely on the lives of people in the churches. The underlying problem arises out of historicity and its attendant historical consciousness. It has been shown how faith and knowing, faith and ideologies, interpenetrate each other. Thus in the course of Christian history the beliefs of Christians have changed, in some cases rather dramatically. Similarly, as Christianity continues to become more and more a truly world religion, and thus inculturated within a wide variety of different thought and behavior systems, pluralism will increase. The question then is whether or not there can remain a common theologically defined identity of Christianity, a principle of sameness and communion. Where and how is such a principle to be located? Practically speaking, in the case of individuals, when their particular beliefs change, so that they do not seem to match the traditional doctrines of the church, does this mean they have lost their Christian faith? In few cases is a thorny theoretical and theological problem matched with such practical ministerial urgency.

The status of beliefs as expressions of faith flows from the definition of terms. Faith in transcendent reality cannot exist without beliefs about the object of faith. Faith always coexists with imaginative portrayals of its object, interpretations of it, conceptualizations and propositions characterizing transcendent reality or interpreting the finite world in the light or on the basis of transcendence. For example, we call God Father, or Mother, or Love. From where do these images, concepts, and interpretative language about the object of faith come? Certainly they arise from knowledge of the world. They are drawn from everyday experience and what we have called knowing this world in an ordinary sense. But their meaning and validity as construals of transcendent reality can only come from faith itself.[33] In other words, within the phenomenon of faith coupled with beliefs the significance of beliefs emerges out of what is deeper than beliefs, namely, the experience of, and the surrender and commitment of, loyalty in faith to transcendence. This is not a chronological priority, as though one could have first "pure faith" followed by a formulation of beliefs. Rather it derives from and resides in the structure of a relationship in which conscious commitment to the object of faith provides the intentionality that transforms language fashioned in ordinary knowledge of the world into faith's objectification. Beliefs then have no real independent status apart from the existential faith which they express.

This does not mean that beliefs, once engendered, cannot have coherence and meaning apart from a faith commitment to them. Beliefs formulated in a public way can communicate intelligible meaning to those who do not share the faith that gave rise to them. They can also stimulate or mediate faith in those who previously did not have it in this specific object. But beyond the question of their notional *meaning* beliefs cannot represent *truth* for any person apart from faith. The affirmation of the validity of beliefs depends on faith. The affirmation of belief statements as true requires faith. This conception of the matter presupposes that the idea of second-hand or indirect faith is wrongheaded. Faith is not reducible to a "pure believing that" what someone else says is true, without any inner experience of or commitment to its value as true. Thus, in the end, beliefs that represent no one's commitment in faith are mere hollow statements, mere notions, with no power to truly express transcendent reality. They become no more than mere thought-experiments.

Granted that beliefs are expressions of faith, how does one show the distinction between faith and beliefs? Arguments for this distinction may be formulated in terms of locating the constant and the changeable aspects of a consistent faith. Faith reaches out and attaches itself to an object which is transcendent. The interpretation of that object employs the concepts and language of knowledge of this world. But the world and human knowledge of it is constantly moving and changing, and thus the interpretative position in relation to the object of faith is always shifting. Beliefs change and should change. One could say that faith changes too, or both faith and beliefs change together. It is true that faith is altered in some measure with different beliefs, but it need not be changed substantially. Faith contains within its attachment to transcendence elements of an experience that transcend every conceptualization of it. The object of faith as it is experienced within the context of faith's commitment to it on a deep foundational level of ultimate concern can remain substantially unchanged despite different beliefs about it. The object of faith which is given to faith and to which faith responds in loyalty may remain constant and one even while beliefs about it are altered.[34]

In short the distinction between faith and beliefs becomes apparent with the acceptance that there can be one faith and different beliefs about the object of faith. Faith commitment to a transcendent object allows for different interpretations and expressions of it, because none of them is adequate or comprehensive of its transcendence and mystery. All expressions of faith, every theological statement, all doctrines or dogmas are partial, relative, limited, and inadequate to their transcendent object. This is recognized within the experience of faith itself. Thus there has been a pluralism of successive beliefs across history which theology has called the development of doctrine. A community, like an individual, may go through a development or change in its belief structure while still identifying a single faith characterized by constancy and sameness.[35] There may be and inevitably is a pluralism of beliefs in one extended community of faith at any given time. This very pluralism of beliefs is found in scripture itself regarding the absolutely central issue of faith in Jesus as God's salvation bringer. This central and unifying faith finds expression in many very different christological beliefs.[36]

In sum, faith cannot exist without some belief, but the same faith need not be wedded to any particular belief. Beliefs are distinct enough from faith that beliefs can be changed even while faith remains substantially the same. This dialectical principle concerning the phenomenon of faith is actually fundamental to the whole discipline of theology. It both frees theology from false problems connected with a fundamentalistic or creedalistic imagination and allows the constructive task of theological interpretation to go forward.[37]

FAITH AS PRAXIS

One last principle concerning faith will prove to be important for understanding theological statements and hence the discipline of theology itself. It will also come to bear on the interpretation of doctrines. Faith is so closely aligned with human action that it falls just short of being identified as action. But faith is primarily constituted by and therefore manifested in action.

It was said that no single faculty or religious sense is responsible for the genesis of faith. Faith can be engendered by a variety of different kinds of experiences. But once generated, faith as it were resides in a locus. The nature of faith was explained as an acceptance of and loyalty to something that commands the whole of human personality in a central and centering way. Faith as such is an existential reality; it consists in the dynamic commitment of the entire person in action. Therefore one has to say that faith exists, it is real and actual, only insofar as one actually receives and accepts a transcendent value or object and actually surrenders one's life to it in committed loyalty. This same existential principle can also be understood in the other direction to make the point at issue. A person's faith really consists in the actual surrender and dedication to value that constitutes that person's life. The real or actual object of anyone's faith lies in that to which one is actually receptive and loyal. Thus the actuality of faith is constituted by human response which, insofar as it is conscious, thematized, and intentionally directed, can be called praxis. Ultimately faith defines its object by action. Faith is faith in that which ultimately guides and directs one's action.

This principle of faith, which emerges directly out of a transcendental existential analysis of it, is so obvious that it is often ignored. New Testament literature is filled with this theme; one's faith is constituted by one's behavior, not by what one says but by what one does. One cannot quite say that faith is action or praxis, but one must say that the object of one's faith is defined by the logic of one's behavior. The object of one's real faith lies in a fundamental option which consists in the radical orientation of a person at any given time as that is circumscribed by the sum total of concrete decisions that make up a person's life. This makes faith the deepest and in a way the most unknown aspect of human life. In many respects human beings cannot know clearly what defines their deepest faith. What do we really live for, put most stock in, count on most, direct our actions by, place our heart in? Depth psychology has shown how hidden are the deepest human motivations that govern human lives, and how conscious intentions often obscure these motivations from the self. Thus faith is not only mysterious in its object; it is mysterious in its source or wellsprings as well. Faith is so deeply embedded in human action that it can often only be brought to clear consciousness by extended reflective analysis of action.

This conception of the inner logic of faith has a direct bearing upon the nature of theology and the meaning of theological assertion. For theology does not consist merely in the analysis of the meaning of Christian doctrines as free-standing logical propositions. These statements about reality are expressions of faith, engendered by faith, and carry the internal logic of a commitment to a transcendent object and a whole way of life. When one recognizes that faith, of which beliefs are the expressions, is constituted by action, it follows that theological statements have a moral substance. Responsible moral action becomes a theme or a dimension of the very meaning of belief. Doctrines and beliefs must then be read as principles of human action, objects of loyalty and fidelity, imperatives for commitment, and guidelines for action. Since moral commitment enters into the substance of the formulation of theological beliefs, one must search the dynamics of the epistemology of moral response to help uncover the full significance of the meaning of doctrine. It is not simply that theology and ethics cannot be separated. Despite the ability to distinguish these two areas of reflection, they become inextricably fused in the interpretation of the meaning of theological assertion itself. In short, doctrines emerge *out of* and are *for* the Christian life, and consideration of only their intelligible meaning as distinct from their moral meaning distorts their significance.

CONCLUSION

This descriptive analysis of faith represents only a first probe into the nature of theology and theological assertion. Since theology deals with beliefs that are the expressions of faith, each one of the aspects of faith brought out here will have a bearing on the nature of theological propositions. The transcendence of the object of religious faith, that faith is not knowing in any ordinary sense, that faith essentially consists in a commitment that is borne in action, all this will help to understand the inner logic of theological doctrines. After some considerations of faith from a social-historical point of view, we shall show at the end of chapter two how these aspects of faith can be converted into general principles for interpreting the nature of theology.

Chapter Two

FAITH AND THE COMMUNITY
OF BELIEFS

The last chapter laid down some very general but fundamental principles regarding the nature of faith. On the basis of a transcendental analysis of the dynamics of faith it outlined qualities of faith that seem to define its universal structure. In the chapter which follows the perspective on faith shifts to a social historical viewpoint. The emphasis will fall less on faith and more on beliefs, but without failing to recognize that beliefs must always be considered as functions of the faith of which they are an expression.

This chapter will delineate the public character of faith, belief, and theology. These phenomena are by no means merely personal in the sense of individual or private. Once the social and historical function of beliefs are clearly entered into the equation, some of the deeper problems that accompany theology and theological interpretation will also become apparent. Finally, against this background of the problems involved in theological interpretation we shall be able to bring to bear some general guidelines and principles for the task of theological interpretation that flow from these analyses of the nature of faith.

FAITH AS A PUBLIC ACT

Faith was characterized in the last chapter in such a way that it appeared to be constituted in the deepest and most intimate regions of personhood. Sometimes one's real faith lies hidden from the self. But that is never the end of the matter. This deep commitment of faith always enters into dialogue with clear consciousness and reflective questioning. In some measure it cannot escape the conscious level of self-understanding. Thus one must say that on the one hand there is a dimension of everyone's faith that is individual and uniquely his or her own. But on the other hand it cannot remain merely or purely private; it inevitably and inescapably shares in the public sphere.[1]

It is not difficult to understand why this is necessarily the case. The object of faith concerns ultimate truth, and both the nature of truth and its ultimacy demand that faith become a public act. For truth cannot remain "truth for me." The inner logic of a search for truth cannot accept and necessarily rejects an absolute relativism that negates the idea of truth itself. This is especially apparent in matters of ultimate importance. They cannot remain purely private matters. Thus two things happen in the formulation of faith into beliefs about its object and about reality in its light: first, the object of ultimate concern is clarified or thematized for individuals; second, this object of faith is rendered public by the use of common language. The necessity that faith express itself in beliefs is the same necessity by which faith is rendered public.

The dynamics of the desire for truth show that faith has an inner tendency to communicate itself. And when the object of faith has been communicated in the form of public beliefs, it tends toward the formation of a community of faith and beliefs as well as a tradition. It would not be difficult to analyze the formation of the Christian community and its development into a tradition in the light of this dynamic of faith. Behind and at the source of Christianity lie persons who had a profound experience of faith. Historically the faith of Jesus and those who became his disciples developed into a distinct community and tradition of faith and belief.

From this social and historical point of view, then, one can understand why faith in the concrete is never a private individual commitment. In fact faith is a public act and usually consists in joining or aligning oneself with a tradition. One could say that people are simply born and socialized into a community of beliefs. Even more strongly one can say that the community shapes, forms, and structures an individual's faith not only by its belief system but also and principally by its action which is the more vital expression of its faith. The identity of any individual, which is fashioned by faith at an elementary level, is in its turn passively constituted by the tradition. But authentic religious faith transcends a passive acceptance or merely social association with a set of beliefs. Insofar as faith is authentic it should involve an entering into, sharing, and participation in a tradition through active commitment. Somewhere along the line people undergo an explicit or implicit conversion, or a series of transformations, through which passively accepted formation is internalized and appropriated, if it is not rejected for another faith and system of beliefs. On the more active level, then, a person publicly ratifies his or her given formation by identifying with the community. The identity of the community in its turn involves a commitment to shared symbols, ideas, values, beliefs, and doctrines that extend far back into the past. In sum, one's most personal faith is necessarily social; it is a public social act and attitude that implies a co-responsibility with a community of other people. It involves a system of shared language, meaning, and values which ideally should involve corporate responsibility.[2]

A recognition of the public social character of faith also contains a strong apologetic dimension with ministerial relevance. Although each person shares some irreducible personal responsibility for his or her own faith, no one is alone in the search for the fitting object of that faith. To many Christians today faith appears threatened by religious pluralism and by Christianity's minority status in relation to the diverse faiths and systems of belief in the world. But we have already remarked that one cannot escape faith; to leave one set of beliefs behind is to accept another community of faith and its beliefs. No matter how insecure or uneasy one may feel in relation to this or that belief, it is helpful to realize that Christian faith participates in a set of beliefs that have defined the identity of living communities of people extending back two thousand years, and beyond that into our own Jewish history. To have faith is to belong to an extended community and a vital tradition.

THE SOCIAL FUNCTION OF BELIEF

In describing faith as a public social commitment we have already touched upon the social function of beliefs. Theological statements, beliefs, and doctrines, by publicly expressing the object of faith, serve as one of the social bonds that holds the community together and gives it a public identity.

It is interesting to compare the different appraisals of beliefs that one can arrive at by considering them from the point of view of personal faith and then from a social perspective. If one considers this or that specific belief in terms of the personal structure and dynamics of faith, beliefs appear to be secondary and derivative. What is primary is the committed clinging and loyalty to the object of faith and its cause that always transcends a particular formulation. A clear, imaginative, reflective, and conceptual portrayal of the object of faith may be important but is still secondary to the reality of faith itself. The commitment of faith can remain consistent while beliefs are refined or even changed.

From the social perspective things are partially reversed. Beliefs are in place before an individual commits his or her faith to the objects they represent; beliefs appear prior to and generative of faith. Since beliefs help to define this identity of the community, they thus touch upon the intimate identity of each person within the community. Since they announce to the world the content of a community's faith, they generate a sense of security that comes with a clear social identity in distinction from other communities. Since they interpret and define the object of ultimate concern, they also tend to share in the ultimacy of the concern itself. Tampering with or changing the beliefs that express the faith of a person or a community can only run into deep and fierce resistance.

A theological appropriation of the status of beliefs must keep in balance these two points of view and what they reveal. The data here is not contradictory, but simply indicates the complexity of religious phenomena. The analysis of the nature of faith shows clearly that beliefs are derivative. But their secondary status does not in any way minimize their intrinsic importance or the generative role they play in the community of faith and through it in the individual's life of faith. But beliefs are not in the long run the primary expressions nor mediators of faith. Much more basic is action, both the ritual action of the community[3] and the action of everyday life, that bear witness to the fact that the object of faith is indeed real, vital, and able to engender ultimate concern.[4] Especially in the lives of individuals, when passively received tradition becomes transformed into appropriated meaning and commitment, the role of significant witnesses, who testify by their action, is paramount.[5] Despite the role that beliefs play in defining the identity of a community's faith, sometimes in very crucial ways when the life and very faith of the community seem to be at stake vis-à-vis deviations within the community, or other communities, or general society, they should never be given the status of faith itself.

THE PROBLEM OF THEOLOGICAL STATEMENTS: BELIEFS MASQUERADE AS FAITH

But this is exactly what happens. Beliefs are given the status of faith and masquerade as faith itself. The phenomenon is so common and prevalent that one needs only call attention to it in order to make the point. By an almost necessary sociological law theological propositions become themselves the object of ultimate concern, and adhering to and retaining them tends to substitute for faith itself.

To describe the phenomenon is to unmask it. Because of the social importance of beliefs and their role of defining the community's faith, faith itself tends to be confused with, collapsed into, and mistaken for holding on to these beliefs. Faith, now seen as holding these beliefs, becomes objectified. For this faith, which is now belief, means assenting to an objective set of beliefs about reality. This objectified faith can be summarized in a set of propositions, because only as such can beliefs perform their rightful function of defining the object of faith and the identity of the community. These propositions are presented as guaranteed by external authority, ultimately the authority of God as mediated through scripture and the church. There seems to be an inherent social tendency toward fundamentalism and creedalism.

Moreover, from an uncritical and narrow perspective within the community, these beliefs, which do not represent knowledge but interpretations and expressions of faith in transcendence, begin to function precisely as knowledge. Beliefs naively appear as objectively true knowledge about reality. They may even be considered as information about transcendent reality. Since they are objectively true, and faith is an assent to them, faith itself becomes a form of ordinary knowledge, one that is based purely on extrinsic authority. Christian faith becomes objective knowledge that Christians possess and others do not, and the formulas of this knowledge must be preserved intact at all cost given their identity with faith itself. Change a proposition, and faith itself is changed. Doubt about a proposition, because it is hesitancy or failure of assent, represents loss of faith because authority itself is called into question. Loss of faith in one belief is infidelity *tout court*, because the whole body of beliefs rests on the single external authority of God represented by scripture or the church which is itself called into question.

At this point it should be clear that the phenomenon of beliefs masquerading as faith is theologically wrong. The error begins with the social tendency of beliefs, because of their important and intrinsically necessary social function, to take the place of the transcendent object of faith. This dynamism serves as a buttress against human insecurity, and it reinforces a kind of natural desire to grasp and control transcendent reality. The result is that the transcendent object of faith in the same measure ceases to be transcendent, to break in upon the passive dimension of faith, and to draw forth ever new commitment to the ever new exigencies of its cause. But beyond the theological confusion involved, this process also has disastrous consequences for the life of faith of ordinary people, especially in a time of radical pluralism when scientific knowledge, discovery, and changing world-views have a high profile. Members of such a community can only be confused and threatened by the growing body of genuinely new knowledge human beings are generating about themselves and the world. These external forces drive a wedge between a community of beliefs taken as knowledge and the competing and seemingly contradictory knowledge of the rest of the world. The result is that many people leave the church, and what is left is a community of closed, eviscerated and impoverished faith isolated from the world on the basis of archaic beliefs. The distinction between faith and beliefs, then, is crucial. So too is the recognition of the historicity of beliefs.

BELIEFS AS HISTORICALLY CONDITIONED

The social historical perspective on beliefs reveals how they tend toward displacing faith and its object as the bond of the community. The same perspective also reveals the historically conditioned character of beliefs. All theological affirmations, all beliefs and doctrines, are historically conditioned, and this implies that they are not absolute, but are limited and relative.

H. Richard Niebuhr described at length the many social and historical factors that together help to bind any religious community into a unity of self-identity.[6] Not merely doctrinal beliefs, but a great variety of social and historical elements flow together to define a church. Region and place, origin of people and thus ethnicity, race, language, social practices, and ethical convictions, all of these may be crucial factors for defining the identity of a church and its members. Beliefs may be simply one more factor added to the others; they are by no means an exclusive bond. Moreover, like the other social sources of denominationalism, beliefs too are generated socially and share in the arbitrariness that characterizes the other factors as well. They are historically conditioned.

The recognition of this arbitrariness of history is the other side of historical consciousness. We have already described how faith as a public act means joining a tradition that unites people in a community that extends backward into the past. But when one considers the past with which one is united, one begins to realize how different that past was from the present. Historical consciousness involves coming to the realization that everything that exists in time and history is individual and particular, something whose individuality and particularity were determined by the unique historical circumstances of time and place. The study of beliefs and doctrines of the past, especially in their genesis, uncovers both the uniqueness of the circumstances in which they came to be and the human and relative quality of the argument and reasoning that established these conclusions. Through an historical consciousness one appreciates that Christian beliefs, even though under the influence of an ultimate and absolute concern, are human productions, human works, human expressions of faith.

Social historical consciousness contains within itself an experience of relativity. All particular beliefs and doctrines that give interpretative expression to the object of faith are relative; they are not absolute, but historical, and the historical implies relativity. The reasons for this relativity are not mysterious but obvious. All theological statements, beliefs, interpretations of the object of faith, and doctrines were formulated by an historically specific group or community. They are formulated in historically specific terms, categories, languages of the day. These in turn depend on contemporary preunderstandings, suppositions, and world-views that are peculiar to a particular culture. Each belief or developed doctrine rests on some form of argument or inference that accepts this or that data as sufficient warrant for conclusions. In every case a certain question or issue that determines the point of view is at work in the formulation of the particular belief. These are all ingredients of relativity. All theological statements, beliefs, and doctrines are functions of these multiple factors and thus are what they are on the basis of these relations.

All beliefs and doctrines may be said to have a double relativity. They are relative in relation to the ultimate, transcendent, or absolute object which they interpret and seek to express. Here "relative" takes on the character of inadequacy as well. Since faith is not knowing in the ordinary sense, linguistic and conceptual representation cannot encompass its object. The very experience of the dynamics of faith reveals the transcendence of its object and the inadequacy of every representation of it to comprehend or circumscribe it. Beliefs are also relative to the culture in which they are generated in the manner just explained. This relativity characterizes all human expressions of belief, including those of scripture and what is called dogma. There is no absolute expression of faith in history, no doctrine of the past or the present with which one could identify faith in an absolute and adequate way.

To some this blunt characterization of religious beliefs as starkly relative may seem to be an overstatement of the case. It is true that there is much more to be said on the matter, and we shall return to the question of the object of faith when dealing with revelation. But many who share an historical consciousness will be more surprised that such attention has been given to the relativity of doctrine and belief. Indeed this hardly needs to be pointed out; historicity forms the very context for theology. It is not something that has to be argued; it is presupposed.

The problem of faith and belief concerns the other side of the equation: What can consistency and permanence of a faith that exists in history mean? Where and how are we to locate the sameness and consistency of Christian faith over time? These issues will be discussed in terms of revelation. For now, let us look at beliefs in relation to critical reason.

BELIEFS AND REASON

By the term reason I refer generally to the critical faculty of human intelligence. "Objective" critical reason is the reflective power of the mind to ask questions, to look for evidence, and to infer answers in the light of data.[7] It is critical insofar as it is reflective; it calls into question inadequate or tentative conclusions on the basis of lack of data or inconsistency and thus may appear negative. But its whole thrust is positive. It operates in the service of truth. By eliminating false leads it discovers new connections. By imaginative insight it comes to see new meaning. By creative inference it builds new understandings. By dialectical argument it approaches closer to the truth. Reason operates critically in any number of different ways. The study of history through critical reason has helped to generate the historical consciousness which has in turn made reason more humble. Perhaps today science represents the area in which critical reason is exercised in its most disciplined and methodical way and is yielding the most spectacular results. But critical reasoning is simply an aspect of the way all human beings come to know. This discussion of reason is then no more than a reprise of the issue of faith and knowing.

The question of faith and reason was pervasive in the history of Christian thought during the Enlightenment and subsequent nineteenth century. For at no time in the west did philosophers and scientists glory more in the power of human reason to judge for itself.[8] The Roman Catholic theology of faith formulated at Vatican I is set firmly within the context of this issue. Interestingly, the theology of faith today does not seem to be preoccupied with the question of the tension between faith and reason in the same way. The adoption of an anthropological starting point for the theology of faith, both existentially and historically, allows an integration of faith and reason without considerable difficulty. The point of considering the issue here is really constructive. Instead of viewing the tension between faith and reason, and between belief and reason, from a defensive posture, one should be able to view the interaction of faith, belief, and reason in constructive terms.

The writings of John Henry Newman on faith and reason are classic. In a way some of his basic distinctions dissolve many of the theoretical problems of relating faith and reason. Often faith and reason were conceived as opposed to each other, so that one had to choose between them. For Newman faith and reason are not opposed or separable activities of the human subject. Indeed, faith for Newman is a form of reasoning.[9] This makes complete sense as an initial premise. The action of the human spirit that is reflective freedom, in its dynamism for an object of ultimate commitment and loyalty, unfolds in and through the human mind. In some measure all human consciousness involves critical and questioning reason; at the deep level of its being *reflective*, it always bends back on itself. Although this dynamism of the human subject has other outlets and channels for its energy, still the basic freedom of the human spirit is always self-conscious and reasonable; the human person is always actively perceiving, thinking, weighing, and judging. Thus the dynamism of freedom that finally commits itself to this or that as its ultimate concern is an exercise of reason; it occurs not apart from reason, but thoroughly within the light of reason.

Having laid down this premise, Newman is now in a position to make some distinctions. Although the dynamism that leads to faith is a form of reason or reasoning, it is not limited to but is rather more than "pure" reason. Pure reason stands for a certain reduction or harnessing of the powers of reason to an "objective" and methodical process of inference on the basis of self-evident or empirical or proven data. The exercise of pure reason is the equivalent of step by step demonstration. The reasonable process that binds human freedom to its ultimate and transcendent object of concern transcends such a process of objective reasoning. The movement toward faith includes a whole host of other subjective dynamisms and responses which therefore are part of faith itself: within the context of reason, but over and above what has been called "pure" reason, faith includes moral openness, preference, bias, temperament, taste, latent presuppositions, conscious and antecedent expectations of probabilities, hopes, affective desires, emotional responses, appreciation of values, exposure to certain experiences, people and events. The kind of reasoning that faith involves Newman calls implicit reasoning as distinct from formal and explicit reasoning. Because of this self-transcending character of reason which is manifest in the dynamics of faith, one can say that faith has a dimension of autonomous validity that goes beyond any explicit exercise of objective reasoning. The implicit reasoning involved in coming to faith contributes reasons for the object of faith, but these reasons transcend the power of "pure" reason. Faith has its reasons which critical reason may not be able to supply.

Many other theologians have made moves analogous to those of Newman. For example, for Tillich too faith would be a form of reason. But one must make distinctions between kinds of reason. The quest for and the reception of revelation which is faith does not emerge out of objective technological reason. Rather a contemplative reason looks within its depths to find revealed within itself the ground of being. Or, changing the metaphor, Tillich speaks of ecstatic reason which stands out beyond itself and all finite beings to encounter the ground of being itself.[10] The basis of these considerations in every case lies in a concrete, existential and anthropological approach to faith as an integral human response to reality. Faith is not mere belief on the word of another; faith is not assent with no evidence; faith is not belief in what everyone knows is not true, that is, against the testimony of objective critical reason. Faith and reason are in no way antithetical. Reason is intrinsic to faith, even though the dynamics of faith exceed "pure reasoning"; and the dynamism toward faith is intrinsic to human reason.

But the relation between belief and reason is somewhat different. It has been shown that reason is intrinsic to faith; faith is not faith apart from reason. But this implies that the beliefs that are fashioned to express the object of faith are not immune from the questioning of critical "objective" reason. It is true that more goes into the production of beliefs than rational analysis. As was said we do not know the object of faith in an objectifiable way. The object of faith is "known" only insofar as it comes to bear on human life, and the fashioning of the expressions of belief depend as much upon human imagination as upon critical "objective" reasoning. But beliefs still must be coherent with what we do know through critical "objective" reason. Faith cannot be considered belief against reason. Therefore critical reason enters intrinsically into the interpretation of the object of faith and of the world in the light of the object of faith. Beliefs must always come under the scrutiny of critical reason.

Often the impact of critical reason upon the traditional beliefs of a community is considered negative, critical in a pejorative sense, hostile, and threatening to faith. Certainly critical reason has been and continues to be critical in this negative sense of some beliefs and doctrines. At times Newman seemed to think that the critical activity of reason is almost always negative and destructive.[11] The historicity of beliefs means that they have always been formulated on the basis of presuppositions, evidence, and arguments that were convincing at a particular time. If at a later time or in a different culture the presuppositions are no longer in place, the evidence no longer provides warrant, and the argument is no longer convincing, then neither a person nor a society can accept the

traditional doctrine in the same sense in which it was originally formulated. History abounds in examples of old beliefs either falling away or
being explicitly reformulated on the basis of new evidence provided by
critical reason.

The view that critical reason has a merely negative and destructive
relationship to the belief structure of the community rests on the confusion between faith and belief. But faith and belief are not the same.
Beliefs can, do, and should change in the course of the historical life of
the community. Yet despite changes in theological formulation, faith
retains a relative autonomy which has its foundation in a dynamism that
far transcends "pure" reason even while it includes it. /

Thus the interaction between belief and reason can and should be
construed in a positive and constructive light. Critical reason may be
destructive of past beliefs that no longer appear credible from the point
of view of what people know through science or other forms of critical
reasoning. But this same critical reasoning enters intrinsically into the
process of theology itself. Its task is to fashion new interpretations of
faith's object, to construct new expressions of faith, to establish new
formulations of belief. These new and critically reasoned reinterpretations actually enhance and strengthen faith, as well as give new force to
beliefs as bonds of the community.

In sum, although faith transcends reason, critically questioning
reason remains intrinsic to the dynamics of faith. It comes to bear most
directly on the interpretations of faith's object and the world in the light
of this transcendent object. These interpretations are contained in theological statement, belief, and doctrine. The interaction between beliefs
and critical reason inevitably involves a calling into question the historically relative conceptions that constitute any tradition. But this critical
dialogue between the interpretation of the object of faith, that is, beliefs, and the understanding of the world at any given time should on the
whole be viewed as a positive constructive interaction in the service of
faith itself.[12]

INTERPRETING BELIEFS AS EXPRESSIONS OF FAITH

It should be clear at this point that the beliefs of the Christian
community need to be continually reinterpreted. The task of theology
consists in this constructive reinterpretation. A first characterization of
the structure of this interpretation can be gleaned from the personal
and social historical nature and dynamics of faith. The following princi-

ples drawn from the theology of faith help to clarify how this reinterpretation is possible and why it is always needed.

First, the self- and world-transcending character of faith means that it shares a semi-autonomous identity in distinction from the expressions of its object which are called beliefs. History clearly demonstrates that beliefs can and do change. This is especially true when the words and formulas remain the same. When words, concepts, and propositions are received in new historical contexts their meaning and significance always change. But beneath the historical change Christians identify their faith with a community that stretches well back into the past. They recognize a communion with Christians living in other cultures with practices and systems of meaning different from their own. This communion can be determined by no single factor alone, not beliefs, not practices. It resides rather in a much more diffuse reality that may be called a way of life. In other words, despite differences in beliefs, Christians can recognize a unity of faith that transcends all the differences.[13]

Second, everything that has been said about beliefs points to the possibility and the necessity of their being consciously reinterpreted. Beliefs as interpretations of the object of faith arise out of the interpenetration of faith and knowledge of this world in an ordinary sense. Since knowledge of this world is historically conditioned and changing, conceptions of the past may lose their usefulness as expressions of faith in a later time. Doctrines formulated in the language of past eras may lose their intelligibility when the presuppositions, the issue to which a doctrine responds, the evidence, and the reasoning no longer appear applicable in a new intellectual culture. Formulations of belief, at that point, no longer open up subjectivity to the object of faith but begin to obscure it. They may continue to bind a community together, but the dynamics of the solidarity become pathological. Beliefs themselves become the object of faith, and human formulas begin to ensure security over against the world to which the Christian message is precisely addressed.

Third, then, critical reason can be considered the ally of faith by being the critic of beliefs that appear alien to what is known to be true or are unintelligible in any given culture or society. Critical reason more positively becomes the constructive agent of reinterpretation so that the formulas of belief come to bear on the community and on human society in an intelligible and credible way. There is no more reason to fear what used to be called rationalism in this formulation than there is to fear a fideism which equally betrays the message of Christian faith.[14] It will always be the case, however, that insofar as interpretation is theological, the ultimate ground for and object of interpretation must be transcendent.[15]

Theological reinterpretation is not easy. Part of the psychological security of faith lies in its attachment to the tradition of the beliefs of the community. Added to this is the radical corporate inertia of any community that spontaneously resists change. Thus the delicate task of theological reinterpretation must be characterized by open dialogue and interchange. The need for dialogic interchange can only increase in the future as the Christian church becomes more and more a truly world church. The demands of inculturation can only result in a greater pluralism of beliefs within world Christianity, so that only open dialogue, and not extrinsicist authority and discipline, will be able to hold the community together.

Theological reinterpretation cannot always be successful in retrieving a meaning from the past that is intelligible today. Every doctrine from the past cannot be salvaged. Some doctrinal positions, by being explained historically, will be explained away. A good example is the following proposition of Boniface VIII which has had a prominent role in the history of Christian doctrine: "Furthermore we declare, state and define that it is absolutely necessary for the salvation of all human beings that they submit to the Roman Pontiff." [16] No one can reasonably hold this doctrine today. But such statements as these cannot be dropped from our history as though they did not exist; they are part of the Christian tradition. Rather they should be explained as part of a past culture, and precisely determined by that culture historically. At best one can appreciate historically the motivations of faith that led to such doctrines.

In a later chapter we shall take up the question of theological reinterpretation directly in terms of the method of theology. But without anticipating that discussion one can still lay down some general principles for theological reinterpretation that flow directly from this consideration of the nature and dynamics of faith. Since theological statements of belief are expressions of religious faith in transcendence, the nature of this faith and its dynamic interaction with critical reason and society yield principles concerning the nature of theological assertions as such. In other words, the nature of faith is itself the first hermeneutical principle for interpreting the generic meaning of the beliefs which are expressions of faith. A consideration of three such principles will serve as a conclusion to the first part of this essay on the nature of theological assertion.

Beliefs as Principles of Action

Chapter one showed that faith far exceeds ordinary knowing; its object strictly speaking is transcendent. Faith consists in a kind of commitment that engages human responsiveness simultaneously at all sorts of different levels. As a fundamental option it fashions the kind of person anyone is by defining what a person lives for. For this reason the deepest locus of the faith of each one lies in his or her action. Faith is constituted in and by human action. The primal expression and manifestation of actual faith, therefore, is an action that transpires not uninformed by conscious intelligence but on a level far deeper than even personal self-reflection can go. The appearance of faith in the form of explicit, reflective, thematic, or conceptual expression, as in belief, is dependent upon and expressive of the commitment borne in action where faith is primarily constituted. Since beliefs are expressions of faith-as-action, when one focuses on the nature of beliefs, one must define them as principles of action, that is, faith's action.[17]

The recognition that theological assertions are principles of action rests on the analysis of what is entailed in the faith they express. This is much more than an analysis of the meaning of concepts through an appeal to perception or historical usage or other forms of objective evidence. The point here is not to minimize the concern for clarity of meaning in the analysis of theological conception. It is rather to insist that this whole structure of meaning is carried to a radically new level when language is used to express faith in a transcendent object. At issue here is not this or that meaning, but the very structure and dynamic of a strictly theological assertion.

For example, the affirmation that God is good has its ground in faith, that is, in the actual lives of people who experience and live out the committed conviction that the ultimate ground of being that supports their existence is personal and benevolent. The life lived in action constitutes that which is expressed in conceptual terms as "God" and "good." The meaning of "Jesus is Lord" simply cannot be reduced to what an historical and philological analysis, or any other kind of objective analysis, will yield. The primary and basal meaning emerges out of faith, namely, that people submit and attach themselves to Jesus with an ultimate commitment or infinite passion as the point where, or the person in and through whom, the power of God on whom they are absolutely dependent is mediated to them.[18]

Theological language therefore always has what can be called a moral substance.[19] This does not mean that theological assertions cannot also be analyzed for their sheer intelligibility and coherence on an objective level. But insofar as language is strictly theological, such analysis will never reach the substance of its theological meaning and truth. For such language is intrinsically an appeal to a response that transcends mere knowing in an ordinary manner. It has been generated by commitment and its naming of a transcendent object cannot but include an appeal to surrender and active loyalty.[20] Of course a division of labor between theology and theological ethics has characterized theological disciplines. But in the end this is an arbitrary and convenient separation which tends to eviscerate theological interpretation.[21] Intrinsic to all strictly theological language lies a normative appeal to responsible commitment and action. Failure to account for this rather fundamental dimension of beliefs and doctrines ignores the deeper inner structure of theological language and is hence inadequate.

A first conclusion, therefore, states that theological assertions are principles of human action. They have a deep moral substance. They emerge out of committed loyalty and action and express or seek to communicate such a faith-in-action. Doctrines and beliefs are for human living and must be interpreted in such a way that includes direction for human life.

The Mediation of Critical Social Reason

We have shown how knowing in the form of critical objective reasoning comes to bear on the formulation of theological statement and belief. Although faith transcends methodic reasoning, reason comes to bear directly on the interpretation of the object of faith, because reason is intrinsic to faith itself. It is generally recognized today that the discussion of faith or belief and reason in the past unfolded within the context of a too exalted and at the same time too limited a view of the power of human reason. The human mind exhibits many ways of knowing, and reason can be employed critically along the axes of many different methodologies and disciplines. Faith too was often narrowly identified with beliefs. With an expanded existential conception of faith, few people beyond fundamentalists should feel any threat to their faith from the natural sciences. On the level of beliefs, for example, the interpretation of the object of faith seems to have entered into a new partnership with the natural sciences. Signs of transcendence are appearing in the amazing new vistas opened up by the new science.

The case is different with critical sociological reason. More than in any other area the critical quality of objective reasoning, in both its negative and positive senses, comes to bear on the theological structure of belief through the social sciences.[22] Social sciences have demonstrated the historically conditioned quality of all human language and knowing, and hence their relativity. History and sociology have confirmed that every a priori and transcendentally mediated anthropology is inadequate in its abstractness; it fails to define the human as it is.

Political science and the sociology of knowledge have uncovered the ideological biases that are written into what are taken to be simple apprehensions of the obvious. In an age of historical consciousness and pluralism, as well as radical social disorder in the world, no area for the exercise of critical objective reason is more important today for theology than the social sciences.

The impact of society on knowing and thus the interpretation of the object of faith has direct bearing on faith itself. For no theological assertion, no doctrine or belief, can be free from social and ideological determinants. Ideology not only reflects action but doubles back again to channel and direct it. The term ideology points directly to the moral implications of understanding. Theological interpretation, therefore, must be in dialogue with critical social analysis and reasoning. Theological reinterpretation of beliefs should consciously attend to the need for deideologization, and for a reideologization of beliefs that are congruent with the moral demands of the transcendent object of faith.[23]

Beliefs and the Community's Relation to Society

Theological assertions are public. They arise out of a community of faith. They are never merely the statements of an individual, for they are engendered by a long tradition and are intended to be accepted within it. Theological beliefs represent a community: they are one of the institutional bonds that holds it together, and they are meant to portray and define it before the rest of society or the world. Thus, because beliefs express the faith of a community, they should represent the community's commitment and action in society and the world.

This conclusion may not be self-evident. Very often theological propositions are simply considered in terms of their intelligibility, and what they communicate about their object. From a logical standpoint this conclusion flows from simply placing the last two principles in conjunction with each other. Is this carrying logic too far? Not if the theology or belief structure of a community of faith is meant to define its faith-identity before the world. The real faith of a community too will lie in its corporate behavior or action in the world. Liberation theology has clearly brought home to us that, because faith lies in praxis, belief statements must reflect the praxis of the church. But the praxis of the church is *always* relevant and responsive to the problems of human beings in history and society. It is so even when it is thought not to be. The question, however, is this: How is it so responsive? What does the faith that is latent in church action say to the common concrete issues of our world today? To massive human suffering, to oppression, to dangerous overpopulation, to the extent of the human misery and death human beings inflict on other human beings socially, to the destruction of the earth itself, to the relation of this aggressive behavior against the planet to human social suffering?

The point, then, is that these issues cannot be isolated or separated off from the interpretation of the object of faith. They cannot simply be relegated to a discrete discipline called Christian social ethics. The sociology of knowledge has shown how bias and class interests come to bear on every level of understanding. The interpretation of basic beliefs has to attend to the implications and consequences of these beliefs in conjunction with the question of what the church's faith-action should be in the social world. In the face of the massive social evils of the world today, the intelligibility itself of theological assertion is at stake. Theological assertions deal with a transcendence that is available only through faith. But the interpretation of that faith must include the dimension of loyalty in action to the cause that is attached to that transcendence. What is God's cause in the world? One cannot avoid this question of where belief directs faithful community action. Theological statements therefore have to be made intelligible in terms of the public social praxis of a community in the situation of worldwide social suffering. If interpretation does not respond to this issue, neither will it supply human life with comprehensive unity and meaning which faith purports to give.[24]

These conclusions represent no more than very general principles stemming from only a first probe into the nature of theology, theological interpretation, and theological statement based on a consideration of faith. What has been said here has been restricted to a purely formal consideration of faith which prescinds almost entirely from the content of the object of faith. The discussion of revelation and specifically Christian revelation will move the investigation further along.

II

REVELATION

Chapter Three

THE STRUCTURE OF REVELATION

We move now to the topic of revelation. The consideration of faith has shown how intimately revelation and faith are interconnected with each other. Faith, insofar as it is genuinely religious and attaches itself to an object that is transcendently ultimate, must have its object revealed to it. Faith is not a matter of knowing in an ordinary sense. Rather faith is faith in what is revealed, and that which is revealed is an object of faith. Faith and revelation, then, are mutually or reciprocally related to each other. As fundamental categories they are correlative and mutually define each other.

The mutual relationship between faith and revelation demands that there be a consistency in the way the two phenomena are understood. The theologies of faith and revelation should correspond with each other. In the analysis of faith we assumed a concrete historical and existential anthropological point of departure. Correspondingly we shall analyze revelation as a common human experience that is an integral part of the human phenomenon of religious faith. But it is impossible to retain an anthropocentric perspective when dealing with revelation. For the phenomenon of faith itself includes a dimension of being acted upon from outside the self and, in authentic religious faith, "from above." The transcendent object of faith is "given" to faith, breaks in upon it, manifests itself, and draws forth the human subject out of itself in a conscious commitment to something other than itself.

The interconnectedness of the human response of faith with its revealed object makes an initial definition of the meaning of the term revelation difficult. It will have to be clarified in the course of the analysis. But the following preliminary characterization of the term can serve as a guide for the discussion and its point of view: revelation means the unveiling and manifestation of the object of faith to human consciousness. It is first of all a dynamic human process. But within this human process and experience a certain primacy lies with the action of

51

the object being revealed upon the self. Thus in Christian theology one speaks of God revealing God's self. Revelation in a dynamic sense is the object of revelation making itself "known" in faith.[1] But this becoming known cannot be conceived apart from the reception and response of the person in faith. The object that is revealed can only be revealed when the communication is actualized by response. Revelation cannot be clearly separated from human inquiry and discovery. The result is that while revelation has an objective dimension, it can never be separated from the dynamic human dimension of response. If the object of revelation is never recognized or responded to, it is difficult to speak of a process of revelation having occurred.

In this chapter I will discuss what may be called a general theory of revelation. Such a theory, first of all, will try to account for revelation as a common human phenomenon corresponding to faith. Second, it will focus attention on a common structure of revelation. To speak of such a universal structure obviously entails a treatment of revelation in the most general of terms. Then, in the light of this general theory of revelation, chapter four will take up the question of Christian revelation and the mutual relation between it and Christian theology.

Finally, as a last prenote, one should bear in mind the logic motivating this discussion of revelation. Since the content of faith, and hence the content of theological assertion, has its source in revelation, the whole discipline of theology tacitly assumes or explicitly rests on some view of this phenomenon. It follows that the generic meaning of what theology is and the intentionality of theological assertion itself should be further illumined by an explanation of the structure and dynamics of revelation.

The Modern Problem of Revelation

Any number of problems must be reckoned with when one takes up the theology of revelation from an apologetic point of view.[2] For example, in a modern secular world the whole idea of revelation appears as at best a weak concept. One can judge that for oneself. If a person responds to the question "How do you know that?" with the statement, "It was revealed to me," one is naturally suspicious. Of course a whole community with a long tradition of revelation has more credibility. But a secular age that looks for evidence in a situation of historical pluralism about ultimate concerns is also bound to be somewhat skeptical about notions of revelation.

In characterizing the modern problem of revelation, I do not maintain that what follows is the only problem with which a theology of revelation must contend. Rather I shall simply focus on two questions that arose in the course of the Enlightenment and subsequently in the nineteenth century. These questions may be regarded as still relevant to Christian theology; they still come to bear on Christian experience.

The first question arose out of the eighteenth century's quest for human autonomy in understanding and its glorification of human reason. When these currents of thought were brought to bear on theology, they seemed to undermine the Christian view of a privileged and final revelation. The problem may have been first raised by a hostile and anti-authoritarian rationalism, but it quickly became a question that theology itself had to address. How can a particular and historically conditioned revelation be the vehicle of salvation for the whole human race? Not only revelation, but also a conception of God is involved in the question. It presumes that God is the God of all, who wills the salvation of all, and acts in a just and egalitarian manner. Can such a God condition salvation on the acceptance of a revelation that is not available to all but only a portion of the human race?

This fundamental question can be seen at work in Immanuel Kant's view of revelation.[3] Kant recognized the validity or truth of Christian revelation. But this positive historical revelation through Jesus was required because of sin, human blindness, and lack of development. The essence of religion and revelation was mediated through reason and was theoretically available to all. In fact the content of Christian revelation merely anticipated and taught what pure religion, mediated through reason, could and would over the long term discover for itself. Whether or not one considers Kant's reconstruction adequate to meet the dilemma, the question itself is a telling one. It does not seem to be possible to conceive of God's historical revelation in Jesus as having an exclusive bearing upon final salvation. Or, if one does, one must also open up the conception of revelation so that it becomes understood as a process that is universally accessible.

The second question regarding revelation is associated with the deepening of historical consciousness during the course of the nineteenth century. In a way the dilemma which arose with the experience of historicity cuts against the grain of the first issue. When one assumes an historical perspective in viewing the human race, what one finds beyond the Christian sphere is not a lack of revelation, but a whole host of different revelations and their traditions. The natural tendency of Christian theologians was to view these revelations as inferior and preliminary to Christian revelation which, in an evolutionary view of things, was the highest and, if not the absolute, at least the final and normative revelation. But by the beginning of the twentieth century historical consciousness had sunk deeper and some Christian theologians simply accepted in principle an egalitarian pluralism of revelations.[4]

The dilemma that historical consciousness has created for a theology of revelation was not accepted in the beginning of this century. In fact there was a strong reaction against it. But there is a deep issue here that can be and is more readily appreciated today. For on the one hand not only theologians but also many Christians generally have come to recognize and appreciate other religious traditions, to value them, and to consider them valid in their own right.[5] We are aware of the relativity of cultures and the fittingness of other religions to these cultures. In effect many theologians and others have accepted in principle a pluralism of many revelations. But this idea has not yet been integrated with the Christian theology of a singular revelation. A completely open attitude to all revelations, which are precisely not all the same, does not sit well with the inner logic and dynamics of a desire for ultimate truth. If all revelations are equally valid, it seems hard to imagine how we have any revelation at all.

THE STRUCTURE OF REVELATION

The two questions, or problems, or dilemmas for a theology of revelation that have just been outlined did not emerge all at once. What I have formulated is an interpretation of an inner logic that has come to the surface over a long period of time. The issues are as real as they are profound; they cannot be dismissed; they have to be dealt with. And in dealing with them the theology of revelation has in turn been deeply affected and changed. So much is this the case, that one can understand the very structure of revelation in correlation with these issues. This can be seen in the shift that each of these problems necessitates.

The first dilemma concerned the impossibility of a single historical revelation mediating God's salvific communication universally. Faced with this problem theologians or philosophers of religion spoke of revelation through nature or rational religion as the only way God could deal with all human beings equally for their salvation. But what exactly is the cause of the dilemma in the first place? The precise problem really lies in an objectivist understanding of revelation. When revelation is identified with an objective content once and for all given in history, the scope of that particular revelation cannot be universally operative.

By an objectivist concept of revelation I mean equating revelation with some particular objective form or expression of it. For example, biblical fundamentalism tends to equate the process of revelation with inspiration, and then equates revelation itself with the scriptures. Scripture is revelation; its words are God's words; revelation is an objective form of knowledge of and about God. Dogmatic fundamentalism which tends to equate doctrines or dogmas with revelation is another form of the same objectivist understanding. Revelation is understood as objective knowledge of God contained in the teachings of scripture, creed, and church. Revelation is closely tied with propositions which in their objective word-forms are that which has been revealed. In the end revelation is so exclusively identified with the particular objective historical forms that most of the human race is excluded from participation in it.[6]

In response to the dilemma caused by an objectivist understanding of revelation, a shift occurred during the nineteenth century to a subjective or existential understanding of revelation. One could almost define modern theology on the basis of this change. Although this oversimplifies things, it may be said that modern theology began to understand revelation as existential experience. A deeper and more elementary process than its objective expressions, revelation consisted in a dynamic process within human religious experience. As such revelation could be recognized as a common phenomenon of human life and as universal. With this move the basis of theology, revelation, shifted from an exclusive focus on the objective forms of Christian revelation to the deeper level of subjective experience that lay behind or beneath them.[7] This conception of revelation as existential experience of transcendence allowed one to consider revelation as occurring outside the Christian sphere and thus had the potential for recognizing the universal and egalitarian nature of God's saving will.

The general acceptance of the arena of human experience and subjectivity as the matrix for unfolding a theology of revelation has itself met with severe criticism, especially during the first half of the twentieth century. Two elements of this reaction have particular bearing on how revelation may be understood today. First, it has been generally held that the move to an experiential notion of revelation, particularly within liberal theology, resulted in a shift away from the object of revelation which is "given to" experience and in a tendency to reduce the object of theology to human experience itself. In H. Richard Niebuhr's expression of this criticism, an anthropological starting point yielded to an anthropocentrism that failed to acknowledge the realism of the impact of transcendence upon the subject.[8] An adequate view of revelation should take account of what in the analysis of faith was called the passive and receptive quality of religious experience under the influence of an action upon the self "from above."

Second, the historicity of revelation has asserted itself as an implied criticism of any merely subjective view of revelation. Since all revelation occurs in history, it is necessarily attached to particular historical circumstances and forms. Revelation cannot be understood in terms of an abstract subjectivity that is in turn detached from concrete history. This critique will have a direct bearing on the theory of revelation presented here. One cannot today view revelation merely as a diffuse subjective experience that is the same in each person, community, culture, or time in history. Although Kant did have a basic historical consciousness, which is illustrated in his work on religion, he did not realize the extent to which reason itself is historically conditioned. The historicist perspective on revelation has demonstrated that there is no "pure" common historical religious experience. Every historical experience of revelation is related to the particularities of situation and circumstance and in this sense objective. It follows that revelation is inevitably pluralistic.

To sum up, the two questions concerning the nature of revelation that arose with modernity caused some fundamental readjustments in the theological conception of revelation. The first made necessary a turn to the subject, to anthropology, to common human experience as the sphere for investigating the phenomenon of revelation. One must begin the study of revelation by assuming that revelation could be a common and universal form of religious experience. The second experience, that of the obvious pluralism and historicity of revelation, seemed to hold the subjective paradigm in check. Revelation is always historically objective at the same time; it can only exist concretely in particular, objective, and historically mediated forms. These two parameters, inseparable and held together in tension with each other, account for what may be called the fundamental structure of revelation. In what follows we shall investigate each of these two poles in turn: its universal and subjective character on the one hand, and its historical mediation on the other.

The Universality of Revelation

We begin by presenting a theory of the universality of revelation. The characterization of this position as a theory means that it is a constructive view that tries to account for revelation in the light of the seeming injustice that revelation be an historically exclusive phenomenon. The theory is also peculiarly Christian and theological. In the course of this discussion I will point out in what measure this theory rests on purely theological assumptions which in turn are only made available to the Christian imagination by revelation itself. In the interest of clarity, I shall present the theory of the universality of God's revelation in a series of reflections which constitute its chief building blocks.[9]

Transcendental Openness to God

The first basis for a general theory of revelation as a universal phenomenon lies in what was already discussed in the theology of faith, namely, the transcendental openness of human freedom to being itself. Transcendental here means universal. The unlimited self-transcending of human existence and a reaching out for ultimate and permanent being characterize all human subjectivity. This first premise is derived from a phenomenological or descriptive and transcendental analysis of human action itself. Whether or not any single human being becomes explicitly cognizant of this dynamism, it is operative as a condition, inner law, and a priori deep dimension of the human actions of knowing, willing, striving, and achieving. One can argue that this inner and necessary drive contains an implicit demand that there be a transcendent and absolute object that corresponds to this urgent and inner impulse toward ultimacy.

The Postulate of Grace

In response to the restless quest of human freedom in action, Christian theologians postulate the grace of God. I say postulate here in order to underline the presuppositions and character of the analysis which follows. It is, as it were, purely theological. It rests on faith and a particular system of belief that interprets the object of faith. Moreover the whole analysis presupposes the revelation whose character it seeks to explain. In relation to the first premise of a transcendental openness to God, which can be substantiated by transcendental analysis, what follows represents a transition, a jump, in terms of evidence. That God is, that God is personal and universally gracious, are not assertions that are based on knowing in an ordinary sense and cannot be demonstrated or verified in any objective way.[10] The apologetic value of what follows, then, does not consist in a mediation of a position that will be convincing on critical rational grounds alone. Rather the analysis seeks a coherence of meaning within the context of a belief-system that itself rests on a faith commitment to a revealed object. The point is not to argue to revelation, but to understand revelation theologically as a universal subjective phenomenon.

Within the context of an experience of revelation grace signifies the love of a personal God for human beings. God is personal, and, as Johannine literature continually asserts, God is love. This love reaches out and engages human existence for its salvation. This is the first meaning of God's graciousness and grace.

The Universality of Grace

Within the context of Christian faith and revelation Karl Rahner has provided a persuasive argument for the universality of God's grace. The premise of the argument, once again, is purely theological and rests on a certain experience of God and God's love. This experience indicates that the love of God is so universal that it intends the salvation of all human beings.[11] God is experienced in the Christian community as the God of all; God is simply God. And this personal Creator-God loves not only God's creation as a whole but each thing in it as God's own. In respect to human beings, who are all subjects and personal, this love comes as a personal love fitting its human object: personal love, from freedom to freedom. This love reaches out in an egalitarian way to all of God's people: God's loving intent is the salvation of all.

It is impossible, Rahner argues further, to conceive of God's love as a will and desire for human salvation without at the same time imagining its efficacy.[12] The loving will of God cannot merely be a wishful thinking, a mere intention that remains untranslated into act and effectiveness. The idea of God's universal saving will, then, necessarily implies thinking about what this love does to human existence, how it affects human beings, and how a response to it might be conceived as universally operative in human life. This requires a more exact formulation of God's grace.

The Presence of God to Human Existence

One way of depicting the real presence and activity of God's love in human life is provided by the language of God as Spirit. This term is operative throughout the Jewish writings and becomes a major category in the New Testament. In the metaphor, Spirit is like the breath of the wind; although invisible its presence is energy, a principle of life, a creative power and force that inspires to activity beyond the ordinary powers of human beings.[13] God as Spirit is God present and active in God's creation, as it were, beyond the immanent sphere of the Godhead itself. God as Spirit, of course, is not other than God's self. God as Spirit is simply God, but God as experienced present to and personally impacting the world, especially the world of human life.

God's love, God's grace, symbolized as God as Spirit, can all be translated into the phrase, God's Presence.[14] This theological interpretation of God as Spirit places a particular stress on God's Presence as personal Presence. Over and above God's creative activity, God as Spirit points to God as personal being who is present to human beings. In a second movement, so to speak, God who has established human freedom in existence also communicates freely God's own self to humankind.[15] Besides being transcendent power, God is also immanent to human personhood and freedom. This presence of God is not reducible to an impersonal creative power that holds human existence in being. God's Presence is precisely the presence of God's own self which actively summons human freedom out of itself in a self-transcending movement toward God.

God's Presence as Revelatory

Are there any grounds for correlating the postulate of God's Presence to human existence and revelation? Does such a theological construction correspond to anything in human experience? It was said that for revelation to be revelation, there must be some conscious response on the part of human beings. How does God's Presence enter into human subjectivity as consciousness of God?

One must understand the manifestations of God's universal Presence to human existence as occurring within the deepest dimensions of human subjectivity. God's Presence to human freedom and action cannot be conceived in terms of the influence of an inner-worldly object. God's Presence is precisely God as Spirit being present to the unfolding of the dynamics of human freedom. God's Presence is merged with and operates within the self-transcending impulse of human freedom itself. There is no way for human beings to analyze and distinguish within the experience of the self-transcending movement of one's own freedom that which is self from that which is the influence of God's Presence. At this level God's personal Presence is merged with and indistinguishable from the dynamics of the self-transcendence of freedom itself.[16]

Thus God's Presence is presence to and operation within human subjectivity. And as such it is conscious. This consciousness, however, is not the explicit and objective consciousness of an object. Rather it is only manifest as the impulse itself toward transcendence and ultimacy in being. This consciousness can become self-consciousness, a reflective awareness and a conscious searching for that which will satisfy the inner desire for permanent being. But whether or not human beings explicitly assume that search, the dynamism is at work within human freedom in a really conscious but unreflected and unthematic way.

The revelatory Presence of God within human freedom itself may be seen to operate as an horizon of all human action. God's Presence constitutes the ontic or existential context of the operation of human freedom itself. God's Presence sets up an a priori horizon of all the concrete and historically conditioned horizons in which each human being operates or acts.[17] This language of horizon is metaphorical, but it is not complicated. An horizon forms a backdrop, a prior context, against or within which any given object can be perceived. So too, God's Presence is a prior given, a personal prior Presence at work in all human knowing, willing, and acting. An horizon is simply the fundamental condition of being in which all human beings exist. In plain language, if God is, as Christians say, a lover of all human beings, and if this love entails God's personally being present to and operative within each human subject, then that moving influence has an effect on human subjectivity. And what transpires in free human subjectivity is conscious, whether or not it becomes a theme of one's explicit reflection.

Revelation as a Universal Subjective Phenomenon

The revealing activity of God therefore is universal. Christians experience by a faith mediated by Jesus a God who is in loving contact with human beings. But the very force of that revelation means that God's loving contact with human beings is not limited by the historical mediation of Jesus. The activity of such a God is operative subjectively in all and available to every human consciousness. Revelation is thus as common a human phenomenon as is faith itself; authentic religious faith is correlative to the universal and revealing Presence of God to human subjectivity. Revelation as a consciousness of God's Presence is available to all.

The dynamics of this revelation can be described in more concrete terms. Whenever and wherever there is experience of self-transcendence, or of an ultimacy that is genuinely ultimate, or of what is absolutely good and valuable and true beyond the self, whenever one reaches for what is truly transcendent, this becomes a vehicle of experiencing and responding to the personal Presence that Christians call God. It is God who draws human freedom precisely out of and beyond itself. In the subjectivity of each and all, or through the conscious freedom of every person, the Presence of God negotiates the possibility, likelihood, and probability that all human beings will respond to that Presence. This means that God will be revealed to them. This is especially true in the religious communities and traditions of the world where God has become objectively symbolized. The very basis of these religious traditions is this postulated structure. Although the experience of transcendence is always conscious and involves a contact with God, this contact with God is not necessarily construed as such. God may remain anonymous and that which is experienced may be given another name. But the theory suggests that God is present to and at work in every genuine experience of self-transcendence.

The conclusion implied by this theory is that theology at this point should accept the critique of the Enlightenment. God does deal with all human beings equally through a common or universal structure of human subjectivity. That common structure, however, is not pure reason; revelation is not "natural" or "general" revelation. The structure is the openness of human freedom for transcendence and a dynamism toward it, on the one hand, and its being met by a universal personal Presence of God called Spirit or grace, on the other. But this also means the breakdown of the primacy of an objective theory of revelation and a triumph of human subjectivity as the place where God is encountered and revealed. As Dulles has remarked, considering revelation in relation to other religions, in the broader context of the whole history of the interaction between God and human beings, has provided the clue to the essential nature of revelation itself.[18]

THE HISTORICAL MEDIATION OF REVELATION

The second element of the structure of revelation seems to run counter to the first. One does not witness a common revelation in history, but a pluralism of many really different conceptions of transcendence. The universal Presence of God can never be grasped in any pure form; it is always historically mediated to human consciousness. The reasons for this can be explained in the considerations which follow.[19]

Human Consciousness as Bound to the World

Let us begin with an axiom that is fundamental to epistemology. All human consciousness is tied to the physical world and to the data of the senses. This view has a tradition that can be related back to Aquinas and through him to Aristotle. It is a position highly favored in our scientific-minded and positivistic age. However this boundedness to the sensible world does not mean that human knowing cannot transcend sensible data; human knowing exceeds empirical data in myriad ways. But knowing in every form is always linked to and determined by the external world. For the human spirit or freedom is intrinsically embodied; human existence is spiritual freedom in matter. Thus it becomes unimaginable that, even in its self-transcendence, human consciousness could escape its being-in-the-world in its knowing or in any of its other actions.

This being bound to the physical world accounts for the historicity of all human action. For the concrete world always consists in a specific social and historical situation. All human knowing is influenced and in some measure determined by particular sense data, a specific social situation, a definite language system, as well as other structures that shape the particular space and time of conscious human action. When human action is conceived as reaction, as always consisting insofar as it is conscious in response to action upon it, the role of the particular world in shaping human consciousness falls into place. There may be a universally common structure or pattern of the action of human freedom and reflection, but it always becomes actualized in the relative historical ways the surrounding world dictates.

Mediated Transcendence

This fundamental anthropological conception concerning all human consciousness and action has a direct bearing on religious consciousness and revelation. It implies that all human consciousness of transcendence, all revelation, is and must be historically mediated. It must be channelled through some finite historical medium, focus of attention, or vehicle for the imagination. The content of the experience of revelation is always influenced by a finite and historically conditioned medium.

The idea of a medium at this point is deliberately very general. A medium could consist in a sacred stone, tree, or mountain where the gods live. A medium could be a sacred event of history or a person whose life and teaching communicate transcendent ideas and values. A book of writings could be a religious medium. Even an experience of nature itself, as a whole so to speak, can become a medium that elicits a religious experience of transcendence. A medium consists in any finite piece of this-worldly and historical reality through which people's conception of transcendence has been determined.[20]

This theory of the mediated character of all religious experience provides an alternative to both a rationalist and a mystical explanation of religion. In the end there can be no universal power of reason to un-

cover the shape of transcendent reality because reason itself is historically conditioned. One cannot reason without a conceptual content that
is historically mediated. And what may appear in the testimony of mys-
tics as direct contact and union with the divine can be seen upon reflection to be a kind of "mediated immediacy." For that which is encountered either lacks all shape, form, and identifiability, and hence defies an
ability to assign it any content at all, or it is recognizable by virtue of a
mediated reflection.[21]

This analysis of mystical experience enables one to pinpoint the
precise role and function of a medium in religious experience generally.
For in a way all religious experience can be characterized as mystical.
The point here is not to deny the a priori religious dimension of human
subjectivity itself, nor to overlook the Presence of God to human experience that was considered in the last section. In the analysis of faith we
saw that the dynamic of human freedom itself contains a reaching out
toward absolute self-transcendence in being. Consequently human subjectivity contains within itself a dynamism that can account for experiences and feelings of transcendence. Moreover the theology of grace
exhibited here implies that God is present to these experiences and
human beings are conscious of that Presence at least unreflectively. But
such a priori experiences are not thematic or clear. For example, the
experiences described by Rudolf Otto as a sense of tremendous power
and fascinating mystery remain diffuse and unspecified.[22] The role of a
medium, therefore, is to specify the object of religious experience. A
medium mediates content and makes revelation the revelation of this or
that conception of transcendent reality, or of transcendent reality in this
or that way. A medium provides categories and predicates that identify
the revealed object or revealing power. Without such a mediated revelation there can be no religion in a social sense, no community, and no
tradition.[23]

The Historicity of Revelation

The mediated character of all revelation explains or really defines
its historical nature. All revelation is historical. This means that it is
necessarily mediated by particular historical conditions and events that
make up the being-in-the-world of any particular group. In a way this
obvious conclusion does not need the extended explanation that has
been proposed to back it up. When one looks at positive historical
religion as a social phenomenon, its being historically conditioned is
almost immediately evident. But the point has to do with the structure of
revelation itself, even the revelation received by some unimaginable

solitary figure. Human consciousness of transcendence in any focused or thematic form is always also a product of historical mediation.

The relevance of this conclusion about revelation may be measured against the error implied in some categories that have been operative in the theology of revelation. For example, this thesis contradicts the Enlightenment bias toward the power of reason, as well as its view that the way God deals with human beings is through pure reason or through a natural revelation that is common to all. The historicist perspective on revelation shows that there is no such thing as a general revelation in which all people share. The only way God deals with human beings is through the finite media of the world and the contingencies of history. All that exists in history is special revelation, or, more accurately, specific and particular revelations. Revelation is a common human phenomenon, but it can only be received in particular, concrete, specific, finite, and relative historical forms.

THE DYNAMICS OF REVELATION

We can conclude this first discussion of the general structure of revelation by examining how these two dimensions relate to each other. We can also draw out some of the consequences that flow from this theory of revelation.

The first thing that needs to be stressed in this view of revelation is that revelation has a single basic structure. To put this in another way, we have not been speaking here of two kinds of revelation, but of revelation as such which has distinct dimensions interacting with each other. These two elements are intrinsic to each other; neither exists without the other. The two dimensions have been uncovered by different methodological approaches. The perspective of a transcendental analysis, combined with a strictly theological premise, opens up the common anthropological basis for revelation. A social historicist perspective yields the mediated and historical quality of revelation. The universal or transcendental dimension of revelation stems from the common human dynamism toward a transcendent reality which is met by God's Presence. The particularity of all revelation stems from this very same structure's being bound to the concrete world and its historicity.[24]

At the risk of belaboring the point, it is important to underline the fact that talk about revelation will remain ambiguous if this differentiated structure is not continually borne in mind. All revelation is categorical because it relates back to historical media that concretize, categorize, and objectify the content of the revelatory experience. But at the same time particular revelations are manifestations of a common human dynamic in which Christian theology sees God's Presence at work. Transcendental and particular revelation are distinct categories, but they do not refer to distinct phenomena, but dimensions of a potentially universal human experience.[25]

It follows that revelation is a common and not a rare aspect of human existence. It is as common and real as the many traditions of religious experience. Surely, private, individual religious experience can be genuinely revelatory, but common sense dictates that there are too many dangers of illusion to count them as such. The case is entirely different with the traditions of religious communities that continue to nourish their adherents with transcendent objects for faith. In principle all religious traditions are based upon some real contact with God that in turn has as its source God's initiative. On that basis one should consider the religions of this world valid, lawful, God-given, and revealed by God's Presence to their adherents.[26]

This theory of revelation, then, provides grounds for the dialogue with other religions from a Christian perspective. More forcefully, this theory impels and demands it. At bottom other religions are to be trusted. Of course all religions, including Christianity, can take on demonic, fanatical, and imperialistic qualities. Human beings can distort the contact with God involved in a revelation; no system of beliefs is adequate to God's Presence. But beneath the distortions that inevitably characterize the media of revelation, one should look toward the fundamentally transcendent values and ideals of any tradition. This trust in the fundamental validity of the revelation underlying any other religion is not arbitrarily asserted from a Christian perspective. It is rather grounded in Christian revelation itself through the notions of God's love, grace, and universal Presence.

With this theory of revelation what may be called the problem of revelation today is radically shifted from the way it was conceived in the past. The nature of the problem can be stated in terms of a tensive relationship between the one and the many. At bottom, in this theory of revelation, revelation is radically one. It consists in God being ever present in personal self-communication with the history of human freedom. God is really present to and enters into real dialogue with human beings. But this one revelation is pluriform; it also is many revelations in history. The problem then is not that of the possibility of revelation, nor of the absence of revelation; the problem is the many manifestations of it.

The pluralism of revelations, however, is not a scandal in this view. Quite on the contrary, the many different traditions of revelation can be read as a confirmation of the theological postulate that God is present to all human beings in history. Far from undermining Christian revelation, the pluralism of religions tends to support the core of its content. Thus one should expect that the universal Presence of God to human beings in history be refracted into different revelations by particular historical and cultural media. The solution to the problem of the pluralism of revelations, then, is dialogue. It is not historically likely, however, that this historical pluralism will ever be overcome in history. Pluralism is historically necessary. Thus what has just been called the solution to revelational pluralism does not lead to its resolution. The solution consists in the dialogue itself, a dialogue that will not end, but which seeks mutual understanding and trust but not uniformity.

In this theory of revelation, involving a universal Presence of God in dialogue with historical freedom, revelation must be viewed as an ongoing existential and historical reality. We shall speak of a very special sense in which Christian revelation might be said to be closed in the next chapter. But the dominant and characteristic mark of revelation lies in its continued changing life in history. The problem for understanding Christian revelation does not lie in the question "How can it develop?" but in the question "How can one determine sameness and continuity in the history of Christian revelation?" The presupposition involved in this theory of revelation is that it changes. This is so because revelation in its primary sense consists in a human, existential, and historically living dialogue with God's Presence. Because all revelation is experiential and historical, it will always interact with new experiences through new media in new historical situations.

Finally, the tension between the subjective and the objective aspects of revelation correspond with these same dimensions in the theology of faith with its distinction between faith and beliefs. These two aspects, the Presence of God to human subjectivity and its mediation to consciousness by the data of the historical world, bear a definite relationship to each other. Of the two the most significant is the existentially lived contact and response to the Presence of God. As in the distinction between faith and beliefs, the existential encounter with God's Presence constitutes the central and commanding aspect of revelation.

It would be too strong to call the objective media and manifestations of revelation secondary within the dynamics of revelation. For media are precisely media of the reflective awareness of God in human life and thus the channels of human encounter with God. They are intrinsically essential to revelation; there can be no revelation without them; rightly or wrongly, more or less adequately, they mediate the very content of God revealing. They distinguish this revelation from that revelation and are part of the very conscious response to God's Presence. But they are not the Presence of God in human subjectivity, nor are they the subjective response to God's Presence, but precisely the media of that response. Thus in interpreting the content of revelation one must be careful not to identify revelation either with the medium that mediates God's Presence or with the objective interpretations of God to which the media give rise. This caution can even be applied in the case of Jesus. Because of a lack of differentiation between God's Presence and its historical medium, revelation became so identified with Jesus' person that the church was led to believe there was no revelation outside of Jesus. It failed to see through the medium to the universal loving Presence of God that is revealed in him.

This general theory of revelation which is the source of all religious affirmations, not only of Christians but of all religionists, obviously contains principles for understanding the structure and meaning of religious assertion itself. These principles parallel those which were arrived at in the analysis of faith. However, we shall delay drawing them forward until after a further discussion of the epistemology of revelation exemplified in specifically Christian revelation.

Chapter Four

REVELATION AND THEOLOGY

In the last chapter the discussion focused on what may be called a general theory of revelation. Although this theory is Christian, because its premise is a concept of God's Presence to all human beings which is derived from Christian revelation itself, still the scope of the position reaches out to revelation as such. With this chapter the focus shifts to a consideration of Christian revelation itself. Although I use the general term revelation, the imagination and intentionality is always directed toward specifically Christian revelation.

The goal of the discussion that follows is to try to understand the phenomenon of revelation in a more detailed analytic way. We shall try to distinguish elements within the process of revelation itself. More pointedly, in relation to the project of this whole essay, we shall try to define the distinction of revelation from theology, theological beliefs, and doctrines, and the positive relationship of revelation to these phenomena. In the discussion of faith it was said that the object of religious faith is "given" to faith by revelation. This revealed object cannot be known in the ordinary sense of the word because the object of faith is strictly transcendent. Yet faith has a cognitive dimension, and people become aware of what has been revealed in such a way that they "know" the object of faith and affirm its reality outside themselves. What does the Christian "know" in or through revelation? And how is it "known?"

The object of this chapter, then, is to establish some rudimentary distinctions for an epistemology of revelation.[1] The direct bearing of this upon theology and theological assertion is evident, since revelation is the source of Christian theology. The discussion will unfold in the following way. The first two sections will describe specifically Christian revelation as an experience of God that is mediated by the historical event of Jesus. Taking that experience as a whole, it may be characterized as an encounter with God. The third section of the chapter will try to distinguish elements within this experience; it is not undifferentiated.

Finally, in the light of these distinctions the last three sections will make some further determinations about the nature of theology on the basis of its dependence on revelation.

CHRISTIAN REVELATION AS EXPERIENCE AND JESUS AS ITS MEDIUM

We begin by situating the understanding of Christian revelation within the general theory. Christian revelation too is a subjective existential phenomenon, one whose central historical medium is the event of the life and death of Jesus.

It was said at the outset of chapter three that the word "revelation" is ambiguous. It can be taken and is often used in an objective sense to refer to the content of faith. The objects of faith are revelations; this truth has been revealed and thus is revelation. But this objective sense of the term is really derivative and in the long run causes confusion. In its primary sense revelation refers to the process of God revealing. This revealing occurs in human consciousness. If it did not occur in human consciousness, there would be no revelation. For revelation to be revelation, there must be communication, and this requires human awareness and response.[2]

Revelation, then, is first of all a form of human consciousness. Revelation is human experience and not other than human experience because it is the experience of human beings. The revelation that is "God revealing" becomes as it were fully revelation when it is received by concrete human beings subjectively and existentially. One could also say that revelation occurs *in* human experience, thus emphasizing the initiative of the revealer. This is extremely important, for the idea that revelation is an existential human experience should not be construed to mean revelation is "merely" subjective. Indeed one should stress God's initiative and the reality of what is revealed to human experience in any account of revelation. But even the proposition that revelation occurs *in* human experience means reductively that the dynamic process of revelation is a form of human experience.

The subjective character of revelation can be clarified by comparing it to the structure of faith. No faith exists without an object, and the object of religious faith is given by revelation. Faith and revelation are thus one; they are materially united in one consciousness. Revelation is received by faith, and faith responds to revelation. There is thus a strict parallelism between the analyses of faith and revelation. But one can also distinguish between the faith and the revelation that together constitute one experience. Revelation corresponds to the passive dimension of faith, faith's reception of its object. Insofar as the object of faith is characterized as transcendent, unknowable, uncontrollable, "given" to us as gift and grace from beyond us, in the same measure the object of faith is experienced as not coming from the self, as coming from another, as revealed. From this point of view, which arises out of the experience itself of faith, one can speak of a certain priority of revelation to faith. Even in the case of faith in impersonal values or ideals there is an inbreaking into consciousness from outside the self to which faith submits through recognition and active dedication. In the case of the personal God who is the "object" of Christian faith, one experiences a God being present to human subjectivity, acting within the self, and drawing human response out of the self. All of this, however, occurs within Christian subjectivity. This phenomenology then is no argument but simply an appeal to that Christian experience.

In a way this first encompassing designation of Christian revelation as a form of human experience may seem obvious and trivial. A moment's reflection would yield the conclusion that revelation could be nothing else than a human experience. What else could it be? Yet it remains crucial because in some subtle way revelation comes to be understood as something different. Like beliefs masquerading as faith, revelation too begins to be thought of as though it were some kind of objective knowledge. The subjectivity of faith and revelation are gradually lost sight of and forgotten. Against this tendency, then, one continually has to recall that revelation does not exist on a piece of paper. Revelation is not a book and is not contained in a book. Revelation exists only in human consciousness.

But like all human consciousness and experience that has some content, revelation is historically mediated. Human consciousness is intentional; it is consciousness *of* something. And the transcendent object to which Christian faith responds gains its specificity through the historical medium that is Jesus. The central historical medium for Christian revelation is Jesus of Nazareth.

The centrality of Jesus' mediation of Christian revelation should be taken strictly. There can only be one center of a circle, and Jesus stands at the dead center of all Christian media. This becomes clear, I think, simply by stepping back, gaining distance between oneself and the whole complex movement of Christian revelation, and asking: From what event does this whole Christian revelation derive? What gave rise to it in history? There may be many other media that provide content for the Christian experience of revelation. In dealing with Christian scriptures we shall propose that these media are indeed innumerable. But all other

Christian media relate to Jesus as the absolute center of the mediation of Christian revelation. They are either derived from him or relate back to him for their peculiar Christian meaning; they are always peripheral in relation to the center. This is true not only of the gospels, but also the media contained or referred to in the other New Testament writings as well as the Jewish scriptures. The fundamental meaning of the term "Christian" when it is applied to revelation is derived from the mediation of the experience of God in history by the life and death of Jesus who is called the Christ. The primary objective referent providing the content of Christian revelation then is Jesus of Nazareth, because reductively he is the central historical medium which makes that content present to consciousness in the specifically Christian way.

REVELATION AS ENCOUNTER

We pass now to an initial description and characterization of the experience of Christian revelation and its content. I presuppose here and will not analyze how Jesus is the mediator of this consciousness. There will be no correlation between the medium and the content of a personal and self-communicating God.[3] At this point I merely reassert the necessary connection between the mediation of Jesus and the content of revelation as it is described here. As the central medium of this experience of revelation Jesus is also its norm.

The content of Christian revelation, its "object" so to speak, is a personal and loving God. And the process of revelation itself may be characterized as an experience of "encounter" with such a God. This paradigmatic analogy of an encounter for understanding revelation is borrowed from the theology of revelation of Emil Brunner. Although this phenomenological analysis is heavily dependent upon Brunner's theology, my intention there is not to reproduce his thought exactly.[4]

An Analogy of Personal Encounter

Since the object of Christian faith is God who is a personal and loving Presence to human existence, one can postulate an analogy between the communication of two human subjects and the communication between God and human beings. Dwelling on such an analogy actually opens up the experience of revelation intrinsically or from within. Most people who have been exposed to existentialist philosophy, or even modern psychology, are aware of the main features of interpersonal or intersubjective communication. I will simply recall some of the salient characteristics of the kind of knowledge that emerges in this situation as an analogy for a descriptive characterization and analysis of the Christian experience of revelation.[5]

One can recognize the obvious distinction between knowing about another person, either one whom one has not met or met only casually, and knowing another person personally. In the one case the knowledge about the other is external and objective; in the other one encounters the self of the other. But this obvious difference between the knowledge of an acquaintance and of a personal friend can be pushed further. One often hears the remark, "I do not really know the person," from one who has had a long relationship with another. This points to what can be recognized as a qualitative difference, a difference in kind, between these two levels of dealing with another human being, the one consisting in knowledge of data about another, the other being interpersonal or intersubjective knowledge.

This difference is worth dwelling on because it has been called into question.[6] The difference, when one thinks of it in terms of a communication on the part of the person who is known, lies in freedom. Freedom here means both the mysterious depths of a human person as well as freedom's self-transcending quality. Such a freedom implies that the real self does and at any given time can intentionally transcend his or her actions, even and especially communicative action. For human beings can dissimulate; they can bear false witness not only in their speech but also in the gestures and behaviors that reveal the self on a deeper level.[7] The point here is not to undermine the basic trust that underlies the whole of social existence, namely, that as a rule this is not the case. It is rather simply to bring to the surface distinctions that are in the end necessary to understand human existence. One can and in the end must make a distinction between the human spirit as self-transcending freedom and the outpouring of human freedom into matter, worldly action, and even the communicative action of speech.[8]

On the basis of a distinction between the self-transcending freedom of the human spirit and the merely physical, material, and mechanistic aspects of reality, one can speak of human freedom using the material world as the media of its self-communication. Not only bodily gestures but also language may be considered as media for revealing the self. It is not necessarily true, then, that what you see and hear is what you really have before you. There is always a deeper level in human communication, and the self always transcends its media. From this two things follow that define the special qualitative difference in authentic self-communication resulting in personal encounter. The first is that it is a function of freedom. Self-revelation is a gift of the self out of freedom that is mediated through the signs of gesture and language. Secondly, from the side of the receiver, one accepts the gift as gift. It is received as revelation of an inner self where what is "inner" refers to the freedom of the other. An encounter with another personal self has the quality of an "event," something that is not necessarily present in the gestures, but is freely given by the other through and within the external vehicles of communication.

Revelation as Encounter

God, as God is revealed to human experience through Jesus, is personal. And one can describe the experience of this revelation by using analogously a framework of intersubjective or interpersonal communication. This is not a deductive move that argues on the basis of the personality of God but rather a phenomenology of the experience of Christian revelation that is responsible for the belief that God is personal. Christian revelation does not appear as knowledge about God as about an object, not even as knowledge about a transcendent person. Rather Christian revelation takes the form of a personal encounter with a divine subject. What are some of the qualities of the experience when it is described within this paradigm?

A first characteristic of Christian revelation consists in its being an intersubjective communication. God is experienced as a subject, so that human contact or awareness of God cannot be a knowledge about God as about an object. In Christian revelation God is experienced as a personal self. God is experienced as being present to and within one's self; God communicates God's self to the consciousness of one's own "being-present-to-oneself." God is personal, and the ground for that affirmation is the experience of God as a personal subject.

Second, in Christian revelation of God one experiences God as transcendent. Because God is God, the personhood of God consists in an infinite subjectivity. When one experiences God within oneself, one knows that one is not simply experiencing the self, but a Presence to the self that infinitely transcends one's own subjectivity. When one experiences God in and through the media of history, the theme of such an experience is that God transcends the historical media, the events, the persons, the language that call God to consciousness. God transcends the physical world, nature itself, the universe or cosmos. God's infinity is experienced in the experience of the very finitude of all that is and of which the self is part. Here one sees yet a deeper reason why knowledge of God cannot be objective knowledge in any ordinary sense *about* God. God's subjectivity is an infinite subjectivity. It cannot be contained, limited, pinned down, defined by an objectivity which is by definition finite, limited, and circumscribed. An experience of God by its nature is experience of that which infinitely transcends one's own subjectivity and the worldly historical media that make God's being present an "object" of awareness.

Third, revelational encounter thus has the theme of giftedness that was alluded to in the consideration of faith. But from within the framework of interpersonal communication the deeper reason for this theme of grace becomes manifest. The self-communication of God is a function of God's inner freedom. God does not have to communicate God's inner self. Revelation always has an "event" character; it occurs unpredictably. The correlate of this event character lies in the freedom of God. Whenever revelation occurs or is experienced as an interpersonal encounter with God, the thematic quality of the experience itself is that it has come about on the basis of God's free initiative.

The significance of this characterization of revelational experience of God lies first of all in its being faithful to the experience itself. Does this not in some measure correspond to what Christians mean when they speak of God revealing? If indeed this description does fit the experience, it also bears some further relevance. It explains why Christian faith is not knowledge in the ordinary sense, and at the same time preserves a cognitive dimension to faith and revelation. Revelation is not philosophical wisdom, not scientific knowledge, not any form of impersonal and objective knowledge, not knowledge of things or historical events, not historical knowledge, not propositional knowledge about God, not knowledge generated by innate ideas, not a priori truth latent within the human person as such. All of these other kinds of knowledge will have some bearing on revelation. But revelation cannot be reduced to any of these forms of human knowing. Rather revelation is *sui generis,* a knowing of its own kind, that is in the end different from every other kind of knowing. We have located it within the analogical framework of personal, intersubjective knowledge. But as the result of God's self-communication, it transcends the analogical framework itself.

Because revelation is a form of knowing that is *sui generis,* it competes with no other form of knowing and no other data of human knowledge competes with it. Since revelation is not objective knowledge at all, it is simply wrong, by an a priori mistake in categories, to look upon scientific knowledge or any other kind of knowledge of this world as a threat to revelation. And yet, despite this qualitative difference from other forms of knowing, revelation is still cognitive. Revelation as a consciousness of God is a form of knowledge of God. We shall now try to sort out more carefully the elements that are involved in its epistemology. This will bring us closer to a consideration of the relation between revelation and theology.

DIMENSIONS WITHIN THE EXPERIENCE OF REVELATION

It is not enough, I believe, to conceive of revelation as a personal encounter with God in order to sort out the complex relationship between revelation and the discipline of theology. One needs to look closer at what goes on within this encounter. In what follows I will propose five dimensions of this experience. These dimensions should not be looked upon as discrete elements serving as building blocks for the encounter with God. They are really no more than aspects of a single experience. What is proposed here are distinctions which will provide a language for grasping differentiations within a complex response to God's being present that makes up God's personal self being revealed to human consciousness. Together these dimensions make up a single experience, and often they may run into each other so that they may not be present as such to human consciousness. In other words, they appear as a result of analysis which will help in distinguishing more clearly the difference and relationship between revelation and theology.[9]

This analysis of revelation is most clearly verified when one considers the genesis of a distinctive revelatory experience, for the first time so to speak. In the case of Christian revelation, then, one might consider this analysis as a theoretical hypothesis concerning the genesis of Christian revelation. But the analysis also holds true, *mutatis mutandis,* of the successive communication of this revelation to later Christians.

The first element of revelation is its medium. There is scarcely need at this point to expand on what has already been said about the necessity and function of an historical medium in revelation. It is sufficient to recall that an encounter of the Presence of God that constitutes a revelatory experience cannot be unmediated. The positive content of revelation, then, is influenced and determined by the medium that mediates the experience of God's Presence and initiative. In the case of Christian revelation Jesus is its central historical medium.

A second factor in a consideration of the dynamics of revelation is simply to underscore the holistic character of such an experience of God. In what follows we shall discuss more particularly and narrowly the epistemology or the cognitive aspects and dimensions of revelatory experience. How is the meaning of what is revealed determined? But this issue can only be one aspect of a totally engaging experience. An encounter with God, a coming to consciousness of and responding to

God's Presence, touches the depths of human personality and stimulates a response of the whole person. This response is not merely a question of mental activity, interpretation, and construal. All of this activity is merely a part of a person's full affective receiving and active responding to the God so revealed.

Third, George Tyrrell speaks of the impression on the imagination and mind that revelation makes within the fullness of the whole experience.[10] This impression could be made in a moment or period of heightened subjectivity. The impression left by revelation may also be that which is recalled in memory when the experience is no longer actual. The historical medium or agent of revelation is a most important factor in relation to this imaginative impression of the "object" revealed. It is precisely through the historical medium that this mental impression is formed. It would be wrong of course to say that God's very Presence has no role in the formation of one's impression of it. But it is crucial to insist again on historical mediation; there is no unmediated immediacy of God-consciousness.

This dimension of revelatory experience, the formation of an impression upon the imagination, underscores the theme of passivity. What is revealed impresses itself upon human subjectivity from outside the self. Revelation is not an experience of the self that wells up from within the self. The impression, the image, the rudiments of the conception of what is revealed comes from an external source. Surely Jesus can give rise to many different impressions about God. But it is important to consider that they come from him as from an external source. Moreover, through this external medium, what is revealed to the self "appears" as both other than the medium and other than the self. What is revealed is precisely a transcendent other.

A fourth dimension of revelatory experience is so closely mixed up with the impression that the medium leaves on consciousness that it may not be able to be distinguished from the impression itself within consciousness. But one cannot speak of a passive impression made by revelation without also speaking of an active interpretation of that impression. All experience, insofar as it is cognitive at all, involves an active response of interpretation and implicit construal. There can be no pure experience that is not already interpreting experience, and no purely passive reception that does not involve an active response of meaning-bestowing interpretation. That which is on the one hand "received" is on the other hand "thought" in terms of a language which contains concepts and religious notions that feed into the interpretation.

The distinction between these last two dimensions in a way only becomes clear in terms of passion and action. Action is always a response to being acted upon. Impression and interpretation then are not chronologically distinct; impression is not first and interpretation second. One cannot isolate active interpretation as separable from the impression left by the medium of revelation. Interpretation is spontaneous, a reaction that is within the impression insofar as it is cognitive; and the impression is within the construal as that which is construed in consciousness. In the experience of historically mediated revelation meaning is spontaneously accepted even as the imagination formulates the meaning of the impression that is experienced.

Fifth, one can speak and think of yet another differentiation within the dynamics of revelation in terms of its "first expression." The difference between impression and interpretation on the one hand, and what is called here a first expression on the other, is the difference between what is spontaneous and what is more deliberate. Of course in some cases it may be impossible to differentiate the two; a first spontaneous impression or interpretation may be lasting. But often a deliberate and more reflective construal of what occurred in a revelatory experience can yield a more organized linguistic account of the object in a variety of genres of expression.

If this first expression is called a "reflective" expression and interpretation of the object of revelation, this does not mean that spontaneous interpretation is not also reflective. Rather it points to a more deliberate kind of reflection that may in this case require time and consideration. For example, the writings of the New Testament are not merely the spontaneous impressions and interpretations of the disciples who first experienced what came to be Christian revelation. In themselves they are the product of a good deal of reflection, and they have a great deal of reflective sources behind them. But from our vantage point they have to be considered as the first expressions of revelation in the practical sense that they are the first expressions we possess. In some cases then it may be difficult to distinguish within these writings this first expression from spontaneous impression and interpretation. In other cases this may be rather clear. This distinction, then, further differentiates what is going on epistemologically within the phenomenon of revelation itself.

All of these dimensions together make up revelational experience. As dimensions of a single experience of encounter they run into each other and one cannot really be separated off from the others. The experience as a whole has been called an encounter; the whole of a person's being is engaged existentially in the encounter of and response to God's being present to human subjectivity. But this interpersonal communication is always mediated from outside the person by an historical medium. The historical medium which interprets for human beings the meaning or quality of God's Presence is in its turn interpreted by the receiving subject in terms of the historical language and concepts available to it. At times this spontaneous construal itself can be distinguished from a first reflective appreciation in which it is rendered more coherent in the figurative language of myth, metaphor, or narrative. But this first expression should not be separated off from the whole experience which generated it.

REVELATION AND THEOLOGY

In the light of these analytical differentiations within the experience of encounter that is Christian revelation it is now possible to discuss the relation of revelation to theology. It is possible to distinguish theological assertions as well as the generic discipline of theology from the experience of revelation itself. At the same time we will be able to establish the inseparable relation and the continuity between them.

Let us begin by distinguishing a theological assertion from the experience of revelation itself. A theological proposition may be considered an intentional interpretation of the "object" of revelation or of reality in the light of revelational experience. Such a theological assertion about reality could be identical with what has been called a first reflective expression of revelation and thus intimately connected with the genesis of revelation itself. But it is still clear that such a theological assertion is different from the total experience that constitutes revelation. For revelation is precisely a totally engaging religious experience, whereas interpretation and construal of its meaning in conceptual language is more narrowly a mental response. The whole revelatory experience is more under the influence of God's Presence as mediated by a specific historical medium; a theological statement such as a first expression of it is more reflective and influenced by all sorts of knowledge gained from other areas of life. The experience of revelation as an encounter is more God-initiated and passive; reflective interpretation is more a human response, a human effort and activity. The impression left by the medium of revelation yields a spontaneous interpretation; a theological interpretation is more deliberate, thought through, expressed in linguistic terms that are coherent with other conceptions of the world. Thus even when theological statements are closely connected with the genesis of revelation itself, as are the first expressions of it, they may be distinguished from the whole experience of revelation itself.

Another way to distinguish theology from the genesis of revelation is to consider theology as a discipline that interprets the data of revelation in a carefully reasoned and methodical way. What is the status of the New Testament in terms of "the data of revelation"? From one point of view, relative to the genesis of Christian revelation, the New Testament appears as theology. The New Testament is made up of theological tracts. Each book of the New Testament is in its own way a methodical interpretation of the Christian experience of revelation. From another point of view, relative to our looking back toward the origins of revelation, these writings appear as the first expressions of Christian revelation that we possess. In this respect theology appears as a second reflection, resulting in a second interpretation and expression of the data of revelation. Theology as a discipline in the ongoing life of the church is reflection to the power of two, or even three, whose goal is to generate a more critical, systematic, and coherent interpretation of that which is contained in revelatory experience.[11]

In short, theology is distinct from the revelational experience of an encounter with God. Theology is not in itself revelation. But although distinguishable, theology is dependent upon revelation, inseparably bound to it; theology cannot be isolated from Christian revelation and remain Christian theology. What is important at this point is to explain the structure of this dependence and the intrinsic connection between the two.

Negatively, it is not a dependence that can argue from the first expressions of revelation, for example, those of scripture, as though they were objective principles or expressions of objective knowledge. One cannot arrive at further knowledge of the object of faith on the basis of an objective deduction from the first expressions of revelation. The expressions of revelation are not first premises for objective reasoning. One cannot decide the solutions to new questions by an objective inference from the propositions of scripture. The reason for this lies in the nature of revelation. Revelation is not objective knowledge, but an experience of encounter with God. "The data of revelation," then, is a phrase that refers back to content that emerged out of a heightened experience *of* but not *about* God. To treat the consequent interpretation of God and the world made in the light of such an experience as objective data is to completely distort the very nature of revelational experience, interpretation, and expression. The ultimate ground of all theology relates back to an historically mediated subjective experience of encounter with a divine personal presence. This is not objective knowledge.

Positively theology must appeal to the experience of revelation itself, to experiential and subjective encounter, as the source of its

meaning. To put it bluntly and yet still accurately, theology and theological assertions do not refer directly to their object, the transcendent God.
Insofar as they are theological, these statements refer directly to the
Christian experience of God, and thus indirectly, through that experience, to the God who is really encountered in that experience. Theological statements are not objective statements or statements of objective
knowledge about God, but expressions that interpret reality in the light
of encounter with God.[12] Although theological reflection is methodical
and reasoned, its reasoning is not about an object that is available to it
objectively. Rather all along the way, so to speak, the reasoning of
theology consistently appeals to the underlying encounter with God
upon which the meaning and ultimately the validity of theological assertion rest.[13]

When theology refers back to the first interpretative expressions of
the object of revelation in scripture, it does not find there an objective
datum in the sense of a commonly agreed meaning based on ordinary
knowledge. Rather these statements themselves are expressions and interpretations of an encounter of God. Thus the sense and coherence of
all theology as second reflection too must check its meaning in reference
to revelational encounter. This does not mean recreating a fleeting
experience of the past, which in a literal sense can never be done. Rather
it means finding the meaning of the current theological statement within
the context of a current encounter with God's Presence.

THE DEVELOPMENT OF REVELATION

Thus far we have seen the distinction of theology from revelation as
encounter with God and the radical dependence of theology upon this
encounter as the source of its meaning. We can further clarify this
relationship by a consideration of development, the development of
theology, of doctrine, of revelation. No problem or topic better illustrates the nature and structure of revelation and the relation between
theology and revelation than this issue.

The distinction between original and dependent revelation provides a helpful framework for this discussion.[14] Original revelation
refers to the first occurrence of a particular revelation. It is the original
and originating experience of God's Presence in a specific way through
an historical medium that stands at the head of a religious tradition. We
have seen that the New Testament, although it is the closest expression
of Christian revelation to its source, is not synonymous with original

revelation. Rather this originating revelatory experience must be postulated at the origins of the development of New Testament literature.[15]
Dependent revelation, by contrast, refers to the continuation of this
revelational experience in history in the form of a religious tradition.
Original revelation is passed on, mediated, or communicated to others,
thus making what is passed on and subsequently experienced dependent
upon the original revelation as upon a source. Within the context provided by the distinction between original and dependent revelation we
can ask: What changes and what remains the same in the history of
Christian theology and revelation?

In one obvious historical sense revelation develops. Revelation is an
ongoing existential and experiential phenomenon. It is the process of
God revealing and being revealed to the vital experience of ever more
people who encounter God in new ways. In so doing they interpret God
differently, understand God with new categorical concepts, relate their
experience to the world in changing historical contexts, use different
languages and language systems, reinterpret the first expressions of
revelation in relation to new problems and in response to new questions.
Not only does the interpretation of the "object" of original Christian
revelation change, but also in myriad different ways the experience itself
of revelation changes in the historical course of dependent revelation.
The sheer historicity of the existential encounter with God's Presence
even within the tradition of the Christian community means that not just
theology but revelation itself develops and changes. To hold otherwise
would somehow mean exempting the experience of revelation from
being an historical human experience.

Yet at the same time but in a deeper sense one can determine a level
of the experience of Christian revelation that neither changes nor develops. To appreciate the radical sense in which revelation does not
develop one has to consider the constant dimensions of Christian revelation. First of all, in Brunner's language, revelation is encounter with
God, an interpersonal initiative from and recognition of a personal,
free, accepting, and loving God within the self. The "object" of revelation is a single subject who is God's own self as Presence to human
existence. Second, in all of Christian revelation, original and dependent,
the central historical medium for this encounter remains the same, Jesus
of Nazareth. And third, using Tyrrell's conception, the experience that
is mediated by Jesus is one that encompasses the whole of human personality eliciting a total response. The wholeness of this experience
transcends its mental impression and imaginative interpretation. This
encompassing experience of encounter remains the primary referent of

the term revelation. On its deepest level this experience of encounter neither develops nor changes. Rather it is repeated over and over again. It may be weak or strong, it can fade and be renewed, but it is the same encounter because it is the same Presence and self-communication of the same God through the same medium to the same kind of experience.[16]

This aspect of revelation should not be viewed as a reductionist interpretation of an essence of Christian revelation that places all the other dimensions of revelation at some periphery. But it is an attempt to name a single and simple inner and radical center of gravity of the whole personal and social reality called Christianity.[17] This center of gravity of revelation is in one sense synonymous with what was called in the last chapter transcendental revelation. But in another sense it is not transcendental because it has been identified or categorized through the historical mediation of Jesus.[18] The point, however, is simple. Beneath the complexity of Christianity as an historical and institutional religion, beneath all the theologies of today and across the centuries, beneath all the dogmas, doctrines, and the varieties of belief and interpretation, lies God's personal Presence mediated to Christian consciousness by Jesus. This mediation elicits an encounter with a God who is boundless love, *for me* as Luther put it, and if for me, then for all and for the whole world. This revelation does not develop. It is the consistent basis for ongoing and ever-new interpretation and expression.

INTERPRETING REVELATION

Theology consists in interpreting revelation. We can conclude then by summarizing the interpretation of revelation itself that has been presented here and asking what this view of revelation in its turn implies for the discipline of theology.

We have tried to set forth the fundamental nature of Christian revelation in a manner consistent with a general theory of revelation and in relation to other forms of human knowledge. Revelation is not empirical knowledge, rational knowledge, scientific knowledge, nor even historical knowledge. Revelation, rather, consists in a form of religious experience. It is a common phenomenon, but one that is different from and at bottom unthreatened by other objective forms of knowledge. Christian revelation is existential encounter with a personal loving God who is personally present to human beings. But this encounter with God present is mediated to Christian experience historically, from outside the self, by the event and person of Jesus of Nazareth.

This interpersonal encounter with God mediated by Jesus may be considered the single, simple, and unifying center of gravity of the whole of Christianity. I do not say the essence of Christianity as though Christian revelation and response to it could be reduced to this in a way that makes other things unessential. Rather I use the image of a center of gravity to indicate the internal fundamental basis upon which other things depend and within which they subsist.[19] It is clear, for example, that all theology and doctrine find their basis in corporate Christian life. But behind or beneath this corporate way of life lies existential encounter with the transcendent but immanent and loving God revealed in and through an historical coming into contact with Jesus. This is the always presumed, ever present, consistent, and unchanging foundation of Christian faith, its basic revelation which is always being revealed to it.

Theology is not revelation. Beliefs, doctrines, and dogmas are theological statements and as such cannot be simply identified with revelation. Although doctrines may share a status of general acceptance within the community different from mere theological opinions, generically doctrines are theological statements. As such they are not revelation. There are no revealed doctrines as such, for revelation is personal encounter with a personal God and not an historically relative interpretation of that encounter in the form of an objective proposition.

The point here is not that one cannot on the basis of revelation make such statements as "God is personal," or "God is good," nor whether or not such statements are true. The issue simply concerns the status, the basis, and the inner logic of such statements. Theology consists in the interpretation of revelation; theological statements are interpretative expressions of reality, God, the world, and ourselves under the impact and on the basis of the experience of revelation. Revelation is the initiative and activity of God within the human subject. Relative to this revelatory dimension of experience the human subject is first of all passive. Stimulated by the revealing contact with God, theology is active, a human endeavor, a human activity. Theology relates to revelation as *actio* relates to *passio*. Within the experience of revelation itself these dimensions can scarcely be distinguished because there is no revelation without response; impression and interpretation run together. Yet in the exercise of theology as a discipline, in the deliberate expression of revelation, in second and third reflection on its content, the distinction is clear. Theology depends on experience; it has no direct access to God. It is totally dependent on revelational experience and all its assertions have their meaning through and on the basis of this existential encounter.

The interpretations of reality in the light of this experienced encounter are ongoing within the historical community and continually changing. What they must be faithful to ultimately is the inner and consistent experience that they objectify, express, and communicate, that is, the encounter with a personal and self-communicating God. This principle is extremely important in what it excludes. The final arbiter or criterion for the faithfulness of theological interpretation relative to revelation does not lie in other theological interpretations. The criterion for the "orthodoxy" of any theology is not another theology. For all such interpretations are human projects, historically conditioned, and themselves relative to encounter with God's Presence. Thus in the end the final criterion for the consistency and validity of theological interpretation is internal to the experience of revelation itself.[20]

From all of this can something now be said generally about how theological statements, particularly those of the past, should be interpreted? Are there any principles for understanding the structure of theological statements and for interpreting them contained in this view of revelation? Four such principles stand out.

First, the structure of revelation provides a criterion for how theological statements themselves are to be understood. Theological statements are interpretative expressions of the content of the experience of revelation. Therefore, to discover their meaning, one must appeal to the revelatory religious experience that is the foundation of that meaning. As was seen in the theology of faith, theological statements based on revelation do not have an objectively verifiable meaning; their meaning cannot be reduced to warrants that may be objectively verified as in ordinary knowledge; their meaning cannot be checked against objective data. Thus one must appeal to revelatory experience. But this revelatory experience does not mean trying to recreate the experience of the consciousness of people in the past. Strictly speaking that cannot be done. Even when one succeeds in an objective characterization of that experience by some sort of hypothetical reconstruction, this still remains a relative and historically conditioned experience of the past. Ultimately, to make sense of theological statements today, one must appeal to the religious experience of revelation today as the basis for their meaning and truth.

Second, one can locate the center of gravity of the experience of Christian revelation and its content. Christian revelation is not the revelation of many things; it is certainly not information about God. Revelation is simply revelation of God; its nature is encounter with God. If this encounter with God were to be interpreted into objective content, that content too would appear to be quite simple. The fundamental reality that is revealed in the experiential encounter with God mediated by Jesus is that God is, that God is personal, and that God is boundless love. This formula is not reductionist nor in any way exclusive of other things that may be said of God, human existence standing before this God, and the world. It is precisely non-reductionistic and inclusive: it contains by implication the whole of Christian interpretation at any given time. This then points to the basic experience to which an appeal must be made for interpreting Christian theological statements for yesterday, today, and into the future.

Third, an example will illustrate the degree to which even theological statements which are very close to this basic revelatory experience still need to be interpreted anew in each age. Jesus is the medium of the experience of God as personal and infinitely caring love, the Jesus who called and related to God as Father. The concept of father is so closely connected with Jesus' life and teaching that it is scarcely possible to consider his person without speaking of this relationship. Thus is the personhood of God mediated by the idea of God's fatherhood, and the fatherhood of God lies close to the center of the content of Christian revelation. Yet suddenly we recognize today that fatherhood as a theological interpretation of God has become ideological, ideological in the classical negative sense of serving and protecting the interests of some over against the interests and rights of others, rights that are grounded in and guaranteed by the boundless love of God. Thus the very fatherhood of God as a theological interpretation of God must be critically examined and reinterpreted in the light of God's personal and infinite love of all. In short, reinterpretation must descend right into the heart of revelation itself.

Finally, one might ask what revelation is for. Why do human beings seek revelation? And why, if we presumed to ask this, does God reveal God's Presence to us? The classical answer to this question states that revelation is for human salvation. But that salvation cannot refer exclusively to eternal life, for God does not need to disclose God's Presence to human existence in this life to effect an eternal salvation. The answer to these questions can be none other than for human beings in this world and the way they direct their lives. The purpose of revelation is to inform and animate human existence in this world both individually and socially. All theological interpretation, therefore, must be informed by this same goal. Theology should conform to the dynamics of revelation by interpreting it in relation to concrete human problems, the issues that human beings face in living their lives. All theological assertions should in some way express and mediate the personal Presence of God as Spirit and grace to actual human dilemmas.

These rather simple but basic principles for theology flow from the consideration of revelation as encounter with God's Presence. In the next section we shall take another approach to Christian theology through the traditional axiom that it finds its source and norm in scripture.

III

SCRIPTURE

Chapter Five

THE STATUS OF SCRIPTURE
IN THE CHURCH

The discussion of faith showed that existential commitment to transcendent data and the social bond of beliefs make up the basic stuff out of which theology emerges. The dynamics of revelation provides the content of theology. But there can be no talk of Christian revelation without a consideration of scripture. For some Christians the equation is simple: scripture is Christian revelation. Whether or not this naive identification can be made, an understanding of the status and use of scripture is intrinsic to every conception of Christian theology.

In the history of Christian thought it has been almost universally accepted, with only few exceptions that prove the rule, that scripture is the norm for theology. Scripture is the *norma normans non normata,* the norm which finally decides and is itself normed by no other criterion. It contains the standard of Christian truth; all else is commentary on it. Scripture is the solid basis for fidelity to Christian revelation which was given at a point in time; without it the community would inevitably wander away historically from God's truth. Thus, as Luther demonstrated, the scriptures are also the norm for reform. Again and again in Christian history, before and after Luther, and most lately in the Second Vatican Council, the church has reached back to scripture as a lever to pry open and expose historical distortions of the Christian message. Today the ecumenical context for theology demands in a new way the normativity of scriptures. If Christian churches appeal merely to their own traditions and the social sources of denominationalism, consensus in theology is ruled out in principle.[1]

It is easy enough to say that scripture is normative for theology, and even to explain why that must be the case. It is considerably more difficult to explain *how* this is possible. In the past theologians were content with a series of notions or doctrines about scripture that served

as an underpinning or buttress for its normativity. Scripture was inspired; God is its author; thus it enjoys the authority of God. Scripture is
inerrant; it is adequate and comprehensive in its message; it is inherently
clear and self-interpreting. With the rise of modernity and especially
historical consciousness, however, these received notions about scripture have been rendered ambiguous at best. For many, including some
Christian theologians, they are meaningless and untenable. In whatever
way one looks at it, it is now impossible to justify the normativity of
scripture in the way this was done in classical theology. One needs a new
theory of the status of scripture and consequently a new understanding
of how it operates in the Christian community. Such an understanding
of the status of scripture should be able to illumine how it can come to
bear on theology in a normative way. In doing so, this view of the status
and use of scripture would illumine still further the nature of theology
itself.

The problems underlying the status and use of scripture today
dictate the strategy of these two chapters. This chapter will be dedicated
to the construction of a general theological theory of the status and
place of scripture in the Christian community. On the basis of this
theory the next chapter will discuss the use of scripture in the discipline
of theology. The point as always is to uncover a bit more of the nature of
theology itself as a discipline and the structure and meaning of theological assertion.

The following proposal for a conception of the status of Christian
scriptures within the community will be put forward in a very simple
manner. I shall begin by simply enumerating some of the serious problems entailed in the traditional concepts about scripture. These problems have to be appreciated before one can accept the need and logic of
reinterpretation. The following three sections will consist in a constructive interpretation of the status of scripture. I will conclude by showing
how this theory, while changing the meaning of the received notions,
preserves their intentionality and provides a basis for the normative use
of scripture in theology.

PROBLEMS CONCERNING THE STATUS OF SCRIPTURE

A variety of received notions, beliefs, and doctrines about scripture
have defined the status of these writings and thus have had a direct
bearing on how scripture was used as a source for Christian theology.
But many of these notions have been seriously undermined in modern
consciousness. It is rather important at the outset at least to enumerate

these problems, for they set the context for a reinterpretation of the status of scripture. One cannot really enter sympathetically into the process and dynamics of reinterpretation unless one grasps the nature of the problems at stake.[2]

We begin with the classical doctrine of inspiration; scripture is inspired by God. God as Spirit put it in the mind of the composers of these writings to write what they wrote. In one way or another human beings were the instruments of God's authorship. Thus, reductively, inspiration implies that God is the author of scripture.[3] Two typical uses of scripture by theologians have been justified by these notions. Since God is the author of these texts, they could be cited as containing God's own knowledge and thus as objective information about God. One could argue in theology by citing texts; the citation of a text could decide a position. Moreover, since the whole of scripture had one author, the theologian could roam around all of the different writings and correlate texts. A text in Numbers might clarify the meaning of a statement in Luke, or be added to it as a corroborating authority.

The single most important factor that has undermined the notion of inspiration is the rise of an historical consciousness. And, ironically, this has been brought to bear on Christian consciousness by the enormous resurgence of biblical scholarship over the last century or two. For it has been precisely the naturalist and historicist premises that have accounted for the new opening up of the meaning of the scriptures. By definition all critical biblical study rests on these assumptions. The scriptures can now be understood with startling new relevance because they are interpreted as works of human beings in a concrete historically determined context. In the framework of this new paradigm theories of inspiration appear to be trying to save something through mystification. Who was inspired along the long historical route of the formation of scripture? Does a theory of generic inspiration of scripture as a whole differentiate Christian scriptures from those of other religions which have also received revelation? But the fundamental problem always leads back to the fact of the thoroughly human character of these writings. Everybody knows that they are the work of human beings, that human beings are their authors.

Second, another doctrine about scripture, which is often associated with and argued from inspiration, is inerrancy. Because it is inspired by God, scripture contains no errors. When historical mistakes in scripture are admitted, the assertion tends to be pushed to another level of understanding, that of religious truth. The subject matter of scripture is not really empirical, historical, or scientific truth but truth about God, God's dealing with human existence, and human beings before God. At some level, then, scripture is said to be absolutely true and to contain no falsehood. But indeed the scriptures not only contain factual error, internal contradictions, and a variety of kinds of inconsistency. They also contain religious sentiments that cannot be squared with accepted religious truths and values commonly held by Christians today. This, too, is so because scripture is a product of history. And if to save the doctrine one isolates some inerrant kernal of religious truth that is represented by the scriptures as a whole, has one really said anything significant?

Third, Christian doctrine about scripture usually implies that its religious truth is universal truth. It is therefore transcultural. Because it contains God's truth about God's self, scripture is truth for all peoples. Coupled with this notion, or implied in it, one also finds the notion of scripture's clarity. Scripture is as it were self-interpreting and self-authenticating; its truth lies within itself and does not need to be bolstered by outside argument. But as clearly as it is a human work, so too is scripture historically conditioned. This implies that it is not transcultural but a particular expression of religious truth. To put it sharply, it is because scripture is not clear, not universally or transculturally transparent in its meaning that, as everyone knows, one must study historians and exegetes to know what it means.[4]

Fourth, scripture is considered as an external authority for the church as a community of beliefs and thus for the theologian. It is the norm, measure, criterion for beliefs, a norm that is itself not "normed" by anything else. Scripture is the absolute authority as far as Christian doctrine and theological assertion are concerned. But this authoritative role is seriously compromised by two aspects of current consciousness. Generally people today are profoundly aware of the changes in knowledge over time. Even outside of an evolutionary framework all sense a certain progress or at least an opening up of vast new horizons in human knowledge. How can an historical document of the past be authoritative into the future? A particular manifestation of this general problem is found in the fact that churches and theologians have from the very beginning interpreted scripture in relation to new historical situations and new questions.[5] And this is necessarily the case, so that across the church today one finds a pluralism of churches and theologies that interpret scripture differently on crucial points. What then can an absolute external authority be or even mean if it is the subject of ongoing interpretation? This problem is compounded by the historicity and pluralism within the bible itself. How can an authority which is saying different things be an authority? Another implication of historical consciousness, then, seems to be that it does not allow for an absolute authority in history. The so-called absoluteness is always relativized by different receptions and interpretations.

Fifth, closely related to scripture's authority one finds the demand that scripture be comprehensive in the religious truth that it contains, or at least adequate to respond to all of a community's religious questions. To be the authoritative norm for the community of beliefs, scripture must be comprehensive enough in what it asserts to be adequate to this task. If it is not, the community will divide over issues not clearly treated in scripture. And this is exactly what appears to be the case. For scripture is a very limited work. It clearly does not answer all our questions. Who does not wish that scripture would have addressed issues that seem crucial for us today? And who is not simultaneously happy that it did not? Such historical considerations would have been severely limited, and one can only marvel at some of the ways biblical data have been distorted by theologians to make it relevant today.

Finally, scripture has been regarded as representing the closure of revelation. It reflects a process of historical revelation that has come to an end; what is revealed in the scripture is final and closed. Revelation ended with "the death of the last apostle,"[6] a statement which implies erroneously that the death of the last apostle corresponded with the term of the composition of the New Testament. The basic idea here is that apostolicity, that is, "from the apostles," is a criterion for what is authentically Christian, for it is first and comes most directly from the source. This idea of apostolicity was at work in the determination of the New Testament canon. But once one assumes an existential, historical, and experiential notion of revelation, revelation appears as intrinsically ongoing, and the whole idea of a closed revelation in terms of written texts becomes problematic. In the past, on the basis of this doctrine, one had to try to explain how revelation developed. Today, on the premise of historical consciousness, one must try to explain what a closure of revelation could possibly mean and how this is related to scripture.

These are some of the problems that cause thinking Christians some embarrassment about merely repeating the received doctrine and language concerning scripture. These problems have forced new theological interpretations of the doctrines which we have not examined here. Some are more cogent than others, but often these constructions seem forced. They look like elaborate theological speculation geared to save a set of verbal formulas. Is there a way to speak about scripture in a more simple and straightforward manner that corresponds to the data of history and our experience today and at the same time retrieves the fundamental values that underlie these received doctrines? Such a theory must respond to these problems, refer to the whole of scripture, and at the same time preserve the point that underlies the received doctrine.

SCRIPTURE AS A RECORD OF RELIGIOUS EXPERIENCE

A good place to begin a constructive theory of the place of scripture in the church is with a descriptive account of the development of scripture. The theology of the status of scripture must at least be in accord with the data of the formation of scripture. Without going into historical detail, one can summarize the processes of how the scriptures emerged historically around four key words: experience, traditions, writings, and selection, or the formation of a canon.[7]

The first genetic source for the scriptures, insofar as they are religious writings, lies in some religious experience. It is impossible to reconstruct what these religious experiences were exactly. Depending on the genre of writings, they lie at various depths underneath the surface of the texts. For example, what really happened in the escape from Egypt and how did it come to be viewed religiously? What really occurred historically and subjectively that gave rise to a story about Jesus in which people were struck by wonder? But this component of religious experience must be postulated as the initiating ground of a religious interpretation. And since there can be no content to a religious experience without some historical mediation, one must presume some specific historical events lie behind the genesis of the scriptures.

Significant religious experiences give rise to traditions. These traditions should be thought of as existing in oral non-written forms. They could be sustained within a community in a variety of different ways as song, poem, story, ritual interpretation, prayer form, myth, law, and so on. But the distinctive element of an oral tradition is that it remains somewhat fluid and open. Various traditions within the larger tradition move forward and are continually adapted to new situations. Since they are not fixed in writing, they will be continually adjusted to new situations and develop open-endedly according to normal human processes of historical change.

The writing down of oral traditions means that they become more fixed. What was formerly more flexible and changing now becomes precisely codified into a written form.[8] Thus a particular focus of the community's experience becomes solidified in this and that writing. Of course the great variety of written genres still reflects a wide variety of interacting religious experiences within the great tradition.[9] One should not conceive of a religious tradition becoming static. But two shifts in the dynamics of the tradition appear with written scriptures. On the one hand, as tradition moves forward, reflective self-understanding tends to double back upon the solidified and objective writings that define the community's experience. The objective writings themselves tend to become the objective focus of attention if not the object of reflection and commentary. On the other hand, and in the same process, what is not written down will tend to be forgotten over time.

Finally, in the cases of both the Jewish scriptures and the New Testament writings, the community decides those works which together form its canon. This is done by a process of selection which, in the case of the church, involves a variety of criteria, such as apostolicity, authorship, age, authenticity, and use in the communities. One does not really need to call upon either inspiration or a special revelation for this historical decision. Since this decision is not made in a moment, since it is itself a process that occurs over a long period of time, it would be difficult to say who was inspired or who the subject of the special revelation was. Rather the criteria together point to an act of self-recognition that is reflected in the writings themselves. In effect the community is saying: this set of writings expresses our foundational religious experience in a classical way.[10]

In the light of this historical and descriptive analysis, one can conclude that scripture is a record of the religious experience of the Jewish-Christian tradition. In other words, the simple designation as the classical record of the religious experience of this community is sufficient as a definition of the reason for the existence of this work and its status. Further implications of this still have to be drawn out. But this initial definition corresponds to both the historical description of the process of the development of scripture and the interpretations of faith and revelation already presented.

Scripture is intimately connected with revelation, but revelation should be carefully distinguished from naive conceptions of inspiration. Given the received notion of inspiration, theology has often confused inspiration and revelation; indeed there is a spontaneous tendency to do this in the popular imagination. Since scripture is inspired, its content in terms of its objective linguistic forms was seen as God's words and God's propositions. Thus revelation is reduced to God's verbal communication or God's theophanic appearances in history which are then recorded.[11] However, once one understands revelation as itself a form of human religious experience, scripture's status as an expression or record of Jewish-Christian revelatory experience defines its intimate connection with revelation. Revelation consists in a primal contact with God's Presence and initiative within human existence and experience which is historically mediated and finds its expression in historically available human image, concept, and language.

The view of scripture as a record of religious experience, however, does not entail any naive identification of scripture with revelation. In this understanding one can admit that scripture is a human work, a human interpretation and expression of a "prior" experience of God's Presence which is historically mediated. Thus this initial characterization of scripture accords with both the shifts that have occurred in the modern period regarding revelation as subjective and historically mediated. It is consistent with historical consciousness which necessarily views scripture as a human work, and thus provides a theological grounding for what scripture scholars already implicitly recognize.

This characterization of scripture as a record of religious experience was initially resisted by the churches because it appeared to reduce scripture to a *purely* human document, one that emerged *simply* out of human experience or *merely* human subjectivity, so that in the end it bore no intrinsic relation to God's initiative in revelation. But this is not at all a necessary conclusion, and it is positively rejected in the position proposed here. For this view of scripture and revelation includes the idea that religious experience is or can be revelatory, that is, a product of God's Presence and initiative within human subjectivity. Therefore religious experience itself is not "purely" or merely human; it cannot be reduced to psychology. Moreover this experience is mediated and governed by historical media which determine the content of revelation. Therefore it is not "purely" subjective but tied to an external and historically mediated bearer of content.

SCRIPTURE AS THE CONSTITUTION OF THE CHURCH

Let us move closer now to an understanding of the place of scripture in the church. What is the status of scripture in the church? And, at least in general terms, what is its function?

James Barr has described the process and the final decision in the selection of a canon as also a determination of "the classical model for the understanding of God."[12] In effect the community is saying that each one of these writings authentically expresses an aspect of the community's faith. Moreover, taken together as a whole, they represent in a classical way the object of the community's faith.

This decision is an historical one, and therefore there is no escaping certain aspects of historical contingency and arbitrariness in it. Each writing is particular and historically situated. And were not some writings that might have been included in the canon lost? But it is far from completely arbitrary. This decision was the result of a long process of discernment and debate, one which employed the criteria mentioned earlier. What finally decided the content of the classical model expressing the community's belief was self-recognition. These writings expressed the faith experience of the community itself.

Thus the scriptures are set up as the constitution of the church.[13] The idea of a constitution at this point should not be understood in a merely legal sense as external and binding laws. The gospels hardly appear as forms of law. Rather a constitution expresses that which constitutes a community in being as a community. A deeper consideration of even a body of law will reveal it to be a corporate written memory containing the deepest values and ideals that internally constitute the self-identity of the community. Thus it is by being the self-defining classical expression of the object of the community's faith that the scriptures become the constitution of the church. The scriptures gather together, sum up, and propose publicly in a written form the paradigmatic expression of the inner faith-life that constitutes the Christian church.

Although the scriptures are not simply law, as the constitution of the church they have a normative character. Although this will be the subject matter of the next chapter, this normative dimension is implied in the ideas of classical expression and constitution. What is being said with these terms is that from a theological point of view Christianity is not simply what Christians happen to believe at any particular time and place.[14] Rather there is an historical norm for what is properly and authentically Christian. To be authentically Christian the church must bear some relationship of continuity and correspondence to its constitution, to the founding and constituting record of the religious experience that brought it into being.

JESUS AND THE SCRIPTURES

In the discussion of revelation it was said that Jesus was the central medium of Christian revelation in the strictest sense. Scriptures as the record of this revelation then become fashioned into a canon that becomes in turn one of the factors that founds the church institutionally by being its constitution. Something should now be said about the relation between the scriptures and Jesus.

Jesus should be seen as the central and unifying element in the whole of the New Testament. Although this is a theological judgment, it reflects a description of New Testament literature and its genesis. What holds all of the New Testament books together, if not the encounter with God mediated through Jesus? The New Testament writings are a unity insofar as they all reflect the Christian experience of God mediated by Jesus. Some books, such as the gospels, manifest the centrality of Jesus more directly than others. But all the New Testament writings reflect the centrality of Jesus implicitly; this is presupposed even when he is not the subject matter. Even the letters that recall to a particular community its ethical, organizational, and disciplinary responsibility rest on the common assumption of the experience of God mediated through Jesus. This centrality of Jesus in no way negates the continuities between the religious notions of the Jewish tradition and early Christianity. It simply means that the religious experience and language of Jewish tradition become refocused, recentered, and reinterpreted through Jesus.

The New Testament, therefore, as part of the constitution of the church, is the ever-present second-order medium of ongoing revelation. It stands in the place of Jesus given his physical absence from history. It stands for more than this as well, because it records in a classical way the "whole" revelatory experience of God that was mediated by Jesus. This conception of the relation of Jesus to the New Testament writings as a whole thus gives the gospels a certain centrality. It also gives the New Testament a certain primacy of place for Christians relative to the whole Bible. But this need not be viewed as an excluding canon within the canon. It simply reflects the very nature and function of the New Testament. Christians read the whole bible through the lens of their faith in God mediated by Jesus.

This conception of the relation of Jesus to the whole New Testament seems to be confirmed by the rapid development of New Testament literature and the relative speed with which the canon was defined, at least in substance. For this view postulates the historical necessity of a rapid closure to the Christian scriptures on the grounds of Jesus' centrality to Christian experience. If the central medium and source of Christian revelation is Jesus, so that he is the focus of the Christian imagination's construal of God, then the memory of Jesus cannot be lost. As history moves forward, and as Jesus, as an historical person, recedes from memory into the past, it becomes necessary to crystallize that memory and the religious experience tied to it lest they be lost in the past. In this view, then, it becomes apparent that the gospels are *biographies* of Jesus, even though they are first century Mediterranean biographies that do not correspond to current standards.[15] It is fundamental here to realize that it is of the very nature of historical revelation that it can be either lost or distorted by history, and that this is the underlying reason for all concern for orthodoxy. What one has in the New Testament writings, therefore, are not just the "first," or "earliest," or the closest writings that we have of the originating revelational event. These notions are of course important to their being constitutive of Christian faith. But the New Testament is also a preservation of the original medium of Christian revelation who is Jesus of Nazareth.

From the Christian standpoint Jesus is also the center of the whole bible. This is a confessional stance, however, and does not detract from the integrity of the Jewish writings themselves, on their own, so to speak. Nor does this centrality of Jesus diminish the importance of the Jewish scriptures for Christian self-understanding. Jesus himself was part of the Jewish tradition and cannot be understood apart from it. Yet, as central to Christian faith, because he is the medium of its revelation, Jesus determines how the Christian encounter with God receives its specific content. Jesus is the ultimate medium that informs the Christian imagination in its construal of God, human existence, history, and reality itself.

REVELATION BEHIND AND IN FRONT OF SCRIPTURE

Up to this point the place and status of scripture within the church has been explained largely, although not exclusively, in functional historical terms. The status of scripture is established, by a decision of the community that it represents, as the classical and constitutional expression of its faith. I now want to underscore the theological component of this theory by dwelling on the relationship between scripture and revelation.

Christian revelation is the experience of God mediated through the historical medium Jesus. This includes Jesus' own experience of God, since Jesus is also a subject receiving revelation. His experience of God is a major factor of his own person and thus intrinsic to his mediation.[16] But in the first place Christian revelation is constituted by the experience of his disciples, those who were with him and came after him, and for whom the encounter with God was mediated through him. This experience is recorded in scripture.

The last chapter introduced the distinction between original and dependent revelation. Original revelation lies at the source of a tradition. It refers to the originating revelatory experience. Dependent revelation refers to the handing down or further communication of this original revelation. We can now ask how these categories apply to scripture.

Strictly speaking the New Testament is a record of both original and dependent revelation. But it would be very difficult to separate out what might be the first primitive interpretations and expressions of the content of revelation.[17] These are embedded amid the expressions of a developed reflection. The period of the composition of the New Testament included the work of first, second, third, and possibly even fourth generation Christians, if one takes into account the work of the redactors and editors of the versions we possess. During this period not only was first-hand experience being handed down, but also new theologically sophisticated and reflectively interpretative experience was being fashioned. Looking at the New Testament, then, from the point of view of its genesis, and in the analytic terms of the epistemology of revelation, it is impossible to say that it is simply the expression of original revelation.

The case is different however when one regards the New Testament from the viewpoint of our own situation. When one looks back at the New Testament and regards it within the broader context of social and historical process, one can say that it is an expression of original revelation in a loose but real sense. In fact, because of its being the earliest and closest record of the original revelatory experience, it functions historically as the expression of original revelation. Christian experience after the writing of the New Testament literature tends naturally to bend back and become reflection upon this record of the earliest generations of Christians. Thus one may regard original revelation as loosely corresponding to the experience of God mediated through Jesus during the first generations of the Christian communities, and the New Testament as the record of this experience. This conception corresponds exactly to the function of scripture as the constitution of the church. Scripture is the expression of the revelation that founds and grounds the Christian movement through history.

What then is the relation between scripture and revelation? On the basis of these distinctions one may respond more exactly to the question of where revelation stands with respect to scripture. Revelation, it was seen, is to be understood in its first moment as an existential, experiential, and historical phenomenon. On this understanding one must say that there is revelation both behind scripture and in front of scripture. On the one hand, the revelatory event of Jesus is the basis of the New Testament and the unifying force of the whole Bible insofar as it is Christian. The primitive experience of God mediated by Jesus to those who encountered Jesus, including Jesus' own experience of God which reaches back into the tradition of the Jewish community, lies behind the New Testament. Revelation is also embedded within it because it is the expression of the revelation behind it. But it should be noted that this way of speaking involves a certain "objectification" of the notion of revelation that can become misleading.

On the other hand, revelation also lies in front of scripture because scripture mediates further Christian experience and revelation as the community moves forward in history. As the ever-present and second-order medium of Christian revelation, and as the constitution of the community of faith and beliefs that is the church, scripture continually mediates new religious experience that is precisely Christian. In history it is scripture that provides the commonly possessed Christian medium of revelation. Revelation as an existential historical phenomenon is always going on in front of it.[18]

REINTERPRETING THE RECEIVED NOTIONS ABOUT SCRIPTURE

The essence of this general theory of the status of scripture in the church is that scripture is the constitution of the church because it is the record of the original revelation experience that generated the church. This theory corresponds well with the historical development of the scriptures. What remains to be examined is whether it can also preserve the point of the received notions about scripture while at the same time resolving some of the inherent problems they face today. Certainly these received notions have to be reinterpreted; but the reinterpretations should identify and reassert the deeper truths and values of which these received notions are the expression. The review of these problems will serve to recapitulate and further clarify the theory itself.

We begin with the issue of inspiration. The main problem with the metaphor of inspiration and its implication that God is the author of scripture is that this language does not do justice to the thoroughly human character and historical conditionedness of scripture. The issue here is not whether or not the initiative and influence of God underlies the scriptures, but rather how one should understand that influence in more appropriate and intelligible terms. If one accepts the theology of revelation presented in the last two chapters, it is not difficult to understand God's influence on scripture even though it remains an historical human work. God's Presence is grace, God as Spirit within human revelatory experience. And the specifically Christian content of revelation is mediated through Jesus. The religious experience of God mediated by

Jesus is thus initiated by God's Presence in human subjectivity and through Jesus.[19] Although this mediated encounter with God influences what is expressed in scripture, it does not completely determine the use of language, the choice of words, the human interpretation and creativity that goes into either "first expression," oral tradition, or the more reflective written word. This is a human work of reaction and interpretation which is historically conditioned. Yet at the same time God is prior to and within this project as gracious presence.

In sum, much of the problem with the concept of inspiration is that it has been allowed to take over and distort the notion of revelation. Revelation was reduced to or understood in terms of special and direct inspiration. The problem that this creates can be resolved by understanding inspiration in terms of revelation. In this way nothing essential that sought expression in the idea of inspiration is lost. From a certain point of view the theory of revelation proposed here might look like inspiration, since it relies on such concepts as God's Presence in terms of God as Spirit. But this Presence is universal, working in a way that cannot be isolated from human freedom itself, and is certainly not a dictating voice. The issue of the distinctiveness of Christian revelation, then, can only be resolved theologically in terms of its medium and hence in christology.

Second, the quality of inerrancy when it is applied to scripture is at best misleading and in the long run counter-productive. It does not solve problems; it creates them unnecessarily. For the obvious fact is that scripture is not inerrant in its statements of historical knowledge or consistent in its depiction of religious sentiment. The intrinsic difficulty with inerrancy as a predicate of scripture lies in the fact that all human statements and propositions are historically conditioned and relative; all are inadequate to their objects; no knowledge of anything is comprehensive; all statements of truth can be modified, corrected, changed on the basis of new knowledge from new points of view; and all of this applies in a heightened degree when statements refer to a transcendent object. Because scripture is a book containing historically relative propositions, the language of inerrancy is inappropriate and misleading.

At the same time, however, the deeper meaning of this traditional notion about scripture can be preserved by transferring this quality from scripture itself to the revelation of which it is the expression. It is not an error to think of the revelation of God "contained in" and mediated by scripture as inerrant. Inerrancy points to the conviction of faith about the revelation of God mediated through Jesus. The God encountered through Jesus is, was, and always will be the same personal, forgiving, and loving God. Inerrancy is a quality of the transcendental aspect of revelation, and is not an inerrancy of "many things." The center of gravity of revelation itself is the quality of God that is revealed in and through Jesus, and the revelation of this is inerrant. This reinterpretation may seem to be a departure from the traditional assertion about scripture itself. In one sense it is; but in a deeper sense this reinterpretation states more directly and exactly what the doctrine intends and is designed to express.

Third, the transcultural and universal character of scripture, along with its clarity, seems to be contradicted by the fact that it is a human work that is historically and culturally conditioned. It is a particular collection of individual works which need to be studied in their historical settings to be understood. These obvious characteristics of scripture cannot be denied within the framework of a critical historical consciousness. But they can serve to shift one's attention to where the real problem lies, which is not in scripture as an historical work but in Jesus who is the central medium of Christian revelation. Jesus is the unifying element of the New Testament and of the whole Bible for the Christian imagination. But Jesus too was an historically conditioned particular person. How can he be the mediator of a transcultural and universal salvific truth?

The paradox and scandal of a particular medium in history of a universal saving revelation cannot be escaped. But it can be softened by three considerations. First, all revelation from God must be historically mediated. If there is to be a universally relevant revelation from God, it must be manifested in some particular medium. Historicity and historical consciousness do not undermine the idea of an historically mediated and universally relevant revelation. Rather they demand it; the condition of the possibility of any encounter with God is that it be historically mediated. The only possible revelation of God is an historically particular revelation of God. Second, Jesus as a human being is potentially recognizable and appreciable by other human beings. There is a transcendental oneness about human existence which grounds the possibility of communication between all human beings. Jesus can be understood transculturally. Third, the message of Jesus and the content of the revelation that is mediated through him have universal and transcultural meaning and relevance that are potentially clear. The God who is revealed in Jesus is the God of all, who is personal, forgiving, and boundlessly loving. Jesus is a particular person, but what is revealed through him is not particular in the sense of a particular tribal God. God is the God of the universe.

In sum, one cannot stop at the words of scripture, the historically conditioned forms of expression, to appreciate its universal relevance.

The point of these qualities of scripture is preserved when the qualities are transferred from the language of scripture to Jesus and what is revealed through him. One must move through and beneath scripture to the central medium of Christian revelation itself, Jesus, and through him to the dynamics and content of revelation itself.

Fourth, scripture is authoritative. We have seen the problems involved in this. Scripture is a non-uniform pluralistic document of a past culture. As such it does not seem to bear sufficient competence in a modern situation of a rapid expansion of knowledge in which it is constantly being reinterpreted. What can the authority of scripture mean in such a situation?

It is quite hazardous to say something about religious authority in general and the authority of scripture in particular in only a few words. But two clarifying principles might help. The first is that religious authority is like no other authority; it must be understood within the framework of the dynamics of faith and revelation. Revelation as personal encounter appeals to freedom, and the response of faith is an act and commitment of freedom. Authority in religious matters is ultimately God's authority which is recognized within the experience of encounter. And *ultimately*, that is, in the end, there can be no external authority that can coerce the self-authentication of religious experience.[20] The medium of religious experience, however, shares in the authority of experience because the medium constitutes the experience. Thus the authority of scripture, although it is external, has to be understood on the basis of the experience of God it mediates. Scripture is not merely an external authority, nor one that forces. Scripture is not extrinsic or coercive, but enters into religious experience and from within the encounter with God appeals to and draws forth freedom. Scripture is authoritative when, and only insofar as, it mediates an encounter with God.

Presupposing this notion of religious authority generally, what can be said of the authority of scripture within the church? Since scripture is the constitution of the community of faith, insofar as one is a member of the church, scripture is the authoritative norm and criterion which governs the reflection of the community on its faith. In other words, scripture defines the faith of the community in an authoritative way by being the community's constitution. It should be noted that on one level this appears to be a completely functional and circular consideration; it is a kind of simple definition of what the Christian community of faith is, namely, the community whose faith is normed authoritatively by scripture. Christian faith and belief, to be faithful to its name, means that it is continuous with its origins as defined by scripture. Scripture thus enters into Christian faith and revelation as a regulating and authoritative norm.[21] But on another level it is more than purely a functional and legal understanding. For Christian faith and revelation are also historical and social in the sense that they had an origin in a particular moment of time. Therefore being a Christian entails being faithful to an historical revelation. Thus Christian faith has always freely desired to be faithful to scripture and has recognized it from within as the intrinsic medium and thus criterion for its encounter with God. Even reform and change within the church, insofar as it remains Christian, always appeals to scripture as its authority.

Scripture however is not the only norm and authority to which theology must appeal. Therefore these two considerations do not address the problem of conflicting interpretations. But that is the topic of the next chapter on the use of scripture in theology and the chapters on theological method.

Fifth, regarding the comprehensiveness of scripture relative to our religious questions, it is clear that scripture as an historical document cannot be a comprehensive expression of the content of revelation. There can be no such thing in history as an historical expression that is adequate to, in the sense of completely comprehending, anything let alone a transcendent "object." But scripture is sufficient to its task of mediating encounters with transcendence. It is adequate in the sense of being an expression of Christian faith and belief that is sufficient to continually mediate to the church an encounter with God by means of the dynamics of revelation. The next chapter will describe that process in greater detail.

Finally, the composition of scripture is often said to represent the closure of revelation, whereas revelation as encounter is an ongoing historical phenomenon, and the content of Christian belief is constantly shifting. This issue was briefly discussed in the course of distinguishing different meanings and levels of revelation. Here we take it up again with reference to scripture. What is the deeper logic that accounts for the idea that revelation was closed with the writing of the New Testament?

At first sight it may appear that the idea of the closure of revelation as applied to scripture is based on the logic of an historical revelation which, if it is not recorded, will be lost in the course of the flux of history. Thus we saw that the canon was established rather quickly, and that this classical expression of the primitive events of original revelation serves as the stable constitution of the church. But this does not add up to a closure of revelation in any sense. It merely provides a norm for

ongoing revelation. Dependent revelation really develops. One could
not consider later doctrinal decisions as really expressions of revelation
unless revelation developed. Many of these simply are not present in
scripture. Scripture as the constitution of the church, therefore, does
not mean that revelation is closed.

It seems rather that the idea of the closure of revelation, although it
is associated with the writing of scripture, really has its basis and referent
in Jesus. The reasoning behind the criterion of apostolicity for establishing the canon helps to show the logic of how the quality of closure
was transferred from Jesus to the scriptures. The idea of apostolicity
implies the notion of "from the source." The criterion of apostolicity
for authentic works intends that the work be a genuine expression of the
source and origin of revelation. Jesus is recognized as an event of history
who is the source of Christian revelation and its central medium. The
further writings or authors get from Jesus, the more tenuous is their
claim to represent the authentic original Christian revelation.[22] The
point of the idea of closure is that it seeks to preserve intact original
revelation, and it implicitly relates to Jesus as its medium.

The logic of the idea of closure is really christological.[23] An analysis
of the notion of closure would reveal that it implies at least two things
about Jesus as the unifying element of the New Testament and the
central source and medium of Christian revelation. First, the idea implicitly makes a strictly christological claim, one that is ontological. It
concerns the status of Jesus as the final medium of God's revelation. It
implies some christological conception of Jesus in his relationship to
God and God's relation to him. It indicates that God is at work in this
mediation in some final or eschatological way.[24] Second, relative to the
content of what is revealed in Jesus, closure implies that God really is the
way God is revealed to be through Jesus. It says that this revelation is
true, so that God will always be the same, and no authentic revelation of
God will contradict this revelation. This deeper meaning of "closure"
also provides the reasons why the community needed the event of Jesus
to be captured in writing, so to speak, and authentically so. Once again,
closure does not qualify the language, conceptions, and propositions
that make up scripture. It does not refer to a revelation of many things
about God so that more cannot be experienced, but to God's personal
and loving Presence to human existence, the true self-communication to
human beings that is mediated through the Jesus-event. Closure does
not mean that there cannot be more revelation of God in a categorical
sense. Rather it is reducible to the finality of the transcendental content
of revelation and the definitiveness of its medium. It refers to the un-

veiling of an, in some sense, ontologically decisive self-communication of God to the human race through Jesus.

This whole discussion adds up to no more than a general conception of the status of scripture in the church. By clarifying the relation between revelation and scripture, and relating this to how scripture functions as the constitution of the church, these reflections provide a basis for the subject of the next chapter which will deal with the way scripture comes to bear on theology.

Chapter Six

SCRIPTURE AND THEOLOGY

In the light of the general theory of the status and place of scripture in the church we pass to the question of how scripture may be used in theology. The problem involved in the use of scripture for making theological proposals in today's world was already encountered in the consideration of scripture's authority. It stems from the historically conditioned character of the work. Once the historical nature of scripture is recognized, even though it is a classical account of Christian faith and belief, its authoritative applicability to later times becomes problematic. How does a group of bishops decide that the Logos is consubstantial with the Father when the writers of scripture were totally unaware of the concept of consubstantiality? How does one propose a Christian moral attitude toward nuclear war on the basis of scripture? Examples such as these could be cited indefinitely, because every assertion in scripture is historically conditioned and related to a culture of the past that was ignorant of current issues. What is needed then is a logically coherent and theologically sound explanation of how scripture can be used in theology. One needs a critical explanation of the possibility of bringing scripture to bear on theological proposals in a new and different situation. This will in turn provide principles both for evaluating the use of scripture by theologians and for a constructive interpretation of theological positions that appeal to scripture. In other words, a theology of the use of scripture provides hermeneutical principles for interpreting theological doctrines.[1]

I will approach this question in two stages. In the first I will make use of David Kelsey's work on the logic of bringing scripture to bear on theology within the church.[2] Then in a second stage, represented by the next three divisions of the argument, I will use the theology of revelation and of the status of scripture in the church already put forward to inject a theological component into Kelsey's logical framework. Then in a final section I will develop the implications of this view for the interpretation of theological assertions and the discipline of theology more generally.

The Logic of Scripture's Use in Theology

David Kelsey's important work, *The Uses of Scripture in Recent Theology*, consists in a thorough analysis of the way scripture is actually used in theology by a number of present-day theologians. In fact theologians use scripture in their theology in many different ways. But his goal is not to advocate any single one of them. Rather he tries to define a common logical structure underneath all of them.[3] In a way, then, Kelsey's work might be called meta-theological, an essay that goes behind actual theological uses of scripture, and brings forward an abstract, formal, and functional structure that governs the use of scripture in theology today. In what follows I will not try to reproduce Kelsey's whole theory. Rather I shall merely isolate three elements of his analysis which seem to me to be central to the whole of it, and which, in any case, will form the framework for the specific theological proposal put forward here.

The first and foundational element for the use of scripture in theology concerns the authority of scripture within the church. The recognition of that authority depends on the recognition that the church is, as it were by definition, a community of faith whose faith is expressed by, crystallized in, and normed by scripture. As Kelsey puts it, the authority of scripture is "analytic" in the very concept of church.[4] In other words, one cannot conceive of what the church is without including at least implicitly that scripture be the norm of this community. As was said in the last chapter, this is not so much an argument, since it would be entirely circular, but rather a functional definition of the church. It simply states what the church is, namely, the community whose faith is authoritatively governed by scripture. It may be said that the idea that scripture is the constitution of the church, which is not Kelsey's phrase, includes the same insight.

Although the notion of the authority of scripture is stated here as a logical presupposition of the church, it is important to realize that this is not merely a question of logical definition. We have already discussed, on the basis of the historical character of revelation, the historical necessity that scripture, as a recognized classical expression of revelation, become the church's constitution. As the church moves away from the event of original revelation in time, it risks its loss in the constant changes of historical process. But over and above even this logic this constitutive role of scripture in the church's faith is empirically verified.

In fact scripture is used in the community to express, communicate, nourish, criticize, and govern the community's life of faith in all sorts of different ways: in liturgy, sacrament, preaching, prayer, teaching, and the continuing and constant reading and study of this book. That scripture is the governing authority within the church seems self-evident from within the church.

From this first premise, so to speak, it may be useful to repeat again a principle that is crucial for understanding the discipline of theology. Scripture and the theology flowing from it have a critical function. Theology does not simply describe actual church behavior and practice, preaching and doctrine. Theology, belief, and doctrine point to more than what the church holds at any given time.[5] Social sciences may analyze what in fact people believe and what the church is teaching at any given time. But there is a critical and normative dimension of scripture relative to the church that singles out theology as a normative discipline. Theology more often proposes to change the church rather than simply echo what the church is saying. It is often ideal in its character and not descriptive of the actual beliefs of the church. Theology has the critical task of saying what church teaching should or ought to be in the light of scripture.[6]

The first principle tells us that scripture has authority in the church and the church's theology. But it does not indicate how that comes to bear on the theologian's use of scripture. It is clear that all theologians do not use scripture in the same manner. According to Kelsey, in each case the way the theologian uses scripture depends on an a priori judgment about the way in which God is mediated to the community of faith through scripture. How scripture is normative thus depends on an a priori imaginative judgment about the mode or manner in which God is made present to human existence and the church by scripture. This second principle is the heart of Kelsey's theory which needs further explanation.

The theologian presumably is a member of the church. By participating in the church he or she experiences the actual influence of scripture on or in the community. From this experience a constructive imaginative conception is formed of how God becomes present and influences the community through the mediation of its use of scripture. For example, a fundamentalist theologian may conceive of scripture as God's inspired words and propositions, and thus scripture comes to bear on the community as information about and knowledge of God. A fundamentalist theologian recites or repeats scriptural texts. An existentialist theologian may see scriptural language as myths which have the function of awakening an experience of a forgiving God that provokes a response of fundamental openness and trust in facing the future. A fundamental construal of how God works through the scripture is at work in each of these uses of scripture.[7]

This foundational judgment about how scripture mediates God to the community is a priori in the sense that it functions as a prior premise and framework for other ideas that flow from it. It is imaginative because the data do not yield it automatically. Rather it consists in a constructive construal of what is going on in the use of scripture in the church. Often this foundational conception is so fundamental that it contains in germ a holistic understanding of the dynamics of Christianity itself.[8] Behind every use of scripture in theology, then, whether or not it is openly put forward in an explicit declarative way, lies some conception of scripture as a medium of God's being present to and influencing the community.

Third, although scripture comes to bear on theology as an authoritative norm, it cannot be said to be the exclusively determining norm. This becomes apparent by a *reductio ad extremum*. Were scripture the exclusively binding external authority for theology, theology could consist in no more than a repetition of scriptural words and propositions. But theology is always more than this, and more than a mere translation of scripture into other terms and languages. For even such an attempted translation is not mere translation but a really different expression containing another meaning from what it purportedly merely translated. The doctrines of the church are different from scripture and not merely translations of it. This is as true of Nicaea and Chalcedon as it is of the theological proposals of theologians today. It becomes eminently clear when one reads and compares contemporary theology with the language of scripture. Bultmann is not saying the same thing as Paul, nor Rahner the same thing as the writers of the gospels. This difference means that scripture cannot be regarded as the sole determining authority for theological assertions.

Besides the authority and norm provided by scripture, theology depends on other sources and norms as well: current experience, a whole range of knowledge from other disciplines, and a critical assessment of these sources also enter into the content of theological assertions. Against this view, Paul Tillich seems to argue that contemporary experience should not be thought of as a source and a norm for theology, but only its medium.[9] He wants to preserve God's initiative in the biblical message as the authority for theology. But it is hard to conceive how this is possible. Current experience not only raises the questions of theology, it is also party to the theological conception of their answers.[10]

The conclusion of this logic, then, is that scripture has a normative

influence in theology, but it cannot function as an absolute, determinative, and objective authority. Such a position would reduce theology to a
recitation of the biblical text. Given the historical nature of the biblical
text, even fundamentalistic theologians, insofar as they make theological
proposals today, exceed a mere repetition of biblical texts. For all theology depends on an a priori theological judgment of how scripture comes
to bear on the church. And all theology today exceeds the limits of the
biblical texts. Rather than viewing scripture as an exclusive norm that
determines theological propositions, it may be regarded as a norm for
the aptness of current theology.[11] Christian theological statements may
also come from sources other than scripture, but scripture remains the
internalized external authority for Christian authenticity and genuineness. We shall return to this vague concept of aptness further on.[12]

This schematic interpretation or appropriation of Kelsey's formal
theory of the use of scripture in theology will serve as a framework for a
further constructive proposal. In it I shall try to integrate the theology
of revelation already discussed with the logic of Kelsey to determine how
one might understand theologically how scripture comes to bear on
present-day theology.

REVELATION AND SCRIPTURE

We begin this theological account of how scripture comes to bear
on theology with a recapitulation of some of the major conclusions that
have already been drawn concerning revelation and its relation to scripture. I shall merely enumerate very briefly these propositions which will
serve as the premises for what follows.

First, revelation at bottom is a form of human religious experience,
and as such it is potentially as common as religious experience itself.
This religious experience is revelation in a Christian sense because it is
construed as initiated by God's universal Presence within human subjectivity. One might say more precisely then that revelation occurs within
human experience.

Second, this experience of revelation is always necessarily historically mediated. The content of revelation always lies at the juncture of its
medium and the transcendental Presence of God to human subjectivity.
In Christianity the historical event of the life and death of Jesus is the
central medium of the revelational experience of God. All other revelational media are subordinated to and illumined by Jesus. As mediated by
Jesus, revelational experience may be characterized as an intersubjective

encounter with God as divine personal Presence who accepts and loves all human beings.

Third, the experience of a revelatory encounter with God is differentiated. One can distinguish between the holistic experience of revelation described as personal encounter and the objective interpretation and expression of what is experienced in the encounter. The linguistic and mental construal of God is historically conditioned, and as an aspect of the transcendental experience as a whole it can never be comprehensive of either the experience or the recognized transcendence of what is experienced. This distinction is crucial, for it enables one to bypass completely naive ideas that theology is translation of scripture.

Fourth, original revelation is the first and originating experience of a revelation that becomes the source of a religious community and tradition. Jesus stands at the head of Christian revelation, and the experience of God, mediated through Jesus, of the earliest disciples constitutes the original revelation of Christianity. In a loose sense scripture functions as the expression of this original revelation that governs the tradition that comes after it, that is, dependent revelation.

Fifth, scripture as the constitution of the church has authority in the church. Since scripture is the expression of the original revelation that constituted the church, so as to become the written constitution for the community of tradition that historically follows and depends on this original revelation, scripture must have an intrinsic authority and normative character for the ongoing life of the community in history, that is, insofar as the community intends to remain Christian. Thus the authoritative mediation of scripture is "analytic" to the concept of church; it is implied in the very nature of the Christian church.

At this point we have caught up with the first major premise of Kelsey's theory of the use of scripture in theology. We have also begun to integrate with his formal theory a theology of revelation.

Scripture as a Religious Medium

Given this view of revelation and scripture, we can begin a constructive theory of how scripture relates authoritatively to theology with a broad characterization of scripture as a religious medium.[13] Scripture, relative to Jesus as the founding medium and historical source of Christian revelation, is an ever-present second-order medium for dependent revelation. The point here is merely to call attention to the kind of medium it is.

Scripture as a book is itself a concrete medium for ongoing revelation. But as a whole it is itself a complex set of many, indeed innumerable, religious media. This becomes clear when one recalls that a religious medium can consist of anything, any person, event, idea, concept, written proposition, or work that communicates to religious imagination and experience. A medium provides theme and content to an experience of transcendence. Scripture, then, in the multiplicity of its books and texts, adds up to a whole collection of diverse religious media.

It is important to recognize the sheer generality of this initial characterization of scripture as a complex set of religious media. The significance of the generalization lies in the great diversity of religious media contained in scripture. The very statement that scripture is a set or collection of different media can be understood in a variety of different ways. Not only is scripture made up of an enormous variety of religious media, these media are different in kind. The various books of the scriptures can be viewed as distinct media insofar as they are unified wholes. But passages, paragraphs, verses, sentences, general ideas, individual words also can function as discrete media. The texts of scripture are also made up of myriad different genres: chronicle, history, gospel, biography, letters, and short story; song, psalm, and prophecy; covenant treaties, wisdom sayings, legends, and myths; revelations, laws, moral principles, practical precepts, and orders of discipline; poetry, liturgical formulas, and rites; sermons and doctrinal instruction. All of these different genres refer to different aspects of things; these different aspects of reality all have a distinct way of being known. Scripture is also open to a variety of different modes of analysis each one of which can deepen an understanding of the various kinds of media: philological, historical genetic, historical social, structural, literary, rhetorical and so on.

Added to the extraordinary diversity of religious media that goes into the make-up of scripture are the many different ways in which theologians appeal to and make use of scripture. First of all, any one of the books, passages, paragraphs, sentences, concepts, or words may be appealed to in any given case. The data, then, in terms of media are practically speaking limitless. Also the way or manner in which the appeal is made, according to this or that analysis, can also be widely variable.[14] For example, in the study of the church one could isolate the religious media, the images, metaphors, and other figures that have the primitive church as their referent.[15] But this cannot in any way be seen as a comprehensive consideration of biblical data. It may be that, since the church gets its character from Jesus, all the scriptural data referring to Jesus have considerably more importance than direct characterization of the church, and so on.

There are two sides to this huge amount of diversity among the religious media contained in the scriptures that relate to each other in a certain tension of ambiguity. On the one hand this pluralism mediates an exceptional richness of content for our construal of transcendence. The enormous variety of religious media means that dependent revelation is readily open to new depths of understanding in new situations into the future. The constitution of the church does not leave the church hamstrung and immobile in its journey into the future. On the other hand the church cannot exhaust the potential meaning mediated by scripture, not at any given time, and not across time. And it is clearly and utterly impossible that any theologian can decide a complex theological problem with a mere citation of some biblical concept or scriptural text. When one simply takes a look at the complexity of the scriptural media, the very idea immediately appears absurd. Therefore one will have to come to a much more nuanced understanding of how scripture actually comes to bear authoritatively on theological proposals.[16]

But this diversity of scriptural data does not mean that it is merely a chaotic mass; the religious media of scripture are not lacking in interrelationships and internal coherence. There is some order in the importance of these media that make up the constitution of the church. For the Christian, Jesus stands at the center of scripture, that is, insofar as the scriptures are appropriated by the church. And the person of Jesus always stands behind the text of the New Testament, especially the gospels. This Jesus is not a figure of speech, myth, or legend, even though his life as it is depicted in the New Testament is often called today a parable of God. Rather Jesus was a concrete human being. As such Jesus is the object of christology and the central medium of Christianity itself. All other religious media and interpretative expressions of God in the scriptures are peripheral in relation to this center. But some religious expressions are closer to this central medium than others, some so close that, as "first expressions" or even reflective, second-order theological expressions, they share in the authority of the medium itself. For example, the idea of the kingdom of God is so close to Jesus' life and message as to be considered a part of his personhood. This does not mean that such a concept as the kingdom of God is not open to new interpretation in new historical circumstances; it simply means that such a religious medium, by being closer to the center of scriptural mediation for the Christian consciousness, bears more weight for that consciousness than others at a further remove from Jesus.

In sum, the complex and pluralistic character of the authoritative constitution of the church means that its authority cannot be brought to bear on the church in a simplistic way. But at the same time there is a semblance of order in the bible, so that within the great variety of religious expressions and media that constitute it, one can assign an order of importance and hence degrees of authority to its media. And Jesus is at the center of this order. Jesus is the central focus of the Christian imagination in the church's faith in God. Not Paul, and not John or Luke, and not what Paul and the others say about Jesus are central. Prior to Paul and the object of Paul's interpretation is the person of Jesus who in some measure can be recovered from behind the text of scripture.[17] This Jesus is the central objective medium and hence authority for Christian belief.

SCRIPTURE AS A MEDIUM OF REVELATION

We pass now to the second key element to be appropriated from Kelsey's formal analysis of the use of scripture in theology. This consists in the prior imaginative construal and theological judgment concerning how God is rendered present to the Christian community by scripture. This is the hinge upon which every use of scripture in theology swings, if it is coherent; this is the centerpiece, because it is the presupposition upon which the various kinds of usage of scripture depend. It arises out of an experience of how scripture is actually used in the general life of the church, but at the same time it is a speculative or theoretical construal of what is going on in that usage.

Given this structure, and borrowing from the theology of revelation presented in earlier chapters, it may be understood that scripture makes God present in the church by mediating an awareness of and an empowerment by God's Presence. In other words, scripture, or really any part of scripture, is the historical medium that makes God's Presence as Spirit or grace encountered in this way or that. In the chapters which follow we shall describe this mediation further as symbolic or sacramental. But the analysis of the nature and function of an historical medium in the experience of encounter that is revelation is sufficient to make the point. Scripture as an ever-present second-order expression of original revelation is the historical medium of dependent revelation. Scripture makes God's Presence present in a conscious, thematic, and empowering way within the community of faith.

In a way this statement appears to be a description of what goes on in the church in its use of scripture. It describes what occurs when scripture is read in the assembly and interpreted by preaching. God's Presence is awakened by this reading, this set of religious media, these words, concepts, ideas. From biblical reading and instruction, through the long spectrum of the various instances of formal use of scripture in the church, to the simple usage of biblical words in ordinary Christian conversation, scripture functions by shaping consciousness into a positive specifying awareness of God's Presence. By mediating this or that quality of the encounter with God, scripture empowers Christian freedom and action.

But this is no mere straightforward description. It is itself dependent on a highly theoretical and theological construal of the nature of God, of God as universal and effective love, a love that in turn implies God's self-communication and personal Presence to each human being. This is coupled with an anthropological analysis which concludes that this Presence of God takes on no positive identity in human consciousness without historical media to awaken it in a specific way. Thus the basis for this premise for understanding how scripture comes to bear on the community is itself a theological construction drawn from the mediation of scriptures themselves.

This theological judgment usually sums up or captures the whole complex reality of Christianity in a single unified root metaphor or notion. In it one can find a foundational and all-encompassing theological conception that governs or controls other theological positions. This too is true of the view that is put forward here. The theory of revelation that sees it consisting foundationally in God's Presence to humankind universally, and its center of gravity consisting in an experience of an encounter with God's Presence as accepting and loving, is also a characterization of the holistic meaning of Christianity.[18]

Still remaining on the level of how scripture functions in the general life of the church, we ask how the authority and normative character of scripture comes to bear on Christian life. In response to this question it can be said, on the one hand, that scripture is authoritative and normative because it mediates God's Presence. On the other hand, it is only authoritative and normative insofar as it mediates in some manner an encounter with God. In other words, the various religious media in scripture are not authoritative "in themselves" so to speak. They do not enjoy a merely external and objective authority. Rather they gain their authority by being the medium of an experience that is implicitly and reductively religious. The words of scripture do not bear any intrinsic authority, for religious authority ultimately is God's alone. Since they are media only when they mediate God's Presence, their authority is completely dependent on the experience of an encounter with God that is mediated by them. The same point can be stated in terms of the theology of faith. Religious authority is a function of faith, and faith constitutes religious authority in its own regard by its acceptance of it and commitment to it.[19] But it is important to recognize in this formulation the priority and initiative of God in the experience of faith itself.

This structure of the authority of scripture in the lives of Christians is verified by the many instances in which scripture is not authoritative. There are many aspects of the laws of ancient Israel that simply do not mediate an experience of divine will for people today. Women see no divine authority in the demand to wear veils in Christian assembly. These and many other media in the scriptures do not awaken any religious resonance or response. And this is understandable when the issue concerns religious authority. Unlike all human political and social authority, religious authority is from a transcendent source, and it must be experienced from within. By definition it cannot be attached exclusively and comprehensively to an external worldly object.

In sum, the controlling concept for how scripture comes to bear on the whole life of the Christian community is mediation; scripture is authoritative by being a medium for an experience that reductively is based on an encounter with God. By being the vehicle of God's Presence this religious mediation has an impact on the whole person; it influences the mind, the will, human affectivity, and the exercise of freedom in decision and action. The dimension of authority, however, cannot be attached to the media of dependent revelation in themselves. Rather these media gain their authority within the experience of God that they mediate. Thus scripture is authoritative because and only insofar as it stimulates or mediates experience of God.

SCRIPTURE AND THEOLOGY

Scripture mediates a conscious awareness of God's Presence in this way or that way through the variety of its languages and concepts. It thus becomes a source and norm for theological proposals, beliefs, and doctrines. How does this occur? More specifically, how is the theologian concretely to make use of scripture in making theological statements in an authoritative or normative way? It should be noted here that theologians often use scripture in a variety of ways, as rhetorical devices, as illustrative of a point, as examples of a past historical belief. But the question here regards the proposal of theological assertions today that may enjoy some measure of an authority derived from scripture. In this context the way scripture functions and the way theologians may use scripture are correlative. In this section we describe generally how scripture comes to bear on theology authoritatively. In the next we shall examine the theological use of scripture.

The dynamics of how scripture influences and exercises control of Christian theology may be summed up in the two terms "disclosure" and "elaboration." Scripture is normative "insofar as it can serve as a starting point [by disclosure] for a process of elaboration over which it exercises control because it is the model for the elaboration."[20] Disclosure responds to the questioning of the religious imagination. The whole dynamism of human existence as the action of freedom leads it to the brink of the religious question. At any given point the human subject may become captive to the religious question. This openness to transcendence is the receptive ground for the mediation of scripture. The mediation of scripture may itself open up this receptivity. But at the same time, in the response to scripture, scripture shapes religious experience in this way or that according to the particular words, concepts, texts, or parts of scripture that are brought to bear. But this experience must be elaborated. The mode of subjectivity determined by the specific, objective, scriptural mediations must be expressed in current language fitted to knowledge of our objective world as it is today. Theology is always written in a contemporary language. But insofar as this language is faithful to the experience that is mediated by scriptural language, it will also be influenced by scripture.

Disclosure

The need for a dynamic concept such as disclosure, as opposed to something like dictation, to describe the first level of the influence of scripture on theology can be seen fairly plainly in the fact that current theological language is different from scriptural language. A simple comparison would show that the languages of current theology are new and in varying degrees radically other than those of scripture. Theology today is obviously not a mere repetition of biblical language, and we will have occasion to show in later chapters on theological interpretation that repetition of a past language in a new situation changes meaning. Nor is theology a mere translation of one language into another language such that the meaning remains identical. Current theological proposals correspond to new experiences, new historical situations, new knowledge, and new languages, and new conceptual systems. From the point of view of its historical understanding and expression across time it was said that revelation really develops and changes. This corresponds to the function of theology. Thus scripture does not and cannot dictate absolutely theological language or proposals for today.

In tension with this newness and difference, however, the idea of mediated disclosure guarantees the influence of scripture on theology and preserves on a deep level the qualities of sameness and continuity of an historically given revelation. It was said of revelation that from another perspective it does not develop but occurs again and again. I refer to the center of gravity of revelation that consists in the sheer encounter with God as gracious Presence mediated through Jesus and the scriptures. In its transcendental aspect this experienced encounter with God is the same as original revelation. From this point of view theology is not a translation of concepts and expressions of this encounter that are given in scripture. It is rather a reexpression and reconceptualization of an experience of an encounter with this God that is disclosively mediated by scriptural language. This is the first and most fundamental way in which scripture comes to bear authoritatively on theology. And although it may remain tacit and implicit, an appeal to disclosure is the first and fundamental act of the theologian when he or she uses scriptures.

Elaboration

We shall speak of the elaboration of a theological position more fully while dealing with the issue of theological method. What is at stake here is simply how scripture comes to bear on the theologian and theology. What influence does scripture have on the elaboration of a theological argument?

The elaboration of the renewed experience of revelation is both free of scripture and at the same time governed and influenced by scripture. It is free because theology cannot be a mere recital of scripture, and is much more than a mere translation of scripture. Theology is a critical discipline that does not repeat but tries to understand and make sense out of its authoritative constitution in new situations using new languages. But it is not enough to say that theology is a free expression of the transcendental dimension of revelatory experience. The vast complex of religious media that constitutes the scriptures also has a bearing upon the specific content and language of theological proposals today. One can see how their influence comes to bear both negatively and positively.

First of all, scripture acts as a *negative* norm for theological proposals. But even this simple statement must be understood with a considerable degree of nuance. It cannot mean that this or that idea or proposition in the scriptures cannot be negated. For the whole of scripture is pluralistic and contains contradictions within itself. Therefore plainly any theological proposal today which may be in agreement with one portion of scripture may also take a position at odds with another. But for the Christian scripture has a thematic center in Jesus and a certain wholeness and coherence in the sum total of its message.[21] It is, when interpreted from a Christian standpoint, not merely an indiscriminate collection of writings. As an ordered whole the scriptures offer limits which a Christian theological proposal today cannot negate. For example, one cannot elaborate a proposal that reduces God to impersonal nature or fated determinacy. One cannot portray God as demonic or malevolent, and so on. The scriptures as a whole, then, in their generalized message about God, human existence, and reality in relation to God, as these are recentered and reinterpreted through Jesus, act as a negative norm for theology today.

Second, scripture offers a *positive* guide for theological assertions today. Scripture urges and moves theological elaboration in a positive direction. This positive influence can be seen at work in at least three distinct generic ways:

First and most generally, by their use in the community the scriptures shape the subjectivity of the theologian. They nurture fundamental values and "school the affections" which have considerable bearing on the fundamental response of the theologian to the world.[22] They shape the imagination by which reality itself is construed. They provide fundamental ideas and concepts that enter into the vocabulary of a reflective understanding of God and the world in the light of God. In short they mediate a whole world-view.

Second, when scripture is viewed as an expression of a holistic vision of God with Jesus as its central medium, it acts as the constitution of the church in a manner that is analogous to a legal constitution in a common law tradition. In such a system, the laws change by application and reinterpretation in new situations. The point here however is not the necessity of reinterpretation; this is presupposed in what was said earlier. The point, rather, is how the original constitution continues to come to bear on new interpretation by being that which is interpreted. A constitution works its own way within the new interpretations of law by being their source of inspiration. Thus the fundamental content of scripture continues to guide, shape, and be present within new theological statements. If one cannot find this positive influence within a current theological assertion, then it is dubiously Christian. In other words, they must be genuine elaborations especially of what is found at the center, that is, the narrative of the life and teaching of Jesus.

Third, what is said of scripture as a whole may also be said of any one of the significant religious media that make it up. The complexity of scripture entails that any one of its diverse parts may guide theological elaboration at any given time. In any period the gospel of Luke or the concept of the kingdom of God, once submerged in the complexity of the whole bible, may emerge with particular relevance for a particular historical situation. Thus any part of scripture, always in tension with the whole, may open up and authoritatively influence a new line of theological elaboration.

In sum, these two terms, disclosure and elaboration, describe how scripture comes to bear upon theological assertions today. They describe how scripture exercises its authority. This is not a literal external authority that dictates the words or language of a theology. Rather it is an intrinsic authority that is mediated through the words, concepts, passages, and books of scripture. In the final section we shall turn these conclusions into critical principles for interpreting theological assertions on the basis of their use of scripture.

THE USE OF SCRIPTURE IN THEOLOGY

These two chapters have dealt with the status of scripture in the church. Together they propose a theology of how scripture is the authoritative constitution of the church by virtue of its being the classical expression of original revelation and the authoritative source of theology by its mediation of dependent revelation. The question now concerns its cash value for interpreting or judging theological proposals in terms of their use of scripture. What principles does it yield for the interpretation of the validity of theological assertions, beliefs, or doctrines on the basis of their use of scripture?

First of all, the theological theory developed here stands opposed to fundamentalism and revelational positivism. Why is fundamentalism rejected? Fundamentalism fails because it is based on an a priori imaginative theological construal of revelation but one that is untenable. The theological supposition of fundamentalism is that scriptural words are God's words, inspired in such a way into human minds that they are not historically conditioned but come inerrantly and somehow extra-historically from God. This revelational positivism now stands contradicted by what appears to be common sense. And this historical common sense forms the premise for the enormous advances in the study of scripture itself.

In our day historical consciousness has undermined and ruled out the mere citation of scripture as an external authority as a method for establishing by itself the validity of a theological position. Negatively, then, in the theory proposed here, a direct objective appeal to scripture or to biblical theology to support a theological position does not of itself establish or validate that position. No citation of an individual scriptural text, no collection of citations, are of themselves internally relevant or directly authoritative for a theological assertion today. This is a shift or change relative to classical theology which operated largely on the premise of the received notions about scripture. Given inspiration, the propositions of scripture, understood objectively in themselves, constituted direct authoritative witness, if not knowledge about God. For example, Aquinas held that the strongest argument in theology consisted in an argument from authority and this meant using data from scripture and the creed as objective premises for theological statement.[23] This is no longer possible in the framework of historical consciousness. Because of the historicity of all human conceptions of reality, theology can presuppose neither the meaningfulness nor the relevance of human conceptions of a past age. One of the tasks of theology is to examine critically what the witness of scripture and past doctrine means. And the more that that meaning is historically determined, the more it will appear as distant from us and a product of a past age. Mere external authority, then, has become the weakest theological argument, for it is no argument at all.

Examples will show that this critical principle is extremely relevant for interpreting and evaluating current theological proposals. If a theologian supports a theological position merely with citations from Paul or John, the first reaction to this evidence should be to question its relevance. Why not another scriptural passage that says something different or even opposed? As was said earlier it is not immediately relevant to us today that Paul thought that women should cover their heads at a Christian assembly. But the same is true and for the same reasons of such statements as "the Word was made flesh." The mere citation of scripture by itself does not establish theological positions for today, because scripture is an expression of faith and revelation that is historically relevant to another age.

This critical principle has particular relevance for the theological interpretation of theological doctrines from the tradition insofar as they appear to be based on scripture. A critical understanding of the doctrines of tradition require an examination of how scripture was used to support them. The mere citation of scripture cannot support past doctrines any more than it can support theological assertion today. A good example of this is the Nicene definition of the consubstantiality of the Logos with the Father.[24] Contrary to appearances, the extensive citation of scripture that abounds in Athanasius' arguments to support that doctrine did not and could not have elicited the conclusion over against the Arian position. Rather that which ultimately was decisive for the position of Athanasius was the experience of God's salvation, itself construed in a certain way, that was mediated by Jesus of Nazareth.

Despite the fact that the mere citation of scripture is not sufficient evidence for a theological assertion today, scripture does not cease to be the authoritative constitution of the church, nor does theology cease to be a normative discipline. The internal logic of theology still lies in an intention to disclose the meaning of Christian faith, to investigate critically church doctrine and practice, to change it when it strays from what is mediated by its classical expression, to display and try to justify its truth. Even in the face of the obvious confusion of theology's sometimes wild pluralism, the internal logic of the discipline seeks normativity even when it fails to achieve it. The issue at stake, then, is not the authority and normativity of scripture in itself, so to speak. It is rather *how* scripture may be used, *how* it can be brought to bear on a theological assertion or proposal for our time.

The theory presented here of how the theologian can use scripture in an authoritative way today contains two fundamental principles. The first is that the appeal to scripture in theology in reality rests on a complex theological judgment of how scripture makes present God's authoritative influence in the community. The second states that, when scripture is brought to bear, it must be accompanied by elaboration and argument.

Regarding the first principle of this theory, the fundamental theological judgment upon which it turns is indeed complex. It involves a theology of revelation which itself balances in tension God's universal Presence and self-communication with the necessity that every positive awareness of this Presence of God be historically mediated. It includes a theory of scripture as the first expression of original revelation and as the constitution of the church. It views this ever-present and second-order medium of revelation continually awakening an authoritative experience of God's Presence in ongoing disclosure. This complexity, however, is not arbitrary. It is forced upon us today by the breakdown of the received notions about scripture in the face of historical consciousness. In this situation every foundation for an appeal to scripture involves equally complex presuppositions.

But the theological complexity of this theory should not blind one to a certain simplicity in the whole thing. Since this theory is drawn from the practical life of the church, it can also be used to describe what happens theologically in the church. In other words, is this not what happens? Scripture is read in the church which is itself in ever new historical contexts. Scripture awakens an experience of God in this or that way that takes on a particular relevance in this situation. Scripture is then brought to bear on this or that issue in this specific context to illumine it theologically. When theologians appeal to scripture, this is what is really going on. Their use of scripture is itself an appeal to an experience in the present that is mediated by the text. In the first instance the use of scripture in theology is disclosive.

The second principle of this theory, however, is that the authority of scripture cannot be immediately received as authoritative without elaboration and argument. It is not necessary to review all the reasons for this: the enormous complexity of scripture, its pluralism, historical conditionedness, and lack of comprehensiveness. This historicity of scripture dictates that every use of it, beyond mere citation, must be accompanied by explanation, elaboration of the experience it mediates, and argument why and how this particular use of scripture is relevant as opposed to other texts, mediations, and data. What are the fundamental values and conceptions that are inherent in and mediated by the text? It must be shown to be coherent with other things that we know; it should be intelligible, plausible, consistent with other theological positions. The theologian should be conscious of a relative order in the Christian appropriation of scripture and the centrality of Jesus in it. He or she must elaborate the connections between the foundational disclosive experience and the way it comes to bear on this issue. All of these processes will be discussed further when the issue of method in theology is raised. But they have a bearing here on how the authority of scripture must itself be mediated in the proposals of theological positions.

Finally, one might ask at the end whether anything is left of scripture's authority after all of these qualifications. Certainly a religious authority that appeals to freedom and is open to dialogue and discussion among different parties in the church and in the world is not the same kind of authority postulated by fundamentalism. It is rather precisely the authority of a God who is self-disclosive in human experience in history, a God who appeals to human freedom through love. Can such an authority really be an authority? In the end, there can be no question about the authority of God in the life of faith of a religious person. God's authority is that by which every religious life is led. The internal appeal to freedom within experience constitutes the very nature of religious authority. It is the only authentic religious authority we have. It follows that such is the very basis of all authentic this-worldly religious authority. The external authority of scripture and the church as a community must be understood in relation to and as mediational of God's authority. Every authority within the church is third-order authority, after the tradition of scripture, and whose function is to mediate God's authority in the tradition of scripture.[25] The way this authority can be brought to bear today will be further clarified in the discussion of religious mediation within the context of symbolic communication.

IV

RELIGIOUS SYMBOLS

Chapter Seven

THE SYMBOLIC STRUCTURE
OF RELIGION

We move now to another category and area of investigation which have a fundamental bearing on the nature of theological assertion and the discipline of theology itself. We have seen a variety of reasons why fundamentalism, a literal view of theological affirmation, will not do. An alternative to fundamentalism, one that does not totally rule out the values which fundamentalism seeks to preserve, consists in viewing the whole structure of religion as symbolic. Theology and the theological positions that are entailed in it will on this view also be symbolic.

From one point of view, the discussion of theology as a symbolic discipline will not advance the argument of this book in a linear way. It will rather serve as a reprise from another standpoint of the nature of beliefs, the structure of revelation, and the authority of scripture. The category of symbol will serve as a vehicle for describing more exactly the epistemology of beliefs, the dynamics of the communication of revelation, and the structure of scriptural language. The understanding of religion and theology in terms of symbol will help to clarify and make more explicit elements that were passed over too quickly in the preceding sections.

Once again the two chapters that follow fall into the pattern of moving from a general theory to a particular application of the theory. In this chapter we shall try to explain the structure of religious symbols and why religion itself is always symbolic in nature. In doing so we shall draw heavily on the theologies of symbol of Karl Rahner and Paul Tillich. In the next chapter we shall deal with the dynamics of symbolic communication, especially as that comes to bear on the nature of a theological proposition.

We shall begin by drawing what has been discussed about faith, revelation, and scripture into the framework of the category of the

129

symbolic. Basic theological issues are raised here: How is awareness of transcendence or a self-communication of God entertained by the human mind? What kind of knowledge or truth are we dealing with here? In response to these questions we shall characterize the dialectical structure of the religious symbol and how this is exemplified in two kinds of religious symbols that have a direct bearing on faith, revelation, and the status of scripture. We shall conclude by pointing out the relevance of this view of religion for theology.

The Symbolic Structure of Faith, Revelation, and Scripture

The area of the symbolic involves issues that are fundamental to religion and theology. Like the notion of sacramentality, which on a generic level is identical with the symbolic, we are driven back to the issue of how any contact at all is possible between transcendence and human existence. To introduce this topic on this general theoretical level we shall begin by positing an initial simple definition of what a symbol is. We will then briefly review what has been established in the theologies of faith, revelation, and scripture in terms of the symbolic. The point is to establish another perspective on the premises of theology so that the whole discipline of theology can be clarified further.

A symbol may be simply defined as that through which something other than itself is made present and known. In some cases the symbol may be the only way through which the thing symbolized is actualized or known. Depth psychology provides an example of a symbol in the sense defined here that has become popularly recognized. A dream may be considered a symbol of a deeper layer of consciousness, a symbol through which what is subconscious rises to the surface. The symbolic dream makes present for analysis that which, except for the dream, may be inaccessible to reflective and conscious awareness. Much more could be said about a symbol and about this example, but at least it illustrates the fundamental nature and function of the symbolic. A symbol renders something else present and actual; a symbol is cognitive by making known something other than itself. With this basic concept one can show the symbolic nature of faith, revelation, and scripture.

The analysis of faith with which we began this work unfolded within an existential framework. The point was to understand faith in its first moment as a common human phenomenon. From this anthropological perspective faith appears as the central, radical, and comprehensive commitment of human freedom. Because of its depth, the actuality of one's faith, what one's faith is really committed to, may be difficult to know directly. Faith is something that engages the whole being of a person and cannot be reduced to a function of the mind or intelligence. Because the object of authentic religious faith must be strictly transcendent and not part of this world, because if it were it would not require religious faith at all, faith cannot be considered as knowledge in the ordinary sense of this word. On the one hand, then, faith is not knowledge because its object is not available to it.

But on the other hand, faith is always faith in something; faith always has an object. Although not reducible to a function of mind or conscious intelligence, these are not excluded from the human response of faith. Thus faith is cognitive, and beliefs express what is known of faith and its object. These beliefs are formulated in ordinary human language whose words have their initial meaning drawn from our knowledge of the world. And yet they are designed to express what cannot be strictly speaking known, and really refer to something other than this world from which they draw their initial meaning.

This simple paradox that is involved in all religious faith and belief can be summarized by the designation of religious beliefs as symbolic. Beliefs, whose formulas are constituted by words, concepts, and propositions drawn from ordinary experience of the world, are meant to make present and disclose to our subjectivity something other than anything in this world. All beliefs, then, insofar as they give expression to religious faith, are symbolic. They make present to reflective consciousness something other than themselves, namely, both faith itself and its object. All theological statements are symbolic. Of its very nature, theology is a symbolic discipline.

In the discussion of revelation we took the turn of all modern theology to the framework of the human subject and its existence in history. God's universal Presence to human subjectivity must be historically mediated. Such an historical medium is a symbol; the term symbol is synonymous in every respect with what has been called a medium. A symbol is any thing, event, or person of history which mediates or makes present to human consciousness God in this way or that way. Thus the genetic structure of revelation is always symbolic; at the origin of every religious community and tradition lies some set of historical symbols. In Christianity Jesus is the originating symbol of Christian revelation.

The differentiated analysis of the dimensions of human consciousness that receives revelation, its epistemology, betrays another level of its symbolic structure. One can distinguish the global impact of transcendence on subjectivity, that is, the personal encounter with God and the impression it makes on a person, from the impression made by a concrete medium together with the active interpretation and expression in language of what is experienced. The logical basis for such a distinction lies in a recognition of the meaningfulness of such a term as "infinite" or "infinity." Infinity is the negation of all limit and boundary. Beneath this logical meaning is the experience of the human mind of infinity in the very recognition of the sheer finitude and contingency of every worldly object and the whole of them together.[1] The background of this implicit awareness of infinity is what gives the term finitude its meaning. Against this background, too, all spontaneous interpretations and all more reflective articulations of an encounter with absolute and infinite transcendence appear as symbolic. Interpretation necessarily borrows from the language and concepts of ordinary commerce with the world in order to mediate into public expression that which transcends the content of ordinary speech. The language, concepts, interpretations, and judgments based on religious experience are meant to mediate consciousness of something other than themselves, namely, encounter with infinite transcendence. All reflective consciousness of revelation therefore is intrinsically symbolic.

It follows that scripture is a symbolic book. Scripture is made up of a complex set of symbols that make present to consciousness something other than themselves, namely, an encounter with God's Presence in the church. Of course this is a gross simplification of the variety of different kinds of content one finds in scripture. Some passages in themselves do not seem symbolic at all, but are statements of fact or narrations of historical events. But in the context of the whole work references to merely historical data are often understood as media and hence symbols for God's Presence and action in the world. Scripture is thus a second-order symbolic representation of original revelation which constantly mediates dependent revelation to the community in a symbolic way.

In sum, the idea of a symbol provides a vantage point for another approach to the very foundations of theology. By examining the structure of religious symbols and symbolic communication one should be able to derive new principles for understanding what is going on in theological assertion.

THE DIALECTICAL STRUCTURE OF RELIGIOUS SYMBOLS

What is a religious symbol? What follows is a descriptive characterization of religious symbols. Working within the framework of the initial concept of something through which some other reality is made present and known, I will try to characterize what may be called the nature of a religious symbol. A theme in this description that deserves particular attention is the paradoxical or dialectical structure that is intrinsic to a religious symbol.[2]

A symbol is first of all a finite reality of this world. Indeed anything in this world could function as a religious symbol. But the point here is that a symbol is in itself a finite something. It has its own identity, its own integrity as a finite being. It can be understood in its own terms, so to speak, prior to being a symbol. It is potentially explicable as an integral finite reality. The dream, for example, could be innocent, no more than a nocturnal flash of memory that bears no revelatory depth. At least it could be regarded simply in itself as merely a dream. On the first level then a symbol is itself and not other than itself.

But, second, as a symbol this finite reality or segment of reality points to and reveals something else. This function or operation is precisely what makes a symbol a symbol. The symbol as it were negates itself; its function as a symbol is a pointing beyond itself to something other than itself. Or it becomes transparent; when regarding a symbol one must look through it and beyond it for that which, other than itself, is revealed by it. The dream is not significant in itself but only insofar as it points to deeper dynamisms in other layers of consciousness or subconsciousness.

Here we have an initial indication of the inherently paradoxical nature of the religious symbol. Although it has an integrity of its own, it points beyond itself to something that is totally other than itself. The finite directs our attention to the transcendent and infinite. The perception or recognition of a symbol, then, is an intrinsically dynamic process. Human consciousness both attaches itself to the symbol in its integrity, and at the same time is directed by the symbol away from itself, for the symbol points to, reveals, makes known not itself but something other and different from itself.

Third, one can say more about this paradox. For the symbol does not reveal simply by pointing away from itself; it also makes present that other to which it points. This quality is frequently drawn out by contrasting a symbol to a mere sign. The contrast lies in the definition of a mere sign as something that bears no internal connection with the thing that is signified by it. Thus a red light means stop and a green go. But there is no compelling reason why convention could not establish the opposite, or that stop and go might not be represented by anything at all. The situation is quite other in the case of the dream. This dream may bear an intrinsic relation and connection to an autonomous, submerged, and long ignored set of memories. This dream expresses, re-presents, and makes present to an objective or reflective analysis what otherwise would not be explicitly known at all. In this case the internal connection is causal. This particular dream is caused by these experiences and memories that have come together in some pattern or syndrome.

The tensive or dialectical quality of a symbol is heightened with these ideas of intrinsic connection between the symbol and that which is symbolized. The symbol makes present that what is symbolized, that is, something other than itself. In the case of the dream this being present is easily understood in terms of causality; the unconscious produces the dream. But the presence of transcendence in the integral finitude of a religious symbol is still more paradoxical.

Tillich speaks of the participation of the symbol in that which is symbolized. In other words, the symbol does not merely make the other reality present, but in one way or another the symbol shares or takes part in the reality of the symbolized. This too can be seen in the case of the dream. The subconscious state has caused the dream; the dream shares in, contains, is constituted by the experiences, memories, emotions, and reactions of the subconscious state. In a way the dream, although in this case it is only relatively autonomous, participates in that other form of consciousness in such a way as to be it but in another form.

The term "participates" at this point is merely descriptive and somewhat vague. It will have to be clarified along the way in different kinds of religious symbols. But it is sufficient to highlight in a further degree the tensive or dialectical quality of the religious symbol. Participation suggests unity of different elements. The symbol so participates in the thing symbolized that what is other than the symbol is present within it, and the symbol makes present what is other than itself, even though it retains its finite integrity. In the case of religious symbols this represents a unity and difference between the infinite transcendent and the finite worldly which is paradoxical.

On the basis of this descriptive characterization of the symbol we can now provide a fuller definition of its nature and the precise qualities that are of peculiar interest in religious symbols. A religious symbol is anything finite that discloses and points to what is other than itself and strictly transcendent, but which at the same time makes that transcendent other present by participation in it.

At the heart of this notion of a religious symbol is what can be called a dialectical tension. By dialectical here I simply mean the unity or coexistence of aspects or qualities that seem to be opposed. This does not mean that in any given case the reasons for the unity and opposition cannot be explained. We are not speaking here of contradictions, but rather dimensions of a reality which are genuinely opposed to each other and thus when maintained together exist in tension. Thus, for example, the religious symbol and that to which it points, makes present, and participates in are not just different beings but qualitatively different kinds of being. This unity of differences, and differences in unity, sets up a situation in which one can say in one sense the symbol is not what it symbolizes, for the symbol in its finitude is radically other than transcendent infinity. Yet the same situation yields a sense in which the symbol is what it symbolizes because of its participation in that greater and other reality which it makes present. This "is" and "is not," when viewed from different perspectives, is what I call the dialectical quality of religious symbols. It will be the theme for the further discussion of different kinds of religious symbols.

Religious symbols can be divided into two different kinds: concrete symbols and conscious symbols. Concrete symbols are tangible elements of this world: things, events, or persons that make God present to the world and serve as media to communicate God to human consciousness. Conscious symbols comprise the variety of different ways in which God is portrayed in human consciousness: the myths, figures of speech, and other conceptions that are the human images of God. In the two sections which follow we shall discuss each of these two kinds of symbols in turn, in each case drawing out their dialectical structure. It should be noted that in the case of Christianity these two kinds of symbols correspond roughly to the media of original and dependent revelation. Jesus is the concrete, central, and founding symbol who mediates original revelation, and scripture is the second-order complex of conscious symbols that continue to mediate dependent revelation.[3] Thus this discussion leads back again to the foundations of Christianity and its earliest theologically expressed self-understanding.

CONCRETE SYMBOLS

Concrete symbols are entities of this world. They are the concrete things, events, and persons who mediate to human consciousness conceptions of God. But even more basically they are considered as mediating God's being present in the world. What follows is an analysis that seeks to explain or at least to give an account of how concrete symbols mediate God's being present in and through them. This account is

appropriated from the theology of Karl Rahner. It is put forward here
with a certain stress on the dialectical structure of concrete symbols.

The Dialectical Structure

The primary analogy employed by Rahner to illustrate a concrete
symbol, or what he calls a real symbol, is the human person.[4] The
structure of the human person is itself symbolic, and this provides a
basic analogy for the nature of concrete symbols. But behind this prime
analogue found in the metaphysics of the human person lies yet another
structure which goes back to Thomas Aquinas and through him to
Aristotle. Rahner's theology of symbol ultimately has its roots in Aristotle.

Aquinas borrowed from Aristotle the hylomorphic theory by which
entities are made up of two distinct principles, matter and form. Form is
the principle that accounts for the kind of any being, its being of such or
such a kind. Matter on the other hand accounts for the individuation of
this entity or that within a given species or kind of being. Form and
matter are completely distinct principles of being, almost in themselves
antithetical. Form is intelligible and contributes the intelligibility of
whatever kind of being that exists. Matter is in itself unintelligible, a kind
of primal stuff that can only exist when suffused by some intelligible
form. In the human person the intelligent spirit is form, but matter is
not quite equivalent to the body. For the human body is human also by
virtue of the human spirit. Matter rather is that latent stuff that accounts
for the sheer physicality and individualization of this particular person.

At work in this theory is a causality which Rahner calls mutual or
reciprocal causality. Reciprocal causality simply refers to two principles
that each cause the other to be but in different ways. Matter and form
together make up one single entity, an undivided and unified being. And
yet these two principles of being are really two; they are distinct. But in
together forming one being they cause each other to be. Form is dynamic and makes matter to be the individuality of this being. Matter is
pure receptivity that causes this form to be actualized in this being. By
formal and material causality each principle of being is the cause of the
other being realized in a single entity. In a human person spirit and
matter are diametrically opposed, for spirit is non-matter and matter
non-spirit. Yet they cause each other to be as one in the single unified
person.

The reciprocal causality of spirit and matter in the human person,
but also in being itself, is a truly dialectical principle that allows for
paradoxical statements. The human person is a differentiated unity; it is

constituted by plurality although indissolubly one in being. Spirit, in order to be, must exist in another; it must pour itself out into what is other than itself. Matter, which is not spirit but a diametrically opposed other, becomes the expression of spirit. Matter is the image of spirit, the very expression of what is other than itself. In a paradoxical way, matter which is not spirit becomes the actualization of spirit, for spirit cannot exist at all except by being and expressing itself in another.

One can bypass Thomistic metaphysics and by a phenomenological or descriptive experiential account of the human person arrive at a similar conception. The human person is a unity, but it contains dimensions that are experienced in tension with each other. The person exists in a tension between nature and freedom, where nature refers to the determinations on the physical, biological, and psychological levels, and freedom consists in the spiritual self-transcendence of reflective self-consciousness and self-determination. Within this tension I can say that I am not my body, because the sense of self transcends the body. The experience of the possibility and belief in the actuality of survival after death also seems to necessitate some distinction between the human spirit and the empirical this-worldly body that is laid in the grave. On the basis of this unity and distinction, then, one can make dialectical assertions about the self. One can say, "I am not my body," or "The human person is not the body." And yet one would also want to say, "I am my body," and, "My body is me." What is the reason for insisting on the unified identity of body and spirit, nature and freedom, when one recognizes their non-identity? It lies in the fact that the two are one, that the human person is a differentiated unity. The body makes present to the world an inner core of transcending self. The body precisely embodies human freedom or spirit. The body causes human freedom to be here and now in this way and that way. The body is no mere instrument of human freedom, but the very expression of the human spirit, even though the spirit is more than and different from the corporeal self.[5] Such an analysis is consistent with and explains the phenomenology of interpersonal communication underlying the analysis of revelation presented earlier.

This excursion into a metaphysics and phenomenology of the human person has a point, namely, to establish an analogy for the dialectical notion of symbol on more than impressionistic grounds. In these accounts this dialectical structure is based on a form of causality, mutual or reciprocal causality, that engenders a unity-in-difference in being. It enables one to conceive how, in different ways, one dimension of being may be the expression and real presence of another element of being or even kind of being. Reality itself is complex and differentiated. Thus one can conceive of various levels or kinds of causality mutually influencing each other, while at the same time not being commingled, confused, or conflated into a single undifferentiated thing, but remaining distinct in their interaction. This is a groundwork for the paradoxical assertions which symbols often occasion.

Examples of Concrete Symbols

One such paradoxical assertion might be that of a people who insist that God lives in that sacred mountain over there. That is God's dwelling place; God is present to us through the mountain's being there. Examples such as this could be multiplied. They show how all things are able to be symbols of God, and do make God present, precisely by being finite creatures. By their finitude, coupled with the doctrine of creation, every being makes God present in the power of God's creative activity.[6] Some things, such as mountains, have qualities that call attention to God's power, awesomeness, eternal permanence, and presence to human existence here and now. But the mountain is not God; nor is any finite reality God. Nor would people insist that God lives in the mountain in the same way they live in their houses. The mountain is still finite, and God still God. Yet it like all things can body forth and make present the infinite power of being itself.

The human spirit animates more than the human body, but extends through and beyond it to influence the world. And this action is always a reaction of the influence of the world on it. Thus the world is continuous with the human body and is itself the body of the human spirit. This analogy can give rise to the panentheistic view that finite reality itself is the body of God's presence and power. The world is not God, however, but precisely other than God. Thus all finite reality participates in the power of God, and every portion of it is God's symbol making God present.

Historical events and persons, however, are able to be the symbols of God in a different way and a higher sense than can inanimate or inhuman created things. Because of the personal and dynamic quality of historical events, they are able to embody those qualities of God in a manner that no mere thing ever could. And as has been seen in the general theory of revelation, God can become present to persons in a personal way. God acts in regard to creatures according to their nature.[7] In the case of free human persons God is a personal Presence through a self-communication.[8] On the basis and under the influence of God's Presence human beings are able to speak of God as a divine person. Human beings can embody those qualities of God in their own lives by virtuous deeds that seem to transcend human capacity. Human beings can be the concrete symbols of God's free action in the world. Thus personal symbols of God are able to mediate God's Presence in the world in a qualitatively higher way than inanimate things.

One can follow these lines of thought for an understanding of Jesus as the central symbol of God's revelation and the authoritative and normative embodiment of God in the world. Corresponding to the theology of grace, this understanding would appeal to the tradition of a Spirit christology in the New Testament. God's Presence as Spirit was within and at work in the life of Jesus.[9] In this understanding of the incarnation of God as Spirit, Jesus' being the symbol of God would be strictly dialectical. God as Spirit would not be a Presence in a body, but in Jesus as an integral human being. Jesus is truly, that is to say, really a human being completely like us in all things except for sin. But Jesus is also really God being made present in the world. Insofar as Jesus is a human being, he is not God; yet he more than points to God as a mere sign or prophet. Jesus is God's symbol that makes God effectively present and manifest in this world by Jesus' being God's expression.[10]

This same dialectical structure, although in a lesser degree than in the case of Jesus, also applies analogously to such conceptions as the church as the symbol of God's Presence in the world, and to the sacraments as practical extensions of this conception of the church. For example, it is the common belief among Christians regarding the Eucharist that God is really present in and through the elements that re-present Jesus. These beliefs and doctrines should not suddenly be understood naively and literally. They should be understood precisely symbolically and dialectically. But at the same time one must understand that the meaning of symbol here is one that implies an ontologically real causality that embodies and makes God really present. A concrete religious symbol is not merely a sign or an arbitrary pointer. A concrete religious symbol makes what is symbolized really present.

CONSCIOUS SYMBOLS

One can ask the same questions of conscious symbols that were asked about concrete symbols. How do the ideas, notions, and concepts of God that we predicate of God because they disclose God as the object of faith "participate" in God? Can this be explained in an intelligible manner?

The issue involved in the problem of religious language is rather straightforward. God is transcendent; God is qualitatively other than and completely different from the whole of finite being. This is how God is experienced, and this experience has been codified in the doctrine of

God's absolute and incomprehensible mystery. Yet we speak about God in language and concepts that are drawn from things known in this world. Insofar as their meaning and intelligibility are tied to this-worldly experience, our predicates about God seem to be radically cut off from the reality of God insofar as God is infinitely and qualitatively other. How are we to understand our language about God in such a way that our concepts are not sheer projection, thrown upward into the air, so to speak, without engaging the reality of God?

Given this formulation of the problem, the natural tendency in religion generally and in theology as well is often to confess the absolute transcendence and mystery of God and then to ignore it. How much theology simply appears to know too much about God to be credible? If the problem is to be faced squarely, it must be handled with some form of dialectical thinking. Symbolic language is dialectical. It is comprehensible language drawn from finite, worldly, and historical experience. The question is how this language discloses God by "participation" in God. What does it mean to say that our conceptual symbols participate in that which is symbolized, namely God, and not merely in a human psychological experience? We shall address this issue first in objective and then in existential or subjective terms.

First and objectively, since conceptions of God are drawn from the world and from concrete symbols in nature, history, or personal lives, they may be said to participate in God insofar as the concrete symbols from which they are drawn participate in God. All human language has a certain reference to the world. In the communication of meaning between person and person, and underlying the social bond of meaning constituted by language, lies a common external world of reference.[11] In the analysis of concrete symbols it was said that the world and any part of it can be symbolic by virtue of its foundation in the creative causality of God. For example, one predicates omnipotence of God on the basis of the experience of the vast complexity of nature and the seeming infinity of space in which this quality of God is entailed by being the infinite ground of these still finite realities. Prior to arguments concerning the nature of God, symbols like the sky and the limitless horizon of the sea frequently elicit experiences of God's infinity. Here the objective qualities of the symbols, on the assumption that they themselves reflect qualities of the ground of their being, are merely echoed by conscious symbols. Conscious symbols reflect the reality of God because God is immanent and present to the concrete symbols from which they are drawn.

In the case of Jesus, what we know of his life, teaching, and action unfolded under the influence of his perception of the reign or will of the

God whom he called Father. His life in turn mediates a disclosure of God the content of which is derived from Jesus' participation in God's Presence to him and power within him. Conscious symbols, then, from this point of view, do not refer as it were directly to God, but to God as God is recognized as present in power within the concrete symbols of the world and a Presence in persons and historical events. Insofar as they are drawn from and determined by concrete symbols that participate in God, conscious symbols may also be said to participate in that which is symbolized.

But, second, this objective explanation is not sufficient by itself. Historical consciousness has made matters much more complicated. In the end there are so many and such contradictory concrete symbols which present themselves as revelatory of God, that one has to ask how one can decide whether this symbol or another really participates in God so as to disclose God as God is. Why not a capricious or sadistic God manifested in the Holocaust rather than a faithful and liberating God manifested in the Exodus? Why is crucifixion a symbol of God's salvation and not God's defeat?[12]

Ultimately the response to the question of how human concepts participate in God can only be existential, subjective, and experiential. In the end religious experience is self-authenticating and its own authority. It is for this reason that theology is always confessional; in religious dialogue with other traditions of experience Christianity can only confess its own. Standing back and addressing the validity of religious conceptions from outside religious experience, one cannot finally demonstrate how they truly participate in God's reality. One can only argue *toward* their truth, because faith is ultimately a function of freedom.

But from inside a religious tradition and its experience one can account for this symbolic participation. Conscious symbols participate in God by causing an otherwise vague and undefined Presence of God to the human person by grace to become an explicitly conscious Presence. There is a reciprocal causality here of a material and formal kind. The real contact with God is constituted by God's Presence within human subjectivity, and symbols participate in that Presence by formally causing it to be a thematically or reflectively conscious Presence. The conscious symbols that are predicated of God, then, are constitutive of the experience of God. And insofar as God is really a Presence within human subjectivity, conscious symbols share in God's being present to human consciousness.

But one should distinguish quite clearly this subjective participation in God's Presence to us from the issue of the adequacy of the symbols we predicate of God. No symbol "comprehends" God. Nor is it epistemologically possible for human beings to form an objective conception of God against which other conceptions can be compared, even though Jesus functions this way in the Christian imagination. Symbols mediate and express an encounter with the infinite God, so that a moment's reflection on the symbol from within that experience will reveal at the same time the infinite distance of our language from the reality of God. Even the concept "Being itself," Tillich came to see, is symbolic of God and therefore dialectical.[13] All symbols of God are inadequate, and at best one may speak of a comparative relative adequacy of the symbols we predicate of God.[14] The way in which this relative adequacy is judged will be discussed in the chapters on theological method.

To summarize, concrete symbols and conscious symbolic language about God are always interacting. But the pattern of this interaction is somewhat different in the genesis of original revelation and dependent revelation. The difference here is one of thematic weight since conscious symbols always influence the primitive experience mediated by concrete symbols, and concrete symbols always "lie behind" conscious symbols. But Jesus is the concrete symbol at the origin and source of specifically Christian revelation. The revelatory experience of God that is mediated through him gives rise to conscious symbols. In dependent revelation, in the handing on of this experience to further generations, it is in the first place conscious symbols that mediate and thus shape our experience of God. But these conscious symbols never have an independent and objective status or validity on their own so to speak. They are always a part or a dimension of an experience of an encounter with God, and they always relate back to some source in a concrete symbol. Within the experience of God conscious symbols must correlate with the object of religious experience. But this correlation or correspondence is not the result of an empirical comparison, as if God were an object already known. Rather there must be, on the one hand, an internal and circular correspondence between what is encountered and the conscious symbols which express or mediate this encounter, such as holy, good, gracious, saving and so on. And, on the other hand, a correspondence must exist between these conscious symbols and the concrete historical symbols that continually mediate religious experience, especially the central historical symbol which is Jesus.

THE SYMBOLIC STRUCTURE OF THEOLOGY

We can conclude from this analysis of religious symbols that theology is a symbolic discipline. From beginning to end it deals with symbols.

Theology is the systematic effort to understand reality, God, the world, human existence, and history through and on the basis of the symbols that express Christian faith. The faith to which it gives expression is symbolic; the revelation that supplies its foundational content is symbolic; its scriptural source is symbolic. The simple division of symbols into concrete and conscious should not be allowed to obscure the variety of scriptural symbols; we have already called attention to the great diversity of genres that make up the Bible. The complexity of scripture consists in an elaborate mixture of conscious and concrete historical symbols. Conscious symbols have historical referents, and what appears as pure history and law is disclosive of God's Presence. It may appear that the Genesis myth and the philosophically wrought formula of creation are vastly different kinds of expressions of faith. But they are both symbolic. All theological reasoning and assertion are symbolic.

The idea that theology is a symbolic discipline is not new. Theologians have always been aware that when they spoke of the transcendent God they were not using language in the same manner as when speaking about this-worldly reality.[15] In classical medieval theology various theories of analogical predication functioned as the equivalent of symbolism. One could probably trace the shift from the framework of analogy to that of symbolic language as running parallel with the shift from an objective cosmocentric theology to the anthropocentric, subjective, and historically conscious approach to faith and revelation described earlier. In any case symbolism deals with the same issues as did analogy, but in a way more fitting to a religion whose revelation consists in interpersonal encounter and historical "dialogue" with God.

In the theory of religion that has been outlined here the central and most important element consists in the dialectical structure of the symbol, whether it be a concrete symbol or a conscious symbol. This dialectical element consists in the fact that in the analysis of a symbol, a statement about a symbol, or the use of a symbol in a predication about the transcendent order, one will always be left with two elements that must be held in tension with each other. These two elements can always be reduced to some form of an "is" and "is not."[16] The concrete symbol is and is not that which it mediates. God is and is not that which is predicated of God symbolically. This dialectical structure constitutes the intrinsic nature of the symbol. The symbol is something that makes something other than itself present; it points beyond itself, because it is not that which it symbolizes and makes present. And yet that which is symbolized is mediated and made present by the symbol so that the symbol is the presence and expression of the symbolized. Every mode of expression that attempts to bypass or leave behind this dialectical structure distorts the religious phenomena it seeks to explain. One must keep the tension between the two poles in the dialectical structure of religious symbols taut; it can never be relaxed.[17]

It should be clear at this point that this dialectical structure is not merely rhetorical. The "is" and "is not" of symbols does not consist in a mere impressionistic assertion of paradox. In a way the "is not" is immediately apparent; the symbol by definition is obviously not the symbolized. On the other side, most of this chapter and the next have been dedicated to something of an explanation of the different ways the identity can be understood. The dialectical structure of a symbol then can be explained as a process of mediation. Not a static structure, symbols are communicative. They mediate another reality. What is involved here is a dynamic process in which something is going on in reality and in the dialogue between reality and human consciousness.

On the one hand, religious symbols point to what is other than themselves, that which the symbol precisely is not, because God is infinite and absolute mystery, holy and incomprehensible. Although symbols mediate cognitive awareness of God, this does not constitute a knowledge of God in the way we know finite reality. This simple statement becomes significant when one reflects on how the whole enterprise of religion and theology tends toward objectification. There is a natural tendency to treat theology and its religious symbols as though they provided information about God, as though we could know about God and deal with the sphere of transcendence as one would with this world. If theological language were construed as literal speech, this would at the same time reduce God to the dimensions of our conceptions of finite reality. This literalization of religious language is more than misleading. It can and often does lead to idolatry, fanaticism, and demonic behavior. The theme or implicit claim to possession of religious truth, especially by those in authority within a community, can corrupt the whole religious sphere. In the end we stand before God largely in ignorance and wonder. We do not and cannot grasp or possess God as an object. God is transcendent; God is God. When God is revealed and encountered this disclosure always has an "event" character to it. The response to this is not a sense of possession but of sheer gratitude.

But on the other hand, one should not regard our language about God as if it consisted in merely gratuitous and arbitrary signs. As Tillich says, symbolic truth is not less but more than literal truth. And as Rahner explains, a religious appreciation of our finite world implies that it cannot be reduced to a two dimensional sphere.[18] The world in which we exist has a depth and a height that are constituted by something other than itself. The world subsists in the power of God's creative causality, and God as Spirit has freely entered into dialogue with human existence as personal Presence. The world as symbol mediates to human consciousness the reality of God as power and Presence.

In sum, theology is a symbolic discipline because symbolic language is the only kind of language that is appropriate to its subject matter. This language is not only dialectical and thus paradoxical; it rests on an epistemological realism that corresponds with a symbolic interpretation of reality. The position here could be called a "dialectical symbolic realism." This implies a cognitive appropriation of the way God really is in a dialectical symbolic way. The dynamics of the epistemology of symbolic language will be clarified more in the discussion of symbolic communication in the next chapter.

Chapter Eight

SYMBOLIC RELIGIOUS COMMUNICATION

The last chapter explored the structure of the religious symbol. The question before us now concerns the way in which symbols communicate. The last chapter dwelt especially on the dialectical nature of the religious symbol, and how they can be said to participate in the transcendence they symbolize. We now move to the dynamics of communication, to a descriptive account of the manner in which religious symbols mediate meaning to human subjectivity. The transition is from the nature of religious symbols to their concrete functionality. How do religious symbols impact human consciousness? What are the conditions that are necessary and allow for the recognition of their meaning? What kind of knowledge and truth do they mediate for human life?

The significance of these considerations is once again fundamental for understanding the dynamics of theology as a discipline. In deciding the manner in which religious symbols communicate, one is at the same time laying down presuppositions and principles for the way religious statements are to be interpreted. In other words, the generic meaning or kind of meaning carried by theological statements is implied in the way they communicate that to which they point and in which they participate. Thus after laying down the premises for symbolic communication culled from the theory of symbols just elaborated, and after an analytic description of how they communicate, we shall be able to recapitulate this discussion of religious symbols in the form of principles for interpreting theological affirmations.

For the most part the framework for this analysis is that of dependent revelation. Occasionally we shall refer to the mediation of concrete historical symbols or speak of faith as the response to revelation. Indeed this whole discussion could unfold in the context of the theology of faith, because scripture and doctrine are symbolic expressions of faith. But the context of revelation places more emphasis on the initiative of revelation in providing the specific content of Christian faith. Within

146

this framework, the issue is this: given a set of religious symbols from the past, either in scripture or any set of doctrines, how do they communicate to us today? By expansion, this same question can be put to any theological proposal or statement. Since all theology is symbolic, what are the dynamics of any theological communication?

THE EXISTENTIAL BASIS OF RELIGIOUS COMMUNICATION

We begin with a foundational principle that will serve as the premise for everything that is said in the course of this chapter. This supposition concerns the existential basis of all religious communication. The principle may be formulated in this way: all communication by religious symbols presupposes and is based upon engaged interest. The kind of knowledge that is as it were transmitted is an engaged participatory knowledge. Thus not only the truth of what is communicated by religious symbols, but also its very meaning rests on a distinct form of openness to participatory engagement with what is potentially communicated. The existential basis for the communicability of religious symbols, then, is an engaged participatory interest which alone can generate the knowledge involved, namely, an engaged participatory knowledge.[1]

The quality of this participatory interest is hardly mysterious and its nature can be easily illustrated by contrast with the kind of knowledge that has as its object simple matters of fact. Subjective life is filled with knowledge of data and information that are viewed in a detached, objective, neutral, and disengaged fashion. A great deal of what we know about reality is accompanied by little more interest than simple curiosity. Knowledge of the data of science, of history, of everyday events need not be thematized by any heightened existential engagement. The difference and distinctiveness of engaged participatory knowledge appears in contrast as a knowledge that involves and may even demand subjective, existential, and experiential engagement. In engaged participatory knowledge the knower is subjectively interested because something is personally at stake in subject matter. The object being communicated is laden with value, so that appreciation of it involves value discernment and value response. Prior to this knowledge, one must be looking for what is being presented, engaged in a search to find it, so that discovery appears as a kind of recognition of what was already anticipated by the quest. The communication of religious truth through symbols is based on and demands as a prior condition of its possibility this kind of existentially engaged openness to, interest in, and quest for a religious content.

This distinction, and hence the distinctive quality of religious communication, is noted by H. Richard Niebuhr when he explains how concrete historical religious symbols are able to mediate religious truth. Niebuhr distinguishes between outer history and inner history.[2] Outer history refers simply to our knowledge of external events as objective empirical events that transpire outside of us. This kind of knowledge lacks any theme of an intrinsic bond that links the events to the self in any important way and thus is disinterested. Inner history is the same outer history but with a crucial difference: inner history is engaged and participatory knowledge of outer history. Because the external events have an intrinsic bearing upon the self, the subjective appreciation of them is completely transformed and transforming. For example, the founding persons and events of a nation are not merely objective and neutral for the patriot. Rather they are appropriated in such a way as to determine the values and goals that direct the patriot's life from within.

Extending the terms of Niebuhr's distinction, one could speak of outer language and inner language, where inner language would be synonymous with symbolic language. Thus in an analogous way symbolic language does not merely communicate external and objective meaning. What is being communicated is not verifiable in an objective way and its meaning is not without bearing upon the inner life of those to whom it is addressed. Symbolic language is like the external events of inner history; they are external forms of language which can only bear the meaning they intend when they are approached and appropriated in an existentially engaged and participatory manner.

Another and perhaps simpler way of making the same point would be to insist that religious symbolic communication presupposes religious questions. If one approaches religious symbols without some form of religious experience or religious questioning, at least of an incipient or latent kind, religious symbols will not and cannot communicate as religious symbols. Religious knowledge is obviously not factual knowledge at all, but neither is it a matter of a reception of objective information about transcendent data. Rather religious symbols, although they are composed of ordinary language drawn from everyday experience, and hence possess a certain intelligibility in their own ordinary and everyday sense, intend to mediate something other than this, namely, a meaning which is intrinsically connected to an experience of transcendence. And such an experience of transcendence is an engaging participatory existential experience.

This premise is so basic that it reaches down below the question of truth to the issue of meaning itself. From one point of view and at a certain level of understanding the thesis here may appear counter-intuitive and contradicted by the facts. For example, does one not have to understand before one can believe something?[3] It appears from this point of view that the role of theology is to clarify meaning, to make symbolic language intelligible, and this does not require faith. Faith as a commitment to the truth involved may follow understanding but is not a prerequisite for meaning.

The logic of this position is important for preserving an objective and critical role for the discipline of theology. But it should not obscure the more basic point that is being made here. The logic of a critical theology always already unfolds within the larger circle of the meaningfulness of religious language itself. This always presupposes at some basic level an experience of, and interest in, questions that involve transcendence. The experience of the question of transcendence is latent in human existence as such and can be raised to a level of explicit inquiry. But if it is not, the religiosity of a religious symbol or text will not be recognized. In other words the entertainment of a religious question is an absolute condition for the possibility of knowing what a religious issue is. Therefore prior to the appreciation of all religious symbols as religious is the requirement of the religious question which is here called religious interest and engagement. That this governs even the question of meaning is illustrated by the obvious thematic difference between a religious symbol and an ordinary weather report, a recipe of Julia Child, and the lyrics of most popular music. The very meaning system within which religious and theological language unfold and seek to mediate presupposes some level of engaged participatory interest.[4]

This principle of the kind of knowledge that is mediated by religious symbols, and hence the required presupposition for their intelligibility, is absolutely fundamental to the qualities that characterize symbolic communication. Because symbolic communication is a mediation to an existential religious interest and engagement, its qualities will revolve around its ability to affect human subjectivity. The ways in which or how it affects the human subject can be analyzed phenomenologically. And these affects in turn will provide a basis for interpreting the generic meaning of the religious symbols that make up scripture, doctrine, and all strictly theological proposals.

THE CAUSALITY OF RELIGIOUS COMMUNICATION

Before proceeding with an analytic description of how religious symbols affect human consciousness, we must insist that symbolic communication cannot be reduced to mere psychology. There is both a subjective and an objective dimension to symbolic communication that can be analyzed within the framework of the theology of revelation already in place and in terms of causality.

It has been a constant theme up to this point that religious symbols, interpretations, theological expressions, and beliefs are expressions of religious experience. But it is also true that symbols cause religious experience. In the transmission of a religious tradition there is a certain priority of the symbol system to the experience of its meaning. Individuals are drawn into a concrete religious tradition by being presented with religious symbols, beliefs, and doctrines. In brief, religious symbols, prior to religious experience, cause human beings, through the experience that they mediate, to participate in God.[5] This priority and causality of symbols to religious experience needs to be clarified.

The causality of the religious symbol can be understood rather straightforwardly within the framework of the general theory of revelation that has already been presented. God as Spirit is present to all human beings personally. This grace is God's self-communication, God's Presence within the personality and subjectivity of each person. But this Presence is not a clear, specified, objective, explicit, or thematic object of human consciousness. It may be manifested as an undifferentiated experience or intuition of the transcendent or the holy; it may also be no more than a virtuality that lies implicit in the dynamic action of freedom. The religious symbol makes that a priori Presence of God to the human subject a more or less clearly conscious Presence. By giving specificity and content to the object of and reason for basic human trust, the religious symbol causes human beings to participate by faith in God consciously, that is, by a reflective consciousness.

In this schema, one can understand the causality of the religious symbol in terms of reciprocal causality. If one were to apply the Aristotelian categories of matter and form in an analogous way, God's Presence within the self-transcending dynamics of human action would correspond to "matter," and the religious symbol would correspond to "form." Thus God's Presence relates to the religious symbol as matter relates to form. In other words, the symbol causes an otherwise uninformed and undifferentiated pre-apprehension of God's Presence to become an objectively informed and specified consciousness. In this view one can understand why the religious symbol really and objectively communicates God to other human beings. For on the basis of the "symbolic realism" of concrete historical religious symbols, these symbols are themselves real expressions of God's activity as power in creation or as Presence in self-communication. As Dulles puts it relative to biblical inspiration, which he, too, understands in terms of revelation:

"Grace is God's vital self-communication, and hence what proceeds from a graced consciousness proceeds from God's self. The symbolic self-expression of the people to whom God communicates God's self, insofar as it signifies what God communicates of God's self, is also God's self-expression."[6]

Symbols therefore cause God's being present to human consciousness in a certain specific way, in this or that way according to this or that symbol, theological construal, or belief. They once participated in God's being present to the consciousness of the people who fashioned the symbols, wrote the scriptures, formulated the doctrines of the Christian tradition. And they cause persons in each new generation to participate in like manner. Therefore religious symbols have an objective realistic validity that is prior to the religious experience of the ongoing life of the church.

But it is not as simple as that. Without minimizing what has been said about the objectivity and priority of symbols to the experience they mediate, for these must be insisted upon, one must also recognize and insist upon the dialectical nature of symbolic causality. This inherent dialectical quality carries with it two sets of tensions that cannot be ignored. First, although the symbol fashioned under the influence of God's Presence is God's self-expression, it also is not. It is a human work, historically conditioned, which by its historical limitation can conceal as well as reveal God's self. Second, although there is an historical priority of the objective symbol in causing the experience of God at any given time, this is not the only cause. The other cause comes from God's Presence in subjectivity, and that subjectivity is itself conditioned by myriad circumstances that influence its own distinctiveness in time, place, and cultural individuality. The implications of this are simple but crucial. The past historical meaning of any given symbol contributes to but does not fully determine the meaning that is generated in experience. Thus no historical, philological, or semantic analysis of the objective meaning of the symbols of tradition fully accounts for its meaning today. In short the experience mediated by objective symbols simply is not the product of symbolic mediation alone. That meaning also has its grounds within present-day historically conditioned human subjectivity.[7]

On the one hand, if, after justifying the objectivity and priority of religious symbols, one then forgets the dialectical quality of religious symbols, one inevitably tends to lapse back into some form of scriptural or dogmatic fundamentalism or revelational positivism. On the other hand, within the context of the tension contained in symbolic mediation, one can still insist on these objective and prior dimensions. And with this as a premise, one can go on to appreciate the effects of symbols on human consciousness, that is, the qualities of this communication that are yielded by a descriptive analysis of how they function psychologically.

DIMENSIONS OF RELIGIOUS COMMUNICATION

What follows is a descriptive account of how religious symbols function in religious communication. What we have called dimensions of religious communication could also be called qualities, characteristics, elements, or functions of a process. Each of these dimensions has its significance, but all are merely aspects of a single process of mediation. Other dimensions might also be highlighted in a longer and denser phenomenology. In the course of this description I will illustrate each quality by two examples. The one is the symbolic doctrine that God is the creator of heaven and earth; the other is the symbol of the kingdom of God which Jesus made the central teaching of his ministry.

It is important to note at the outset that this description is itself a function of a critical consciousness. In other words, it attempts to get at what is really going on when religious symbols do communicate and are appropriated as they should be. This does not mean that religious symbols necessarily communicate on a religious level. When two people read the gospel accounts of Jesus, one may be moved while the other is not affected at all. Like many of Jesus' contemporaries, anyone can turn away. So too, it is certainly the case that many people receive religious symbols as a communication of factual information about God. This is not what is described here. It thus becomes apparent that this so-called description is really also a critical and constructive portrayal of how this symbolic mediation should be received and conceived.

Symbols Open Up Levels of Consciousness

Symbols open up levels of awareness in human consciousness that would remain hidden were they not awakened by symbols.[8] A good example of this is that of the dream which was advanced at the beginning of the last chapter. Symbols thus illumine the self; they reveal hidden structures of human life that can only be expressed through the language of symbol.[9] What needs to be recognized here is that the human spirit has these layers and depths. Paul Tillich has described at length the depth of reason. At this level a meditative or contemplative reason can confront the power and ground of being itself as the source of its own being. Tillich also describes an ecstatic reason in which human freedom as it were transcends itself to stand outside of itself by an experience of participation in infinite being.[10] The function of the religious symbol is to reach into these layers of consciousness. Moreover their real power to communicate religiously depends on their ability to touch and call forth into a reflective awareness these depths and heights. Of course these experiences may not be actual at any given time; they may have been past experiences which are implicitly remembered. But the meaningfulness of religious symbols depends on some sort of experience of transcendence or the memory of it.

For example, creation means to fashion out of nothing, so that what is fashioned depends completely and in every respect from the creator. Creator of heaven and earth simply means creator of everything. To say God is creator mediates the experience of one's own creation, the consciousness and realization that one is totally dependent in one's being on the power of God. One experiences the self as absolutely dependent on God, as supported over against nothingness, non-existence, or what Tillich calls the abyss, by the power of God who is the power of being itself. The symbol of creation comes from this experience and it can mediate this kind of experience of the power of God to another person.

The symbol of the kingdom of God is not totally unrelated; it refers to the rule of God as sovereign. It communicates a sense of God's will. The symbol of the kingdom of God can mediate the experience that as personal and as creator God has a will and intention for creation and that, as a creature, the self participates in that intention. The kingdom of God is "the living reality of God's present rule, not only in human spirits but also in the world of nature and of human history."[11] One can experience a sense of obligation, of being bound morally, of a need for obedience to what the will of God might be. In analogous ways, religious symbols, because they mediate transcendence, appeal to and open up the deeper layers of human consciousness.

It will be noted that in describing how the meaning of such religious symbols is communicated no appeal was made to an exegesis of the opening chapters of Genesis. Nor is there a need at this point to try to determine what Jesus meant by the kingdom of God. In the chapters on method in theology we shall insist that such an appeal is necessary in an integral theological method if the normative role of tradition that was justified in chapters five and six is to have any meaning in the discipline of theology. But that authority is not and cannot be literal and apodictic. Ironically, the closer one gets historically to Jesus and his message, the further distant he appears relative to our own cultural experience.[12] Therefore the past historical meanings of religious symbols and doctrines always have to be reexpressed in a contemporary idiom.[13] Moreover, when the symbols of the past are laid bare to the best of our historical ability, they still function in the way that is described here. They still have to awaken deep and self-transcending levels of present consciousness within which they become transcendently meaningful.

Symbols Open Up Levels of Reality

Symbols disclose levels of external reality that are not available to empirical observation.[14] This aspect of the communicative power of the religious symbol is strictly correlative with the former one; the two are simultaneous. In Tillich's conception of this function, reason or human consciousness is simultaneously both subjective and objective. Thus the levels of consciousness that are opened up by symbols correlate with reality, and reality is disclosed in the levels of consciousness that are opened up.[15] Reality cannot be reduced to a factual report of external phenomena and processes. An obvious example of how the human mind transcends neutral data is seen in the perception of, response to, and judgment of values. Here human consciousness transcends empirical data to a deeper level of reality. The function of symbols is to call attention to and open up the transcendent dimensions that are latent in external reality.

Many theologians correctly see a close relation between faith and the power of the imagination.[16] Symbols too are obviously linked to the imagination. By mediating to consciousness the object of faith, symbols release the imagination as the power of the mind to construe reality in dimensions that far exceed their empirical appearance. The imagination, by projecting and injecting deeper meaning into reality, also discovers dimensions that are already there. In their turn symbols evoke sets of meaning that genuinely illumine reality; they shed light on and reveal dimensions otherwise invisible. In sum, symbols bestow meaning on the external world by allowing human beings to see with their imagination what would otherwise remain hidden.[17]

For example, those who experience radically their absolute dependence in being, the experience that is mediated by the symbol of creation, cannot but see the whole world as created, as radically finite and contingent in its existence, without any sufficient reason for being or power of being in itself. One's own contingency is shared by all finite beings and the totality of being itself. This realization is not a new empirical experience; no new external fact is learned. Rather the whole of what is experienced is construed differently; a new dimension of reality has been opened up. The hidden structure of finite reality is disclosed as finite. In its finitude it is sustained by the infinite creating power of the transcendent God.

The symbol of the kingdom of God also responds to a transcendent question about the nature of reality, especially historical reality. Is there any unity or coherence in the world, any direction in its evolution, any goal in human history? One cannot find any unity of meaning in human history except on the basis of some transcendent principle.[18] The symbol of the kingdom of God provides its answer by informing faith and hope. It suggests that the creative power of God is also providence, an oversight that provides an overarching cohesiveness to history despite its evident and chaotic arbitrariness. Such a unifying conception can only come from some revelatory symbol that points to such a principle of unity, a symbol that opens up the possibility of faith and hope in such a reality.[19] As an appeal to hope the symbol of the kingdom of God is utopic. By depicting history in its ideal future the kingdom of God reveals human sin as sin; by contrast it shows that human history does not conform to God's will. It provides a framework for thinking about the direction which history and one's own life should take. It stimulates hope for partial realizations of God's values in the near future and stimulates energy in that direction. It draws forth courage on the basis of a confidence that the kingdom of God defines the final shape of things in an absolute future. In all of this the symbol of the kingdom of God points to these features as dimensions or possibilities of the actual world.

Symbols Transform

Symbols mediate transcendence, and by so doing they transform. This transformation is multifaceted and has many objects. We have already spoken of the transformation of consciousness. The category is especially important, for it indicates that what goes on in symbolic communication is not the learning of new data, but the transformation of the consciousness of old data. The breaking in of an awareness of transcendence alters the appreciation of reality outside the self and the very consciousness of the self. Transformation does not occur by addition; it is a new way of being conscious under the impact and light of transcendence.[20]

Thus symbols transform persons. They mediate conversion. Religious symbols make present to consciousness transcendent reality in a way that can only be appreciated by existentially engaged participation.

This premise of the way religious symbols communicate already implies openness to change, conversion, transformation. But the encounter itself is transforming. One cannot quite imagine an encounter with transcendence, especially an encounter with God as personal, that would not entail a transformation of the encountering person.

This transformation reaches into a person's action. Symbols influence action.[21] This transformation of action is the exact measure of the degree to which the symbol has been a communication which effectively transformed the person. If a religious symbol mediates an experience that really transforms a person, it must flow into personal behavior. Thus action is the criterion for the appropriation of what is mediated by a religious symbol. One could express the same quality of symbolic communication in terms of faith as its responding reception. Symbols appeal to and elicit a total response of a person. Thus they appeal as well to the will; they motivate and empower action; they influence and direct behavior. Symbols are principles of the action which in turn becomes the most elementary bearer of the response of faith.

For example, the symbol of creation transforms consciousness and thereby the whole person. This becomes apparent when one considers by contrast complete ignorance of creation, and awareness of it, and the transition between the two states. It is hard to imagine someone who would be unmoved by awe and reverence when seized by an experience of creation, since this implies that God is one's creator here and now, holding one in existence by power and love. The *"pro me"* of Luther's view of salvation applies intrinsically to creation as well. Consciousness of the self and the world are thus transformed; conversion of one's consciousness becomes a conversion of the whole tenor of a person in existence and in facing the world. The appropriated symbol of creation cannot fail to move a person toward the actions of contemplation and worship.[22]

The symbol of the kingdom of God as was said is not unrelated to what is disclosed by creation; the creator is sovereign of heaven and earth. The special note of the kingdom of God is that the one encountered, God, is encountered as having a divine intention for the world and human history. The symbol thus appeals more directly to human will and influences more pointedly human action. An appreciation of its transcendent meaning fairly demands a conversion to a desire to be in conformity with God's will. The symbol thus transforms natural ethics into an expression of God's will.[23] It transforms a person's responses to the world into simultaneous responses to God.[24] It transforms goals and ideals into the goals and ideals of God. It can thus have an impact on the transformation of the world. The kingdom of God is of this world and transcendently more than that.[25]

Symbols Introduce into Mystery

Symbols introduce one into mystery. This flows from the premise that the object of faith is transcendent and hence incomprehensible mystery. When God is revealed, God is revealed as absolute mystery. This function of symbols, their drawing of human response into mystery, is called mystagogical, a category which gets as close as any descriptive term to the epistemology involved in religious symbolic communication.[26] This is an epistemology of transcendence, or a transcending epistemology. It has its grounds in the power of the human spirit to transcend itself and to stand out from and above nature and finitude itself. This is supported and informed, in the Christian vision of things, by the simultaneous Presence of God that draws human consciousness toward and into this Presence. Thus the focus of attention in symbolic communication does not rest on the symbol in itself; attention moves through the symbol and reaches beyond it. The symbol serves as an instrument or vehicle by which the human spirit is drawn out of itself, and through the symbol beyond finite reality as a whole, in a quest for and then a dwelling in the transcendent sphere of absolute mystery. In Tillich's language, the fact that symbols point beyond themselves means that their "proper meaning is negated by that to which [they] point"; myths communicate by being "broken" in their literal sense; symbols mediate paradoxically by becoming transparent.[27] Consciousness does not rest on them but moves through them and is raised up to dwell in the boundless sphere of absolute infinity.

This mystagogical sense is illustrated well in Karl Barth when he speaks of the world of the bible as the world of God.[28] The symbols of the scriptures are laden with transcendence. Law is God's will; wisdom is God's wisdom; events are covenant fulfillment; escape is God parting the Red Sea; victory is God's action in holy war; Jesus is a man of God, God's wisdom is incarnate in him, God as Spirit moves him. Reading the Bible means entering God's world, that is, allowing human attention to be drawn through the finite world and into the sphere of that to which the symbols point, the world of God beyond the paradoxes and contradictions that may appear in the symbols themselves. But one must also note that symbols are dialectical, so that without denying Barth his say, one can, like Bonhoeffer, reverse the mystagogy. God is not only transcendent and in another world; God is within this world, and symbols make God present. By creation, incarnation, and grace God becomes the very within of things. Thus symbolic mystagogy means that the transcendence of God is also God's otherness which is immanent. The world itself is mystery because God is found at its core.[29]

God is the creator of all things. This symbol expresses the immanence and transcendence of God. The epistemology begins with the experience of one's own being as created. Within the experience of the contingency of one's own being, coupled with the fleeting intuition of being itself, one encounters through the symbol "Creator God" the one upon whom and in whom one's own being depends and subsists. This experience of being from inside being itself is extended or transposed outside the self. The symbol creation has a double sense: objectively it is what is created or all finite reality; subjectively it refers to the action of creation. The one becomes the symbol for the other. The focus of the attention of consciousness is drawn through the sheer finitude of the world and everything in it to rest in the power that causes it to be and the one who is that power. The symbol of creation gives the reason for the undifferentiated sense of awe and attraction in the face of the holy.[30]

The kingdom of God reverses the mystagogy. The creator is the within of things, their reason for being, their intelligibility, their order, their logic. God's will is written into being itself. The focus or attention of consciousness ascends and then descends to experience the intelligence, design, and will of God in the finite order of nature. A similar ascent and descent can occur negatively in the sphere of human affairs. By a negative contrast experience one is shocked into a recognition that a certain human situation should not be. One knows with an absolute certitude that this killing of the innocent is wrong. But why? What is the positive grounding for judging human conduct or human arrangements of oppression perverse? The symbol of the rule of God gives form and shape to what is implicitly apprehended in the human experience of revulsion in the face of innocent suffering. Through it consciousness is awakened in a positive way to the transcendent norm for human affairs. This negative contrast experience is the very ground of theological ethics. Without it there would be no need for ethics at all.[31]

Symbols Generate "Objective" Statements

On the basis of symbolic communication one can fashion objective statements about God. The contact with God that is mediated by symbols enables one to make general statements about God and finite reality in the light of God that are true.[32] But at the same time it is important to see what is going on here dialectically. The objectivity involved here does not entail translating symbolic statements about God into non-symbolic propositions. Objectivity in the sense of affirming something about God that mediates the reality of God has been justified in terms of symbolic realism. Symbols affirm something about the way the reality of God is. But such affirmations always remain symbolic. The function of theology is to explain, conceptualize, and criticize religious symbols.[33] This involves "translating" what they point to into seemingly objective, coherent, and intelligible language. But the content of theology cannot cease to be symbolic. The objective truth of symbols is always derivative from and always leads back to the experience that is mediated symbolically; this objective truth is grounded in existential and engaged participatory knowledge. Theology can never transcend its origin and source which consists in this experience of God mediated through symbolic communication.

The issue here is sufficiently subtle to merit further consideration. Let us move from the existential and subjective quality of symbolic communication to what its objectivity can mean. Because symbolic communication consists in existential engaged participatory knowledge of transcendence, symbolic theological statements cannot function as objective premises for deductive inferential reasoning. Such objective reasoning presupposes an adequate correspondence between concept and the object it refers to, such that reality corresponds also to the logical manipulation of concepts. The content of the symbols of transcendence is never objective in this sense. The meaning of religious symbols is always found within religious experience itself, and inferential conclusions must always also be thematizations of experience that is existentially participatory. Even when one recognizes the objective priority of symbols in causing and mediating experience, the final meaning of what is mediated depends on and is a function of religious experience. Otherwise religious symbols are distorted by being reduced to literal and comprehensive information about God. But at the same time one cannot argue on the basis of this existential quality of religious meaning that religious symbols bear only a private, confessed, non-objectifiable, or non-universalizable meaning.[34] Why?

The objectifiability and universalization of the content of religious symbols can be illustrated with the examples of creation and the kingdom of God. The individual person does not merely stand outside the reality of this world and regard it as a spectator. The human person is a part of this world so that the world is within the human person. And human existence is shared with other human beings. Thus reflective human consciousness is not simply a single person being conscious of himself or herself. Rather, as Rahner puts it, human existence is being-present-to-self; human consciousness is a being-conscious-of-itself of being itself.[35] Being is conscious of itself in any person's reflective awareness of his or her own being. Consciousness of being and statements about being are made from within being itself. Thus the experience of my being held in being by the creative power of God is a reflection of the whole status of the finite being of which I am a part. The experience that there is a will outside my own that rules and norms me, and that that is the will of a sovereign God, cannot but entail the universalization of that sovereignty. One should not confuse the necessity of individual experience for the recognition of meaning with a limitation of the applicability of that meaning. Symbolic communication yields general and true objective statements about God.

Symbols Objectify Corporate Consciousness

In the first two chapters on faith we discussed theological beliefs as the objective expressions of faith and their social function of helping to hold together a community of tradition. On the basis of these beliefs being symbols we are in a better position to consider how symbols objectify corporate consciousness and function to unite the church. Although we shall be referring here principally to doctrinal symbols, what is said here applies analogously to sacramental and ritual symbols.

It is well known that symbols are polysemous and polyvalent. Symbolic language is not literal language that mathematically binds meaning to neatly defined and conceptually limited denotation. Because their object-referent is transcendent they must appeal to the experience of the whole person. Meaning is thus generated not only as a function of critical intelligence but also in relation to will, emotive response to values, and the creative input of imagination. Consciousness is awakened on many levels in any person and in many different ways in different peoples and groups. As was said earlier, there are limits to the meanings and values that any symbol can bear; they cannot be construed to mean anything at all. Yet within the limits that are constituted by the structure of any given symbol, it as it were intentionally provokes a plurality of interpretations.

This richness of meaning and value that characterizes religious symbols makes them peculiarly apt in their function of objectifying corporate religious consciousness and binding the community together. Because religious symbols can bear a plurality of interpretations and meanings, they can unite a religious community over time. A symbol unites past and present by being able to support the meaning or meanings attached to it then and now. Religious symbols can also unite various subgroups of the whole Christian community across cultures at any given time. In other words the polyvalent and polysemic quality of symbols allows them to express and promote a unity amidst differences. Pluralism is the necessary condition of the church in history. But the openness of religious symbols to multiple interpretations allows them to unite a community in diversity. Literal doctrines divide; symbolic doctrines unite.

However, the openness of religious symbols to a plurality of interpretations means that they are also vulnerable to corruption. This is particularly true because of the social function they fill. Religious symbols can be controlled by a segment of the church in its own interest and against the interests of others. Particular interpretations may be a function of group bias and be used by those with power to dominate other groups. Old and outdated interpretations may be clung to when they are no longer warranted on the basis of motives other than the deep meanings and values that symbols represent. Religious symbols are not less but probably more subject to the corrupting influences within the socio-political sphere of church and society because of the themes of ultimacy they imply. They can and often do become ideological in the pejorative sense of the term.

But religious symbols can also yield prophetic reaction and criticism. When the authentic meaning of religious symbols is compromised by social manipulation, they frequently at the same time and in the same measure generate a reaction. By their mediation of transcendence and a transparency that opens up an encounter with God and God's values, religious symbols provide a basis for a critique of those interpretations that legitimate injustice.[36]

For example, the doctrine of creation has its anthropological basis in the transcendental experience of contingency in being and a sense of dependence on a power of being that is transcendent. When this is coupled with an encounter with God, one has the ingredients for the symbol creation. This doctrine finds its classical biblical expression in the narrative myths in Genesis. These symbols are teeming with religious meanings and values. Moreover they are open to a great variety of philosophical and theological interpretations of a cosmological and anthropological nature. The doctrine can be resymbolized in a great variety of conceptual ways. Theoretically any one of the formulas of the symbol might do as a bond of the unity of the church so long as it is recognized that it is symbolic. But it is also important to realize that historical and cultural forces are very relevant in the public formulation of symbolic doctrines. There is little need at this moment in history to dwell on the fact that the doctrine of creation has been interpreted and functioned in an ideological way in the course of the history of the church. Feminist theology has simply demonstrated the variety of historical corruptions of the doctrine. By contrast what one also learns from feminist theology is that the doctrine of creation, when coupled with the doctrine of God's Presence to and love of all, means that equality among human beings is an absolute concept. There can be no qualification of it because the slightest distinctions seem inevitably to lead to discrimination and oppression.

The kingdom of God is a good example of a symbol that has supported a great variety of interpretations and meanings. There is the foundational meaning that stems from Jesus and is found in the New Testament but is so difficult to pin down. The kingdom of God bore a distinctive meaning in the development of American Protestantism, one that also shifted in different periods.[37] The kingdom of God has another social interpretation that is analogously found in the theology of the social gospel and liberation theology. By contrast, for some liberal theologians of the late nineteenth century, the kingdom of God lies within each person. The Roman Catholic Church identified the kingdom of God with itself, but that interpretation seems overruled by Vatican II. Despite the great variety of these meanings, Christians still refer to the kingdom of God in their conversations with each other, even across cultures. In other words, there is something elementary about this symbol that every Christian understands. It can still unite even while the conversation goes on about the distortions of its meaning and its authentic interpretation for today.

Symbols Live and Die in Culture

Finally, symbols live and die in culture. The organic metaphor suggests a kind of symbiotic relationship between the symbols of a religion and the wider culture. This is obvious with symbols that are more concretely imaginative, but it applies no less to conceptual symbols. Of course church tradition tends to perpetuate its own symbols within a culture. But they must be continually interpreted in the terms of any culture to be meaningful to it. In so doing theology must be attuned both to the intrinsic meaning of the traditional symbol and to the culture being addressed. Ordinarily theology reflects the culture in which it unfolds. The inculturation of symbols, however, need not mean that the values of the religious tradition are reduced to and absorbed by culture. Often the relevance of Christian symbols to culture is negative; a critique of culture is also a form of inculturation. However theological interpretation at times may drift so far from the original symbol that it no longer seems appropriate. At other times there may be no possible correlation between the symbols of a tradition and a new cultural context. Then they either die and new symbols must emerge to preserve old truths, or they lie dormant to be revived in a new context. It is interesting, for example, how Paul can comment so extensively on the significance of Jesus while referring so little to the kingdom of God.

Neither the symbol of creation nor the kingdom of God appears to be dying. Rather they seem to be taking on new life and relevance in the context of new world cultural crises. Today there is a new scientifically informed sense of the complexity of creation with its delicately interwoven balances of forces. There is also a new sense of human freedom as something more than a power of choice. God has created freedom as an analogous power of "creating" the new. The doctrine of creation thus has a bearing on how human freedom can collaborate with divine energy in co-creation according to the patterns of nature or be a force of destruction and self-annihilation. The kingdom of God points in the same direction but with the special accent on the need for moral norms in the creation of just social structures as opposed to structures of human oppression.

This description of how religious symbols communicate helps to further clarify a religious epistemology. Given this symbolic theory of religious knowledge, we are now in a position to comment on its relevance for the discipline of theology.

INTERPRETING RELIGIOUS SYMBOLS

We conclude this discussion of religious symbols with an attempt at formulating some principles for the interpretation of theological statements. Theology is a symbolic discipline. We have proposed a theory of the structure of religious symbols and the dynamics of symbolic communication. The elements of the theology of symbol should in turn yield some fundamental generic principles for how theological data are to be interpreted. By theological data I mean the concrete and discursive symbols of scripture, the statements of the creed, the propositions of the classical Christian councils, the confessions of churches, the set of teachings of any given church, the theological positions of past or present theologians, the common popular beliefs of people in the church. In every case, insofar as these statements intend to express the object of faith which has been given by revelation, they are symbolic statements. If they are not symbolic statements, neither do they point to objects of faith, nor are they theological in nature, but simply disciplinary proposals, rules for regulating church life.[38] What principles have emerged for interpreting these symbolic data as a result of the theology of religious symbols?

First, and negatively, it scarcely needs repetition that the symbolic statements that make up the sources for theology are not statements of information about the transcendent order. They do not refer to data that could be confirmed by neutral, dispassionate, or disinterested investigation, let alone empirical observation. Although they may be connected with historical facts, theological statements are never statements of historical facts; statements about historical facts are *ipso facto* not theological. When theological statements do involve historical data, the data themselves function as concrete symbols.

Second, in every case religious and theological symbols were generated by religious experience. In every case they communicate from and are intended to communicate to an engaged existential and participatory religious experience. This principle simply states the epistemological structure of religious and theological statements and the dynamics of how they communicate. They communicate when they open up consciousness to transcendent levels of reality by expanding consciousness to be attuned to them. And in so doing they draw consciousness into absolute mystery. Recognition of mystery as mystery cannot be understood in any other way than existentially and experientially.[39]

Third, symbolic realism means that these participatory experiences and the symbols that correspond to them, because they are real experiences of God, can be and are translated into objective statements. In other words, theological symbols and doctrines participate in and mediate reality in a true way. To say that they correspond with reality is too strong because it begins to suggest an objective adequacy of finite symbol and human conception to what is transcendent mystery. Rather the realism of symbols should be thought of in terms of the dynamics of participatory consciousness called mystagogy.

It seems fairly clear that the vast majority of people most of the time construe religious symbols as objective statements of information about a transcendent order of reality. We referred earlier to the masquerading of beliefs as faith. The very objectification of religious experience in symbols makes their religious truth appear as information; theology appears to state objective data; theology frequently argues from symbolic statements as though they represented verifiable data; theology too often "deduces" from scripture and received doctrine. Thus symbolic realism that justifies "objective" statements about God is often misleading. The fact that theological data are often taken as objective information should not be taken as license for theology to make such a fundamental mistake in categories.

Fourth, because religious and theological symbols are generated by existential and participatory experience, both their meaning and the acceptance of their validity or truth really depend on this experience. This too is a principle of critical evaluation and interpretation, and not a description of ordinary behavior. To understand what religious symbolic propositions mean one must in some measure participate in the experience that they mediate. In other words the very status of the meaning of theological language is existential; it represents engaged participatory experience and knowledge. Therefore to explain the meaning of past theological data, one must as it were get behind it or, better, beneath it to the experience that it thematizes in its present usage.[40] In the end, theological interpretation consists in further mediation by descriptive phenomenology and critical analysis of the experience on which the symbol is founded and in which the symbolized is given.[41]

This principle, it seems to me, is the crux of critical theology. It can be clarified further by what it rules out. The symbols that mediate dependent revelation are "objective" and they are prior to the experience that they awaken in every age. But they do not and cannot exclusively determine the meaning that they give rise to in subsequent generations. In fact, by a *reductio ad extremum,* one could say that the experience they give rise to is literally unique and different in every individual who receives them meaningfully. Such is the nature of historicity; such is the complexity and uniqueness of every human consciousness. It follows, therefore, that the past objective meaning of symbolic theological assertions cannot exhaustively determine what they actually do mean or even can mean today. No amount of philological or any other objective historical determination of meaning in the past has the final word on meaning at any given time.[42] Meaning for today must be finally culled from an analysis of the meaning that common human experience in the present can yield.

Fifth, because the intentionality of religious symbols is to transform persons and their action, this dimension of symbolic communication must enter into their interpretation. Since the very logic of symbolic communication consists in their having a bearing on transformed Christian life, their interpretation cannot rest with some theoretical interpretation without a drawing of the consequences for Christian action. In fact some consequences are always latent in whatever interpretation is given, so that the question of interpretation really consists in making them explicit. But since religious symbols are so susceptible to social corruption, this must be done with a certain suspicion. Giving an account of the direction in which religious symbols point human action must always bring to bear the critical moral dimension that encounter with God always implies for social existence.

We can conclude then with the following general statement concerning Christianity as a whole and Christian theology. Christianity is a symbolic universe or a symbolic world. We mentioned at the outset concerning faith that with faith a person joins a community with a tradition. That tradition of the Christian community is symbolic; it is a corporate construal or interpretation of reality in symbolic terms. This set of symbols which theology interprets, explains, conceptualizes, and criticizes is one that, first, discloses reality for the community and each person in it. The classical doctrines of the church, in its scriptures and history of doctrines, communicate; they shape or form the experience that comes after them. Scripture and classical doctrines may be seen as "the lenses through which human beings see and respond to their changing worlds, or the media in which they formulate their descriptions."[43]

Secondly, this set of symbols empowers the community. It engenders a certain way of life. This is of course the whole point of symbols and of God's revelation, to empower human living. Without this dimension the whole meaning and purpose of religious symbols and church doctrines is completely lost. In the next section we shall examine in more detail the method of interpretation. That discussion will reveal further the nature of theological assertions and the dimensions of theology as a symbolic discipline that empowers life.

V

METHOD

Chapter Nine

THE STRUCTURE OF INTERPRETATION

We move now to the final major topic of this book, the question of method in theology. How does the theologian go about the task of theology which is to interpret or reinterpret reality on the basis of the received symbols of the past? This question is fundamental. One could unfold comprehensively the entire subject matter of this book within the framework of this issue. Therefore many of the considerations that appeared under the headings of faith, revelation, scripture, and religious symbols will reappear as suppositions or premises in this discussion of method.

Theology is a pluralistic discipline. There are many different theologies in terms of content; all Christian theologians are not saying the same thing. But the pluralism extends much further than content, for there is no common agreement on the method of theology. As a discipline theology is quite unlike what is commonly meant by the English word science. Theology, like philosophy, does not have and probably never will build up a large set of common assumptions and premises that constitute a more or less universally accepted paradigm within which all practitioners of the discipline work.

In view of this situation, every account of method in theology in one way or another takes a stand in contrast to other methods in theology. In the case of these two chapters the extremes that are being rejected are clear enough. On the one hand, to the right, lies a fundamentalism or revelational positivism that does not account for reinterpretation. In other words, it is so bound to the words and formulas of the past, as found either in scripture or dogmatic creeds, that it fails to reflect on either the necessity or the actuality of change in meaning. On the other hand, to the left, stands what may be called a radical liberalism. By this I mean either a theoretical or practical reduction of theology to anthropology, that is, the retrieval of meaning from human experience at any

169

given time that excludes the initiative of God's revealing and admits no normative or authoritative role to the tradition from the past.[1]

In contrast to these two extremes I shall not try to delimit in detail any particular method of any school of theology. What is sought are principles that are general enough to be inclusive of a variety of methods in theology, yet specific enough to provide guidelines that may be direc-tive in the concrete task of theology. Once again this is done in two phases. The first of these chapters deals with the structure of interpre-tation; the second deals more specifically but still generally with how this structure is played out dynamically in the method of theology.

This present chapter is an essay in hermeneutics, that is, the disci-pline that deals with the principles of interpretation and whose litera-ture is vast. The intricacies of this discipline, however, have been se-verely limited here by a single overarching framework and issue. The framework consists in the tension between historical consciousness on the one hand and the Christian fact of a revelation given in a point of time in history on the other. Historical consciousness involves the ne-cessity of development and change. A revelation in history involves something given in a specific way that can be lost but should be pre-served intact. The issue underlying Christian interpretation, therefore, may be stated bluntly in the form of a question: How can continuing interpretation of original revelation preserve original revelation? To put it even more crudely: How does theology, by saying different things, mean the same thing as that which is contained in original revelation? Within this limited framework, then, we shall try to establish basic princi-ples concerning, first, the necessity of interpretation; second, the possi-bility of interpretation; third, the structure of interpretation; and fourth, the goal of interpretation. On the basis of these four principles we shall be able to conclude by enumerating three basic methodological criteria for the discipline of theology.

THE NECESSITY OF INTERPRETATION

Christianity is a religion of tradition. It is shaped by the set of symbols which is its foundation and constitution. These symbols have been authoritatively interpreted for the community in a certain number of classical doctrines formulated in its relatively early patristic period and afterward. But these foundational symbols are necessarily reinter-preted. This is not a moral imperative but an historical necessity; the community cannot not reinterpret even its most fundamental and self-identifying symbols or doctrines. The reason for this is that experience today, and at any given time after the generation of these symbols, is different from the original experience that gave rise to them.

This thesis concerning the necessity of ongoing reinterpretation of traditional symbols is counter-intuitive. By that I mean that it is not immediately evident. Why cannot the same doctrines be simply repeated? Why is it necessary that their meaning be reinterpreted? The response to these questions is equally straightforward: the reason is that repetition of past doctrines in new situations already interprets and changes their meaning. But the recognition of this principle is a function of historical consciousness, and, as such, must be mediated or explained. What follows, then, is simply a series of considerations which draw out from a variety of viewpoints the inherent and necessary changes of meaning which history itself imposes on the data of tradition.

A first area of consideration lies in the *anthropological grounds* for the necessity of interpretation. The necessity of ongoing reinterpretation stems from the way human existence is bound to the world, the concrete, material and historical world, for all of its knowledge. It is this contextuality of all human knowing that grounds the historicity of all linguistic expression and construal of meaning that in turn gives rise to historical consciousness. The sacred symbols, the traditional texts which contain its most central ideas and values, and the very kernel of the community's specific genius are always being received in ever new contexts and situations. This inevitably entails that new meaning is always being extracted from the symbols of the past and added to them by the very fact of their being received in and adjusted to new conditions. Our past is continually being modified by new discoveries, reforms, renaissances, and experiences, by a series of successive "nows," so that "our past never stops changing its meaning."[2]

The movement of history thus carries with it changes of meaning that are strictly speaking necessary. And from this follows the necessity of pluralism within an extended community. This pluralism of interpretation stems from differences of historical experience within the community, and it characterizes the community as it moves through time as well as its existence in any given time insofar as it subsists in different cultures.[3] Because experience is a function of historical situatedness, the differences of contextual experience show that the meaning of the basic affirmations of Christian faith inevitably changes; the same affirmation in a different context will not mean the same thing and may have little meaning at all. A commonly cited example of this in our own time is the doctrine of the Trinity which is classically expressed in the terminology of three persons in one God. To current western culture this classic doctrine almost inevitably communicates an understanding of three au-

tonomous persons, sometimes as forming one community. The classic
doctrine thus communicates to many a tritheism which is simply meaningless to their lives. The shift of meaning also implies that the classical
formula has thus become effectively and kerygmatically heretical.

The historical nature of human existence, then, carries with it the
necessity of reinterpretation; one cannot not interpret and the repetition of traditional language is itself reinterpretative. In the discussion of
scripture it was remarked that fundamentalism implies a theological
position on how God is made present to the community through scriptural symbols and doctrines, a position that appears untenable today.
Here we see that fundamentalism, which refuses to reinterpret the symbols and doctrines of tradition, is really reinterpreting them by merely
repeating them, although it may not be aware of it. The reason for this is
simply that historical human experience changes, and the differences
generate meanings different from what was originally intended.

A second area of consideration on the necessity for reinterpreting
the doctrines of the past can be summarized under the *principle of
analogy* for understanding past or other historical cultures. The principle states that one cannot really affirm as true, nor can one really
understand, data of the past unless they bear some analogy with what is
experienced as meaningful and true within one's own ken. In other
words, this principle postulates a certain consistency and homogeneity
of human experience across history, so that data and meaning which
falls completely outside current experience really has no basis for being
comprehended or affirmed. This principle can be and has been used in a
radically skeptical way on the basis of a rather narrow empiricist or
rationalist epistemology. One needs to question the premises upon
which the analogy is based. Yet at the same time it is actually always at
work in every form of critical inquiry. One needs some form of analogous experience in order to situate meaning. This principle, then, has its
bearing on the reception of Christian symbols and the need to interpret them.

One of the best known uses of the principle of analogy in twentieth
century theology is Rudolf Bultmann's method of interpretation which
he called demythologization. A myth, according to Bultmann, consists in
a depiction of God, transcendence, and the other world in terms that are
of this world.[4] It is true that the term myth tends to have pejorative
connotations in Bultmann which it need not have. Since all language of
God is drawn from this world and is symbolic, one could speak of
remythologization. But despite the many critiques Bultmann's project
has received, it still remains true that in many biblical symbols myth and
history seem to blend. Thus the point of biblical symbolism seems to be

obscured by antique conceptions or forms of expression. These can only release their meaning by an interpretation of the cultural forms in present-day existential and historical terms.

The issue that Bultmann raises can be expressed in terms of a question. Let us suppose that there are people, perhaps even a large group forming a subculture, who cannot accept that God intervenes in history in an overt miraculous fashion, that is, by contravening the ordinary workings of nature and human events. These people cannot accept a virgin conception or birth, nature miracles, raising people from the dead, or resuscitated corpses rejoining the living. In other words, these people cannot accept at face value or in a literal way the many recitals of miraculous events that abound in the New Testament, because they fall so far beyond their experience as to contradict positively their understanding of how nature and history unfold. Can such people still be authentic and integral Christians? Insofar as such a mentality is, as Bultmann says, characteristic of a modern culture, it does not seem correct to exclude such a culture from authentic Christian faith on these grounds. Without having to maintain that an appropriation such as this need be raised to a status of normativity for other cultures, one can still see how every culture has to interpret Christianity in terms that somehow do not simply contradict basic premises such as these. For in this case these premises are taken as matters of knowledge of this world supported by science. Bultmann's proposal, then, simply opens up in specific terms the view that religious expressions are symbols that mediate an encounter with transcendence which itself must be interpreted within the context of the experience of those who receive it.

Third, the necessity of constantly reinterpreting Christian symbols can be seen from the very *nature of foundational documents,* whether they be scripture or universal doctrine. Foundational documents are meant to be open to the future. We have already seen the analogy between the New Testament and a legal constitution of a society. The New Testament canon was assembled not only to be the foundation of the church in the early period, but to be its constitution as it moves forward in history. Thus the very nature of symbols that are meant to have universal relevance requires that they be open to future peoples in diverse cultures and situations. The ability to fulfill the function assigned them requires that they be interpreted to supply meaning in response to new and different situations. In other words, the foundational symbols of Christianity are intrinsically designed to be reinterpreted.

Looking forward from the composition of the founding scriptural or doctrinal symbols, one can describe how this interpretation actually happens. Once a symbol becomes written, it becomes independent of the original intention of its author as well as the meaning that was received by its original audience. Once an idea is as it were frozen in a textual symbol, it takes on an autonomous life of its own.[5] It becomes read in different contexts and received by different audiences, with problems and questions different from those originally addressed. Phrases, ideas, propositions take on new relevancy different from what any author had in mind. Once again, then, the very reception and repetition of a symbol with a specific intent relative to the situation in which it was generated necessarily generate new interpretations in different communities in ever new situations.

This same logic can also be illustrated from the point of view of the person or community today which, looking backward so to speak, is confronted with biblical or ecclesial symbols. What is sought from the symbols of tradition? The deepest answer to this question is surely not what was meant in the past. Rather the community necessarily seeks in the symbol a response to its own questions that is meaningful to its own situation in the world. The point of returning to scripture and the tradition of doctrine is not historical curiosity—"What did they think back then?"—but meaning for today—"What is the truth of the matter for us here and now?" Thus, once again, historical distance imposes the necessity of drawing meaning forward through reinterpretation.

Finally, the *hermeneutics of suspicion* provides a fourth set of considerations that necessitate a constant reinterpretation of Christian doctrine. In some ways the principles here run counter to the principle of analogy and must be held in tension with it. The focus of attention here rests on the social function of religious symbols. We have seen how doctrines shape and express the corporate consciousness and behavior of the religious community. Since the Enlightenment a number of important thinkers have suspected on anthropological grounds that religion in general is alienating. They have criticized Christianity in particular for distracting people from life in this world by projecting their true home as another world, for undermining human freedom by postulating a radical dependence on God, for nurturing the values of passivity, obedience, and humility, and thus undermining human responsibility. Others show on social historical grounds that Christianity has tended to align itself with the forces of law, order, and the dominant classes of society at the expense of the poor and exploited classes. In these analyses Christianity appears as radically dehumanizing because it undercuts the creativity of the human spirit or positively lends sacral support to oppression and structures of inequality.

There is an ever growing body of Christians today who realize that these criticisms have some merit not in principle but in fact. We have already pointed out that like any other social structure the symbols that shape Christian consciousness can become socially corrupted. There is no shortage of historical examples of Christian symbols lending their weight to social oppression and structures of inequality even in our own day. In some areas of social thinking and conduct, such as relations between the sexes and the control of population, the examples are blatant and scandalous. When Christian symbols become oppressive and begin to contradict the Christian message itself, the only way to solve the problem is by criticism and reinterpretation.

In sum, then, reinterpretation is an historical necessity, and repetition itself is reinterpretation. Traditional symbols necessarily change their meanings as the community moves through history. This historical necessity imposes a moral demand that the task of reinterpretation be consciously, reflectively, and critically appropriated. But this raises the question for the Christian theologian of the possibility of new interpretation that is both different from original revelation and yet faithful to it.

THE POSSIBILITY OF INTERPRETATION

Granted that interpretation of the tradition is a necessity, is it possible? Can ongoing reinterpretation be faithful to the meaning of original revelation? The problem arises because of the historical nature of Christian revelation. Given in time and codified into classical formulations that are also historically specific, this revelation can be corrupted and even lost in historical process. If Christianity is not to be conceived as a movement in history that is completely open and subject to any possible new conception, one must explain how new and different interpretations of Christianity can also preserve the intrinsic meaning of original revelation.

The thesis proposed here is that interpretation is possible, that one can reinterpret Christian doctrines and remain faithful to their original and intrinsic meaning. This is so, first of all, because Christian doctrines of the past are expressions fashioned by human beings, and therefore they can be understood as such, that is, as human assertions. Second, these Christian affirmations disclose realities that can be and are experienced today. But, third, these realities are transcendent and are mediated symbolically. Therefore, the dialectical structure of symbols and symbolic communication allows one to account for sameness and difference in new interpretations when compared with the original symbols. Once again this response seems counter-intuitive. How can what is different be the same? Reinterpretation of classical Christian symbols is often fiercely resisted. In what follows, then, I will explain this initial response to the problem in the three stages just outlined.

First, the most radical form of the problem of whether reinterpretation can be continuous with the past appears as the question of whether or not one can communicate with the past at all. For example, is our current cultural experience of reality so radically different from that of other past cultures that there can be no communication at all between them? Even in the world of today we frequently have occasion to experience the vast gulf that separates experience and understanding in the West from that of other cultures. The sense of historicity and historical relativity can be so all-encompassing that it does not allow any recognition of commonalities in the way two very diverse cultures experience reality. In this situation cultural anthropologists and historians may be very reluctant to admit even the possibility of communication between cultures, let alone any question of homology or sameness of experience.

In the face of these experiences, one must still affirm the possibility of human communication universally across whatever cultural differences. It is possible because in fact it happens however infrequently. And it happens because in some fundamental way all human beings share a common humanity. Behind human inter-communication one must postulate a unity of the human race. At some foundational level, human beings have been said to share a common human nature. If the idea of a human nature appears too static a concept, then one may speak of anthropological constants that typify human existence at every point in history. Although these common characteristics can only be generally formulated, they are still so essential to human existence as such that they serve as transcendental bonds of unity and communication. For example, all human beings desire to know and all think, understand, and make judgments; all human beings are contingent and must face death; all are in history and must face the future and the question of their ultimate destiny; all human beings experience suffering which can call into question the meaningfulness of existence itself; because of the radical freedom that constitutes a reflective human spirit, all are open to the possible experience of transcendence; all are religious in the radical sense of having to decide what is of ultimate importance and concern.

This recognition of common or transcendental aspects of human existence is essential to all hermeneutical theory. They define the basis of the possibility of human communication and thus the possibility of understanding the symbols of another culture and even our own distant past. Transcendental anthropology is the bridge, as it were, across cultures and between the present and the past, and all interpretation crosses it.[6] In the next chapter on theological method we shall consider how these transcendental aspects of human nature can be considered as an anthropology which opens up the meaning of past symbols and also provides a criterion for the adequacy of their construal.

Second, the religious symbols of the past express and mediate transcendence. The specific nature and function of a religious symbol lies in its ability to open up this level of experience. The interpreter of these symbols can experience transcendence. All human beings are open to the religious question. But beyond this the interpreter *must* bring to the task of theological interpretation such an experience at least in the rudimentary form of a question. This is so because only a religious interpretation of religious symbols will be an adequate interpretation. Thus by the principle of analogy the possibility of accurately interpreting religious symbols presupposes that the interpreter comes to the task of interpretation with some experience and preunderstanding of that which is being communicated by the symbols. One could neither appreciate nor understand them as religious symbols without some experience or interest in transcendence. But with such an experience one already has a measure of understanding of that which they mediate. In other words, that which is mediated by the symbols of the past can be and is encountered today in the present world.[7]

This general principle applies *a fortiori* in the case of the Christian interpreter or theologian. No Christian theologian comes to the symbols of the tradition without some prior experience and understanding of the transcendent meaning and content of the symbols he or she interprets. This derives of course mainly from membership in the tradition.[8] But it also comes from the fact that the theologian is a human being who is open to transcendence. The theologian's own experience of transcendence is conditioned and determined as well by his or her being in the world, by the general historical situation, and the immediate context of life. Interpretation, therefore, does not entail deciding the meaning of past symbols from outside the functioning of the symbols themselves. Interpretation unfolds from within the context of an experience of transcendence that characterizes the consciousness of the interpreter. The Christian theologian has a preunderstanding of, a rudimentary belief in, at least in the form of a question about, and a commitment to, at least in the form of a concern for, what the symbol points to, even though this response is also determined by the theologian's own cultural situation. In sum, the interpreter experiences today, now, the reality which the symbol mediates.

Third, one still has to explain the sameness and continuity between present theological interpretation and traditional symbols and doctrines. Since it is rather clear that current theology is different from that of the past, and necessarily so, it is impossible to claim simple identity. The sameness of meaning can only be a sameness in difference. Such an idea of sameness and difference requires that distinctions be made. A common way of making such a distinction is in terms of form and content, where form is the finite form of the human expression, and content is that which is transcendent. The same content can be expressed in different forms, manners of presentation, languages, or genres. One can communicate the same material or subject matter in different ways. Although this distinction is not complete or is complete only on a formal abstract level, for content is always carried and influenced by the form, still such a distinction is possible. It is moreover helpful in illumining what is going on in faithful interpretation. Difference lies in the conceptual form of a new interpretation, but the content, that which is expressed, is the same.[9] But at the same time this distinction has inherent problems, because it tends to deal with the content of Christian symbols, that is, their transcendent meaning, in objective terms. But one cannot really isolate and distinguish the content of religious symbols from its form of expression in objective terms.

The key to the issue of sameness and difference in the reinterpretation of traditional symbols lies in the dialectical structure of symbols themselves. This dialectical structure must be understood in terms of a dynamic process of communication. The symbol is not the thing symbolized, for that is transcendent and other. Yet the symbol makes present and mediates the transcendent which is encountered in religious experience. The element of sameness cannot be reduced to any objective formula. Its content in the end must reside in existential experience, an encounter which transcends every linguistic symbolic formula, and thus is open to be expressed in a plurality of symbolic formulas. Thus traditional symbols are open to critique, reinterpretation, and different explanations in which the new symbolization mediates an experience of the same encounter with a transcendent, personal, loving, and forgiving divine Presence.[10]

This distinction which allows for reinterpretation can be illustrated by examples from New Testament christology. Is Jesus the final prophet, or the miracle worker, or the anointed by God as Spirit, or the incarnation of wisdom, or the messiah, or the Son of Man, or the new Moses? All are quite different. Yet all express in different ways and therefore mediate to and in Christian experience that Jesus is himself the mediator of God's salvation. And if one says today that Jesus is liberator and means by that that Jesus is the mediator of *God's salvation,* one has faithfully expressed the same experience as the New Testament writers.

In sum, the distinction between the symbol or doctrine and the experience that is mediated and communicated by it is an absolute requirement for Christian theology. Without it people will always be distrustful of the theological enterprise. But without it, too, there can be no theology at all, no reinterpretation, and Christianity is condemned paradoxically to both an unintelligibility associated with archaism and indiscriminate change. However, when this understanding of the possibility of faithful interpretation is coupled with the recognition of the necessity of interpretation, it becomes apparent that traditional symbols must be reinterpreted in order to preserve the sameness of the truth of Christian revelation. The point of interpretation is not simply to reproduce or repeat traditional symbols, formulas, and doctrines, but to reexpress and communicate that to which they point. The fidelity of reinterpretation, therefore, must be judged in terms of the experience of the transcendent which symbols mediate and not exclusively in terms of the traditional symbols themselves, although not without reference to these, since they are the data for reinterpretation. Let us consider now in more detail the structure of this reinterpretation.

THE STRUCTURE OF INTERPRETATION

In a way the difference and sameness of interpretation relative to past tradition represent its structure. Because of historicity, the meaning and understanding of Christian symbols and doctrines necessarily change and become different. Yet, because original revelation is historical and should be preserved, interpretation seeks to grasp the essentially same transcendent meaning and truth despite the new construal of the symbols themselves. In the discussion which follows, this structure will be schematized further in terms of elements or dimensions involved in the process of interpreting. The same structure will be described more dynamically in the next chapter on method in theology. To provide a context for the enumeration of the dimensions of the hermeneutical process I will first provide an example of interpretation and second a theoretical model for the whole process.

An Example

We begin with an example of interpretation from psychology that should be fairly recognizable and clear, and which can serve as an analogy for the discussion of theological interpretation. A young man, eighteen years old, was referred to a clinical psychologist. The history and symptoms of the case were fairly straightforward: the boy hated his father; he said so clearly and was able to explain why. This hatred had begun six or seven years earlier and had been testified to by his general behavior, his conversations with his personal friends, his diary, and his relationships within his family. The psychologist worked with the man for six months on a regular basis: he had questions about all the symptoms; he critically reviewed and analyzed the behavior of the man leading up to and during the six year period of the most intense feelings; he knew that there was an inner knot of response that involved all sorts of reactions, interpretations, desires, and emotions. At the end he put all the data together and realized that the young man did not hate his father but actually loved him passionately. In a two hour session the psychologist explained this to the young man. The sessions continued, and at the end of three weeks the young man announced that he wanted to stop the therapy. He had changed. He had indeed hated his father all these years, but now that hatred had suddenly dissipated. He was able to get along well with his father now and all of the previous symptoms seemed to have disappeared.

This case is an example of the hermeneutical process, although some adjustments will have to be made in comparing it with the interpretation of past religious symbols. In itself it raises some interesting questions. Let us presume that one can distinguish hatred and love, which may be difficult at times. Did the young man really hate or love his father? The symptoms and symbols are there, but they can be construed in very different ways. What is the truth of the matter? Is the historian or biographer to accept the direct witness of the data? Or on studying the analysis of the psychologist should his interpretation be accepted? Should one say it does not make any difference since only the witness, only what was said, is important? Or does not one want to know what was really going on beneath the surface? This case illustrates that interpretation is a matter of construing the data. It also illustrates that an interpretation that may seem to contradict the overt historical meaning of the data may be more adequate to it.

A Dialogical Model of Interpretation

The narrative just put forward is an example of the process of interpretation. It unfolded through consultation, conversation, and dialogue. In the light of this example we can describe the structure of the process of interpretation as dialogic; the process unfolds in dialogue; its structure is dialogical in the sense that it is mediated through a give and take, the back and forth of conversation.[11] The analogy of a conversation or interpersonal dialogue provides a framework or context for understanding the process of interpretation itself; in it are revealed many of the fundamental mechanisms at work. First of all there is the subject matter of the conversation itself. Second, this subject matter is governed by an issue or theme that focuses the interchange. Third, the dialogue consists in a give and take, a back and forth, a mutual informing about the subject matter. Fourth, the point of the dialogue is convergence on a fuller understanding of the truth of the matter. Thus, fifth, the result of the dialogical process is a new and more adequate understanding of the reality involved. The following brief development of each of these points should be understood within this overarching model of dialogue. They can be exemplified analogously in both psychological interpretation and theological interpretation.

The Dimensions of Interpretation

The first element of interpretation concerns the subject matter. It is absolutely crucial to take account of exactly what the subject matter is. From the point of view of the psychologist, it may appear that the subject matter to be interpreted are the young man's words and actions. It is true that in a dialogical situation each should attend carefully to the other in order to understand what is being said. But the further intention of that limited goal is to understand that about which the conversation is had. In this case that subject matter consists in the deeper syndrome and the man's words and actions are symbols and data for getting at that reality. So too in the interpretation of the theological symbols of the past. Although one speaks of interpreting past symbols, the real intent is to interpret the reality to which they point. The subject matter of theological interpretation is not the symbols of the past; they are the witnesses, the symbolic testimonies, for interpreting the object of interpretation which is reality itself.[12]

It would be difficult to overemphasize the critical importance of this insight. In a way the error of fundamentalism can be situated precisely at this point. For the fundamentalist or creedalist believes that truth lies in the symbols themselves, on pieces of paper, in texts, in revealed propositions, in beliefs masquerading as faith. The objects of interpretation are the symbols themselves. But truth is an existential category; truth is a quality of the way human subjectivity relates to reality, that is, in a way that corresponds to the way reality is. The symbols of the past testify to that reality. The intrinsic meaning of past symbols bears witness to how that reality is to be construed. The process of interpretation means listening to the past concerning the object to which they point, that is, the subject matter.

Second, interpretation is always guided by a question which thematizes the dialogue about the subject matter.[13] We have said that some form of participatory experience is a necessary precondition for understanding the very kind of subject matter that religious symbols mediate. In the hermeneutical dialogue this foreknowledge is directed by a question. It may be a question out of ignorance, but never a total ignorance, for the question itself betrays awareness of the subject matter. The question may also emerge from a large pool of participation. In either case the question arises out of some form of negativity, some lack of knowledge, some anomaly, some incongruity.[14] Thus interpretation is always thematized and the subject matter approached from a certain direction. The question governs interpretation because the data about the subject matter is asked to yield an answer to a specifying question.[15] The questions asked by the psychologist were not neutral requests for random information. And theological interpretation will always reflect questions that arise out of the historical life situation of the interpreter. Even when they are not focused, they are operative.

Third, the dialogical character of interpretation involves attending to the testimony of the other. One could say that there is a mutual questioning going on in the process of interpretation.[16] In the case of the psychologist, what the client is really saying makes up the very data that need to be interpreted to understand the subject matter; in the case of theology, this involves transcending the self and as it were placing the self in the situation of the past in order to appreciate the other as other.[17]

A truly dialogic interpretation of the religious symbols of the past therefore requires historical and exegetical knowledge. One cannot interpret the content of these religious symbols without first studying them historically. Religious doctrines must first be understood within their own historical context, in their background, genesis, and full flowering forth.[18] This is the function of history in relation to theology, in whatever variety of forms such an historical study of scripture or doctrine may take. Exegesis and historical reconstruction enters into the systematic interpretation of the meaning of these symbols for today by determining in the first place the original meaning of the symbols to be interpreted.[19] In other words, interpretation is not free interpretation but interpretation of these data. One cannot interpret Nicaea without knowing what Nicaea said and why it said it on the overt historical level. If interpretation is to be faithful to the past, the symbols of the past must be first understood in their own terms and context. The psychologist must study and analyze the historical data of this young man because this is the case he is trying to understand.

The historical study of the religious symbols of the past must be critical. The attempt to understand religious symbols in their own historical context must itself be a questioning, reflective, and analytical study. Study of the past is not mere passive reception and chronicling of data, but itself an attempt to understand what was going on in the formation of religious symbols. During the months of rehearsing the history of the young man's case, the psychologist was not merely passive, but always attentive to causes and effects, to reasons and reactions, motives and interpretations.

Criticism in the study of history is crucial for interpretation. In a way this criticism is what allows interpretation to occur. On the one hand critical history establishes a distance between the religious symbol of the past and the interpreter in the present. The more a symbol of the past is understood in its past context the further distant it will appear from the interpreter. The interpreter may have become familiar with the language of a tradition. But when the language is revealed in its past historical context, it takes on a more distant quality of otherness; it becomes both better understood and less familiar in the measure that it is located in its own historical context. It is a product of the past and can be regarded more objectively. On the other hand, critical historical retrieval enhances the symbolic aspect of past religious symbols. What on the surface may look like explanations or straightforward historical accounts are shown to be symbolic representations. For example, the story of creation naively appears to explain how the world was created and why there is sin in the world. The story of a virgin conception naively appears to explain how it came to pass that God is the Father of Jesus. Criticism may appear destructive because it undermines this naively conceived explanatory function of religious symbols. But by destroying this explanatory function it underscores the symbolic nature of religious symbols and thus further allows the possibility and necessity of a new critical interpretation.

In the case of the psychologist interpreter, this critical distance, objectivity, and the recognition that symptoms are not explanations but symbols give him the freedom to begin to think about an interpretation that may be different from the one that is initially attached to the data. In the theological interpretation of religious symbols an analogous mechanism is at work. The language and reasoning of the past stand out as different from the language and reasoning of the present. Symbols are shown to be symbols which do not explain but express and mediate an experience of transcendence. Like parables they are meant to disclose a transcendent reality which, because it is transcendent, cannot be reduced to historical reality in the terms of cause and effect. The symbol is not the symbolized; a symbol mediates something else other than itself. To understand a religious symbol as an historical narrative robs it of its symbolic and transcendent value.[20] What is true of symbolic narratives is also true of argued doctrines. They may appear to be theological explanations, but in reality they are symbols. Nicaea is not an explanation of the divinity of Jesus, but a theological symbol that expresses and mediates publicly the experience of and belief in this transcendent reality.

In sum, this third moment or element in the process of interpretation is as subtle as it is crucial. The effects of critical historical study are paradoxical. On the one hand this study guarantees fidelity to the past, and on the other it creates the distance that allows for new interpretation. It is one of the steps that guarantees sameness, yet in the same measure it provides the grounds for newness and difference in current understanding.

Fourth, the interpreter cannot but interpret from the standpoint of the experience and world-view of his or her own situation. This means that in the dialogue the data are always being drawn into the horizon of the consciousness of the interpreter and his or her world.[21] This fact is as crucial as it is self-evident and inescapable; we cannot live in another world than the world that is ours. But this means that interpretation is a taking of a position in the present regarding the subject matter mediated by the symbols. The issue of the final meaningfulness and truth mediated by the symbols cannot be determined by past testimony; it can only be finally interpreted and judged now and in the context of the horizon of today's consciousness.

This fusion of horizons is manifest in the case of the psychologist's interpretation. After attending to the testimony of the other and understanding it in its distinctive otherness, this data is drawn up into the world of his expertise and knowledge. His world of experience is expanded by the interchange. And what is communicated is reunderstood from within the context of a broader expanse of experience, consciousness, and knowledge to yield a more adequate understanding of the truth of the matter. His interpretation is informed by both the history of the symptoms and a modern critical familiarity with the workings of the subconscious. The case is analogous in the current reinterpretation of the testimony of past religious symbols. By the fusion of the horizons of consciousness the reinterpreted understanding of the subject matter does not leave the past behind, but draws it forward in an interpretation that preserves the truth affirmed in a limited framework of the past within a broader and still open present-day framework of consciousness.

Fifth, the final element in interpretation is the interpretation itself, a reexpression of the transcendent data in new symbolic terms. This reinterpretation is on the one hand an imaginative, constructive, theoretical act. On the other hand, it is also a concrete and practical act.

Paul Ricoeur sums up the process of interpretation as a theoretical exercise with the aphorism that symbols give rise to thought.[22] The basis of Christian theology are the symbols of its past tradition. These symbols are a given; they are accepted as intrinsic to Christian experience itself. They communicate on the primary level by informing our memory and experience. But they also give rise to thought, and in our historically conscious culture this can only be critical thought. With criticism the symbolic character of the symbols of the past is highlighted; they become received now not uncritically but on a deeper reflective level as symbols. Their giving rise to thought also means that they stimulate further interpretative insight. They become critically reinterpreted in a way that fits experience and knowledge of the world today. The critical conceptions of the world that make up the furniture of intellectual consciousness, the categories and language that define experience today, become the new vehicles and symbols of new interpretation. We also critically evaluate our present world in the light of these symbols and in so doing reinterpret the symbols themselves.

But this imaginative and critically reflective act is also preeminently practical. Gadamer likens theological interpretation to the act of the judge in interpreting the law.[23] After the history of the genesis and meaning of the law has been studied, the interpretation of the judge has to do with its applicability. But this applicability is not merely consequential to the integral, universal, and comprehensive meaning of the law that can be established historically by study of the past. Rather the very meaning and value of a past law which is still valid lies in its applicability in the present. In other words, understanding the meaning and truth of the past is constituted precisely by understanding its significance and relevance for life in this situation here and now.[24] The truth of the symbols of the past is decided by the judgment of their practicability for life today.

To summarize, the dialogical process of interpretation yields a dialectical structure. The dialectical structure is one of sameness and difference, continuity with the past and newness, preservative of the original transcendent meaning and change in that meaning. This structure is strictly dialectical because these two are asserted at the same time. One cannot assert simple identity between the original and the reinterpreted meaning of symbols; one cannot assert complete otherness and difference either. Sameness, however, must be located "below" or "above" the level of thematic understanding. It subsists in the experienced encounter with transcendence as transcendent, because conceptual understanding is precisely that which is changed in reinterpretation. This dialectical structure cannot be broken or overcome. Attempts to do so always lead to the incoherent extremes of fundamentalism or revelational positivism on the one hand or the reduction of theology to psychological anthropology on the other.

THE GOAL OF INTERPRETATION

Having described the structure of interpretation we conclude now by considering the goal of interpretation. The goal of the discipline of theological reinterpretation must be tied intrinsically to the very nature of Christian symbols. To determine the goal of theology one must turn to Christian symbols themselves and draw out of their nature and logic the intrinsic intentionality of religious symbols generally and more pointedly the original Christian symbols.

To begin, religious symbols are meant to communicate. More specifically they intend to mediate transcendent reality. The point of religious symbols is not to communicate facts about this world nor historical events. Were this the case they would not be religious symbols. It may be that transcendent meaning is tied to certain historical data, as is especially true in the case of Jesus. But insofar as one is dealing with religious symbols, historical reference always includes an appeal to a recognition and the participation of inner history in transcendence. Religious symbols as such always intend to mediate an experience of transcendence. Moreover this mediation of transcendence is always oriented to the future, not only the immediate future, but especially the long term and indefinite future. Religious symbols are not meant to exhaust their significance in the past. They are intended to continue to communicate into the ongoing future of the community, to the historical life of the community as it continually faces new situations. The purpose of religious symbols is therefore to generate new understanding and empower new life continuously in ever new situations. This is both their inner logic and their function within the community.

In accord with this inner intention and historical logic, one should speak of the meaning of religious symbols as not simply lying behind them but also and most significantly as in front of them.[25] The meaning that lies behind a symbol, text or doctrine stems from the historical experience that generated it. As was indicated earlier, this experience can be uncovered by critical historical study, not in the sense of psychologically reproducing it, but in the sense of understanding it in terms of the objective historical situation and causes of the past.[26] What is thus determined is that to which the symbol points but in the historically conditioned language or conceptual form of a past age. The meaning in front of the symbol, by contrast, lies in the experience which the symbol opens up to others in the immediate and ongoing future. But that to which the symbol points and which it makes present is always experienced in new circumstances. This necessarily entails newness and difference in the experience itself as conditioned by the historical situation. Thus ever-contemporary understanding and truth are coincident with applicability and relevance, and the meaning in front of past symbols is constituted by ongoing interpretation.

Given the intrinsic qualities of historical symbols and their function in the community, we can now formulate the goal of interpretation. Since symbols look to the future, and yield ever new meanings for the community in every future, the goal of interpretation is to illumine and to empower the community in each new era. Religious symbols themselves are meant to communicate transcendence and thus illumine and empower the community. The goal of interpretation then is to unlock that which is symbolized from the past and to release it into present-day consciousness. The symbols of the past are a given within the community. Through them the community understands the object of its loyalty and commitment. The role of interpretation is to construe the present meaning of that which is symbolized within the consciousness of the community today. Insofar as interpretation makes sense of the symbols, it allows them to work in the imagination of the community to flood present experience of reality with significant and relevant meaning. Thus the goal of interpretation is also to transform and to empower action. It seeks to open up new possibilities for human life, for human freedom, and human action. This goal of theological interpretation is intrinsic to the religious life of the community itself. It does not come from outside the community to be imposed on it. Rather this intentionality of theological interpretation arises out of the inner nature of the community and its symbols themselves. Interpretation is meant to open up human freedom from within by putting into intelligible terms what is already present implicitly within the freedom of the community insofar as it is shaped by the symbols of its tradition.

In conclusion, one can see from this account of the structure of interpretation three principles which will serve as criteria for theology within the Christian community. Interpretation must be faithful, intelligible, and empowering: faithful to the symbols of scripture and the history of doctrine that are constitutive of the community;[27] intelligible within a present-day horizon of consciousness;[28] and applicable to the present and immediate future of the community in such a way as to engender and empower its praxis.[29] All three are necessary. Interpretation that is faithful and intelligible but does not empower human freedom is irrelevant. Interpretation that is faithful and empowering but unintelligible is demagogic and a contradiction of Christian freedom. Interpretation that is intelligible and empowering but unfaithful to Christian origins is, by definition, in that measure non-Christian. But these criteria for theology will have to be developed further in the next chapter on method in theology.

Chapter Ten

METHOD IN THEOLOGY

With this chapter we move from considerations of the theory of interpretation to the way theology actually goes about interpreting. In the last chapter we discussed the structure of interpretation; in what follows we shall examine in more detail the dynamics of interpretation. What is said here about the method of theology should thus correspond to the general theory just laid out and be consistent as well with the positions taken on faith, revelation, scripture, and religious symbols.

The question of the method of theology is absolutely fundamental to the discipline itself. Often the discussion of method is received with a certain frustration: "Get on with it." Yet since the way one understands governs the understanding itself, since understanding itself is generated by its method, the "getting on with it" without a reflective grasp of what is going on can yield rather superficial results. By contrast, once one grasps what a given theologian is up to methodologically, one can have a fairly accurate appreciation by anticipation of what his or her conclusions will be. For method reaches into the content of theology to shape the very understanding of the subject matter. An appreciation of the way one understands theologically is in part a foundational theological understanding in its own right.

The centrality and importance of the question of method is compounded when one considers for a moment the extravagant pluralism of methods that reigns in current theology. Theology in fact is far removed from those sciences which share a large set of common assumptions, axioms, and working principles. At best it is a discipline of many methods. But these methods seem so diverse that one may wonder whether Christian theologians can communicate with each other. Theology is what theologians do, and they are doing such a variety of different things that anyone coming to the discipline for the first time can only encounter a seeming confusion.

Some theologians are biblical theologians who assume that a critical

189

understanding of scripture is immediately relevant to our times. Some biblical theologians combine exegesis with a complex theology of revelation that attempts to explain how the past record comes to bear on life today. Others use reflections from linguistic philosophy and hermeneutical theory to open up past symbols as mediators of a truth that can be experienced today. Some theologians rely on the discipline of history to lay bare the movement of Christian theology across the centuries, to situate and relativize it, and at the same time to draw forward forgotten historical possibilities for current understanding. Some theologians are narrowly confessional and tie Christian theology to their particular church community. Others are ecumenical and eclectic; they survey the possibilities in the variety of traditions, schematize it in abstract models, and try to maintain a balance of positions. Others see the confrontation of Christianity with other religions in dialogue as the axis for unlocking a new meaning for distinctively Christian self-understanding. And still others see the dialogue and interaction of Christianity with the world, including especially its social arrangements, as the matrix for relevant Christian understanding that leads to praxis. These theologians thus focus their interpretation of Christian truth in terms of its social meaning and significance. Others move in the same direction by using the technical language of a critical sociology of knowledge to unlock the implicit ideology and social corruption that creeps into seemingly innocent theological formulas. Feminist theologians react against hardened patriarchal structures in society and church by radicalizing God's value of equality and allowing it to recast Christian self-understanding and practice. Liberation theologians see the test case of the Christian understanding of the meaning of salvation in its relevance for the poor who suffer innocently from oppression. Other theologians, however, mediate Christian understanding through some form of philosophical understanding. Some are concerned with an appropriation of Christian truth in terms of the existential question of dealing with life itself. Others are concerned with the coherence of Christian truth with an organic theory of cosmos and history. Some theologians want to integrate Christian truth with the deepest human aspirations reflected in human culture broadly defined; they try to envision a universal horizon of human consciousness. Other theologians, especially in non-Western cultures, are completely dedicated to reinterpreting Christian expression in such a way that it begins to fit or represent cultures that are distinctively other than Western or Christian. Finally any of these different assumptions and methods may be combined in one respect or another with others.

The point of this impressionistic *tour de force* is to make sure that the *de facto* pluralism in theology be recognized for what it is. Christian theologians are doing many different things. Our aim in this account of theological method is not to overcome this pluralism. Rather we shall seek to analyze what is going on in Christian theology in such a way that it includes these different projects. We shall try to pitch the description of methodological principles in such a way that they describe what a great variety of theologians are actually doing. Yet at the same time we shall try to give these principles enough specificity to exclude the idea that any theologian can say anything that he or she wants to say at any particular time.

We shall begin with the characterization of method in theology as a method of correlation. The structure of such a method is dialogic, and in the next two sections we shall analyze the elements of method that are involved in each pole of the interchange. From this analysis we will be able to develop further the criteria for theological interpretation.

A METHOD OF CORRELATION

Method in theology may be called a method of correlation. A method of correlation finds its basis in the distinction between original and dependent revelation. Original revelation lies at the source of the religious tradition and is codified in the scriptures. Dependent revelation is the ongoing communication and reception of revelation in the community. Although dependent revelation is dependent, that is, a receiving of the tradition, it is at the same time an existential and social historical experience. Revelation is always received and experienced now, within human consciousness at any given time.[1] Thus revelation cannot but be filtered within and through the historical cultural experience of those who receive it.

A method of correlation rests on this necessary fusion of past and present in the reception of revelation. It consists in distinguishing and then bringing together original revelation as mediated through its traditional symbols and the situation of human consciousness in which it is received at any given time. What are correlated are the meaning of original revelation and present-day human experience. Thus a method of correlation makes explicit what happens spontaneously in the community's ongoing appropriation of tradition. The term correlation points directly to a duality or tension: correlation means distinguishing and then bringing together the meaning of the symbols of tradition and current experience in such a way that they mutually condition each other in generating an understanding of the object of Christian faith.

The point of this chapter is to describe more fully method in theology. But simply on the basis of this initial characterization it can be seen that method in theology *per se* is a method of correlation. In other words, a method of correlation is not *a* method of theology, but *the* method of a discipline that seeks to preserve the meaning of the past but understand it in a distinctly present-day manner. This is the case as long as we are dealing with theology and neither fundamentalism or revelational positivism on the one hand, nor the reduction of theology to a psychological anthropology on the other. This will become clearer in the light of four qualities of a method of correlation.

First, method in theology should be, and a method of correlation is, apologetic. Apologetic here does not refer to proving the truth of Christianity; theology is always also confessional in the sense that it depends on a particular revelation and tradition. Apologetic means rather that, first of all, in terms of *meaning*, theology should address the issues of the culture to which it is addressed in the terms of that culture. Theology seeks to explain the meaning of Christian assertions in a language comprehensible to any given age. Unless it does, it cannot be intelligible to that age. Second, the apologetic dimension of theology implies an effort to display the *truth* of Christian revelation. The logic of truth itself implies universality. Therefore Christian theology unfolds within the horizon of the whole human race. Theology involves asking critical questions and generating a self-critical understanding vis-à-vis the wider world. It is an effort not to demonstrate but to display the universal relevance of Christian meaning even in the context of a discussion with other traditions of revelation. But it is also important to realize at this point that this principle from mission theology also has a direct bearing on Christian self-understanding. Since Christians live in the world of everyday affairs, in ordinary society and culture that reflects an historical consciousness, that culture is within them and thus becomes a living dimension of the church itself.[2] The apologetic dimension of a method of correlation, then, is necessary for the *self*-understanding of Christians at any given time.

Second, a method of correlation is dialogical. It reproduces the dialogical structure of interpretation. The data of traditional symbols are explicitly brought into a dialogue with the cultural experience and consciousness of any given age. Current consciousness confronts the world of traditional symbols; and the symbols of tradition confront the present world of experience. On the one hand one could say that interpretation begins with the interpreter: the interpreter makes sense out of traditional symbols by interpreting them. On the other hand one could say that interpretation begins with the subject matter to be interpreted:

the symbols of the tradition illumine and make sense out of current experience. In a dialogue interpretation is mutual; interpretation goes both ways.

Paul Tillich explains the dialogical structure of a method of correlation from the point of view of the interpreter. The theologian always and necessarily comes to the data of Christian symbols from his or her present situation. The consciousness of the theologian is necessarily filled with the problems, concerns, questions, and preunderstandings that define the present situation. The goal of theological method is to understand the Christian message in a way that illumines the present situation; thus these questions must be thematized and clarified and then addressed to traditional symbols. In the dialogue present-day questions become fused with the responses yielded by the symbols to create "a mutual dependence between question and answer. In respect to content the Christian answers are dependent on the revelatory events in which they appear; in respect to form they are dependent on the structure of the questions which they answer."[3] In other words, the questions determine the answers, but with respect to the form of theological interpretations and not the content which is mediated by revelation through its foundational symbols.

But this dialogic structure can also be understood in exactly the reverse fashion as was seen in the consideration of the causality of religious symbols in symbolic communication. The interpreter comes with all the questions just referred to and confronts the world of religious symbolic tradition. But the goal of interpretation is also to understand and make sense of one's present consciousness of the world, history, and God in terms of the biblical message. Thus in the fusion of present-day consciousness and the data from the past the mutual dependence between question and answer can be understood the other way around. In respect to content the Christian answers are dependent on what the theologian experiences to be the case here and now; in respect to form they are dependent upon the Christian symbols that are allowed to shape human consciousness and inform it with Christian meaning from the past.[4] In other words, present-day questioning and experience is also a genuine source for theology; one encounters God's Presence here and now.[5] But in the dialogue with traditional symbols these symbols shape and give specific form to current experience. Dialogue goes both ways; the symbols of the past question, call into question, and then shape present-day religious experience and experience of the world.

Third, a method of correlation describes in very elementary terms how human beings learn. Learning is not simply a question of information and gathering data. Paulo Freire has shown that learning begins when people objectify their experience, gain a certain distance from it, and then call it into question by asking critical questions about it.[6] Thus any and every understanding of the Christian message presupposes that the symbols of the past are responsive to certain basic human questions. The method of theology thus proceeds by formulating the questions that arise out of actual cultural life because "human beings cannot receive answers to questions they never have asked."[7] This rather simple insight is also basic because it formulates something of a universal psychological law. Without a question, without inquiry, scripture and tradition remain mere data. The only way to mediate an understanding of the religious symbols of the tradition lies in the passageway of the mutual critical questioning of dialogue.

Fourth, in the light of this last reflection, one can understand why some form of a method of correlation characterizes the method of theology universally. This is how theology has always been done. One can accurately describe the history of theology as the raising of new questions and a critical or reflective interpretation of the symbols of Christian faith in response to these questions. When anything incrementally new appears in the history of Christian thought, the reason for it lies in a new situation that raises new questions that in turn cause a new understanding of received data. Indeed all the methods of current theology listed earlier display the same structure. All of them gain some leverage on the religious symbols of the tradition, either through some central, privileged, and encompassing experience, or through some historical problem, or through a discipline other than theology which provides a new and distinctive understanding of our current experience. This lever is then used to raise critical questions for the understanding of the religious tradition, and this in turn yields a new appreciation of the meaning of traditional symbols for today's situation.

Finally, a method of correlation is not a mechanical process, but an historically relative and pluralistic process. It is a function of human freedom. The many different uses of a method of correlation will yield different results. An identical method of correlation, if such were possible, in different cultures will yield different results. Thus the dialogue in theology must not only be between the interpreter and the data, but also between interpreters. A method of correlation should also include a mediation between the conflict or complementarity of different interpretations.[8] This horizontal or synchronic dialogue will not and is not meant to overcome pluralism. It will however engender communication between interpretations. No single leverage of critical questioning is sufficient or adequate to the data; every employment of a method of correlation is itself particular. But the dialogue between methods of correlation can help to secure at least a relative adequacy of any particular interpretation.

In what follows I will try to describe more fully what goes on in the process of a method of correlation. I will do this within the Tillichean framework of the formulation of the question or questions and the interpretation of the responses of the tradition. This will be done in a way that is conscious of the fact that interpretation also goes the other way, that the symbols of tradition also question the interpreter. The point, however, is not to design a particular method of correlation but to describe what goes on analogously in any critical method of correlation if it is to be adequate to its task.

THE QUESTIONS

Theology consists in the attempt to understand the world, human existence, history, and God in the light of the religious symbols that make up the tradition of the community. This essay at understanding is a critical discipline; it involves the asking of critical and reflective questions. Where do these questions come from, and what kind of questions are they? In this section I will describe the various kinds of questions which give rise to theological reflection and the different levels of experience that give rise to these questions. Many methods of correlation deal with one or other kind or level of questioning. A relatively adequate method of correlation should deal with all of them in order at least to approach comprehensiveness.

Negativity and Salvation

We begin with a consideration of where these questions arise and the kind of question we are dealing with. The questions which thematize theological reflection stem from some experience of negativity. Without an experience of negativity there would be no question and hence no need for theological reflection or reinterpretation. Some form of negativity in human experience is the very condition for religious understanding and theological interpretation.[9] I will first describe dramatic forms of this negative experience of contrast and then show how the most fundamental form of the questions to which they give rise always concerns the issue of salvation.

An experience of a negative contrast consists in a reaction to something, an event, a situation, a set of relationships, that should not be.[10]

That which is experienced is experienced precisely as negative. What is experienced is, but there is something wrong. It is not simply that there is something lacking, that there is an open space; what is should be different. One may not know exactly what the right order of things should be, but one knows that what is in place is out of whack and distorted. Such an experience, however, presupposes at least some preapprehension of a right order of things, for without that there could be no experience of negativity. It may be that it is precisely the experience of negativity, of a lack of coherence, of disorder, of unintelligibility, that mediates the horizon of insight into what should be.

One can summon up many examples of negative experiences of contrast from the moral and religious spheres. The experience of Job is such an experience of negativity which calls into question the orthodox theology of his time. Since he is innocent, what is happening to him is simply wrong, and no theology can make it right. The positive message of the prophets about God is generated by a contrast experience of social injustice. Our own century witnesses to dramatic and powerful corporate experiences of negativity. The experience of the holocaust is one that will never be forgotten. The experience of nuclear buildup is an experience of something that simply should not be; it has begun to stimulate a universal reaction against it and a positive search for an alternative way of handling an international balance of power. The negative contrast experience of women began in the Western world and is becoming worldwide. The fundamental intuition of liberation theology lies in outrage at the sub-human conditions of poverty and oppression that characterize the lives of so many human beings. But these dramatic examples of such an experience should not blind one to the commonness of such experiences. Some form of an experience of negativity, of a distorted order, coherence, and intelligibility, lies behind every deep human question, especially religious questions. Such human questions in turn seek to overturn the negativity, to negate the negation, and discover and establish what should be.

The most basic form of all religious questions is the question of salvation. One could say that the question of salvation is *the* religious question itself, so that all the other kinds of questions we shall consider are either subordinate to it or derivative from it. For the question of salvation is the question of the nature of being itself. The question of salvation arises out of the experience of negativity, of finitude, frustration, the incoherence of history and society, suffering, diminishment, and the anticipation of final death and extinction. All of these experiences are radically negative and appear so against the implicit background of the dimensions of human spirit and freedom that in their transcendence seek salvation: the quest for infinity, wholeness, and permanence in being. The experience of sin as sin is a good example of how the negativity of experience is already a revelation of the positive ground that makes evil sin. Because the sinfulness of human existence must be revealed, the implicit horizon of what we could be and should be by a power that exceeds our own capacity has already begun to make itself known.[11] The sheer negativity of all these experiences only appears as negative against an expanded horizon of other possibilities or at least desires. The deep desire beneath all these desires is for salvation, the negation of these negativities by a transcendent source of power not our own. This question of salvation, in one form or another, is an anthropological constant because the negativities of existence are intrinsic to human existence itself. Is there salvation? Where is it? What is it? How is it accomplished? At bottom all theological questions are soteriological in their grounding. They derive from here and must always be led back to this issue. This logic will become very important in the discernment and interpretation of the precise point of revelational encounter that is mediated by the symbols of tradition.

In sum, all theological questioning arises out of some form of an experience of negativity. At their deepest level, the negative experiences that give rise to theological questions ultimately concern salvation. At bottom they involve human beings in their relation to transcendence. But these experiences themselves can be differentiated. They are not generated at the same level of existence or experience. Rather different kinds of negativity correspond with different dimensions or planes of human existence and yield different foci of attention.

Dimensions of Questioning

Beneath all theological questioning lies the fundamental question of salvation. The question of salvation does not merely concern *my* salvation. By an internal necessity the question of individual salvation is tied up with that of the whole human race. The question of salvation is inherently social and not less personal and individual because of this. But in the discipline of theology this deepest theme is challenged practically by a variety of negativities that call into question the adequacy of the understanding and actual appropriation of Christian revelation at any given time. What follows is a delineation of dimensions or areas in which negative experiences are stimulating theological questioning today. The following schematization of the kinds of negative experience and questioning is not meant to be exhaustive. But it will show that theological questioning itself must unfold within the context of a variety of different dimensions of experience in order to generate comprehensive understanding of the religious symbols it interprets.

A first level of specifically theological questioning arises out of the negative side of historical growth, change, and the acquisition of new knowledge. Religious symbols and their theological rationales no longer make sense, and the salvation that they once mediated seems threatened by a lack of coherence with other experience. What makes sense to a child no longer satisfies the adult. What adults believed in the past no longer appears credible or tenable in the present. New knowledge, the relentless quest of science to dispel sheer ignorance, the changes in the very assumptions with which we view the world, turn what appeared to be simple religious beliefs into nonsense. In the face of new experience and knowledge theology always seems to be retreating and marshaling a new defense before retreating again.[12] The negativity which gives rise to the question of intelligibility may be slight, calling for adjustments in our understanding. But it can also be dramatic as in the case of a classical consciousness giving way to an historical consciousness. In the world of historical change the repetition of past symbols simply does not make sense. One question for theology then is simply that of coherent intelligibility. But behind it always lies the question of salvation.

Another distinct level of theological questioning regards the social meaning and function of religious symbols. We are only now coming to realize the degree to which religious symbols have an impact on society. How one conceives God sanctions social structures. How one depicts Jesus and the salvation accomplished in him overflows into social behavior patterns. Religious views of sexuality have enormous ramifications in the social order. The meaning of theological conceptions cannot be restricted to a framework in which they are viewed as carrying meaning only for individuals. What we are realizing today is that theological symbols *always* have a social function and a social meaning even when this is not intended. They can have as much impact by what they do not say as by what is said. This meaning and the way it functions are distinct from their individualist interpretation and must be attended to directly.

The issue of the social meaning and function of religious symbols also arises out of negative experiences. We have discussed earlier the corruptibility of religious symbols and doctrines on the level of their social function. The objectification of religious symbols may be congruent with and benign relative to a given social order. But societies are always shifting and the meaning of religious symbols will always tend to reflect the interests of those in power. Thus suddenly religious symbols are experienced negatively because they have become one of the vehicles of oppression. There is no need to chronicle the history of Christian oppression of other groups outside the Christian fold as examples of this. It is enough in our own day to point to the eruption of the poor, women, and other groups within the church itself to show the degree to which religious symbols can assume a negative and oppressive function. But the issue goes deeper than function to the level of religious meaning itself. One has to ask the fundamental religious questions again on this social level. One has not grasped the meaning of salvation until one can answer what it implies for the social existence of human beings. When there is so much dehumanizing poverty and death in Christian cultures and societies, and such overt discrimination and oppression within the church itself, one has to ask again: What is Christian salvation? Where is it? In sum, the social level of human existence is a distinct and quasi-autonomous dimension of function and meaning, and it is beset with distinct experiences of negativity that raise distinct religious and theological questions.

Still another whole set of questions has arisen in our time from the negative side of the experience of historicity, relativity, and pluralism. These questions have to do with the universality of the meaningfulness and the truth of Christianity itself. It has always been assumed that Christian truth is universally relevant. Our experience of the world today calls this into question.

The negative side of the experience of pluralism and relativity operates in several spheres. Regarding Christianity itself and its religious symbols the empirical historical data seem to indicate that they are not universally relevant. The pluralism of vital religions seems to contradict it. At the very least this raises the question of whether or not these symbols are construed in such a way that this universal relevance is apparent or credible. Within the church itself, further, the experience of the pluralism of cultures raises the question of whether there can be a single universal theology. Since all human experience is particular, all points of view limited, and all focused concerns peculiar to a culture, it is difficult today to imagine a single theology or construal of Christian symbols that can unite the church. Most theologians who seek a culturally relevant and thus inculturated theology would agree with this proposition. But this is merely the definition of the problem. For once again one must presume the universal relevance of Christian truth insofar as it is true. At some level one must strive for a Christian theology that is comparable or analogous with all other Christian theologies because the unity of Christian revelation reaches out and strains for universal relevance. The theological question, then, concerns a construal of Christian symbols that is both particular and yet open to all Christian experience and ultimately to the context of the human race as a whole.

Finally, there is the question of empowerment. The negativities experienced on the fundamental level of the human and which give rise to the religious question are not removed by mere revelation and understanding. Revelation does not merely appeal to the passive needs of humanity. It also addresses the human potential for activity and unleashes the creativity of human freedom. Against the background of human suffering and diminishment, theological questioning must look for the positive ideals and values that appeal to human freedom and give an account of the lineaments of the hope that stimulates action even in the face of death.

Such are the levels and dimensions of questioning that initiate theological inquiry, understanding, and affirmation. Many of the various methods in theology that together comprise the discipline today unfold along the line of one or another dimension of meaning. They use one or other or a combination of disciplines and questions as levers for critically examining and thus drawing out the meaning of traditional theological symbols and doctrines. The comprehensiveness of theological questioning and the adequacy of interpretation depends on the measure in which all these levels of meaning are addressed. At least the outline of these various levels and dimensions shows that adequate theological interpretation cannot consist in a reduction of meaning to one of these axes to the exclusion of others.

THE FRAMEWORK OF AN ANSWER

Method in theology is a method of correlation which consists in a dialogue between the questioning of the community and the traditional data of the community's religious symbols. We pass now to the second pole of that dialogue. We assume that this is a genuine dialogue, that the traditional symbols shape, inform, and thus structure the consciousness of the theologian. This assumption is founded on the presumption of the critical historical inquiry that is a necessary component of theological method and which was described in the last chapter. The stress in this account of the design of the answer, however, falls on the activity of the theologian. What is being described here is precisely the creative activity of the theologian in the process of theological interpretation. The point of view then is that of the theologian and the description is phenomenological.[13]

The Salvific Point of Traditional Symbols

Theology is inquiry. Theological investigation as we have just shown begins with questions and is looking for answers. But the one who inquires and investigates already possesses the answers in some rudimentary form, at least in a preunderstanding of the religious dimension of the symbols being investigated. The very interest and desire to interpret this meaning indicates some awareness of what they mean. It is more likely, however, that the theologian is a member of the religious community whose symbols he or she investigates. In this case the theologian has a concrete, existential, and engaged participatory knowledge of the meaning of the symbols investigated. As a member of the church the symbols of scripture and creed have shaped the theologian's consciousness. Like everyone else in the community the theologian understands existentially the creed which he or she now begins to examine. But the theologian is looking for a different kind of knowledge, a critical-minded and reflective interpretation of its meaning. By asking critical questions theologians display a vague knowledge of that which is lacking in the church's understanding of its symbols. The experience of negativity points to a preapprehension of the kind of understanding which up to now has been missing.

The theologian brings this preunderstanding to the historical study of foundational religious symbols. There is no reason to repeat all that was said in the last chapter concerning the necessity of critical historical study for a genuine dialogue between the interpreter and the constitutive testimony to what is to be interpreted. But it is important at this point to stress the phenomenon of distantiation that occurs in historical study because it is critical for theological method. The more thorough the historical study of traditional symbols is, the more one's initial preunderstanding of them is undermined. The more one succeeds in an historical understanding of traditional symbols, the more distant does their meaning appear from the engaged participatory knowledge one brought to the task, especially when it is naive and untutored. The more critical history determines the meaning of the symbols of the past within the context of a past culture, the more they appear alien to present-day modes of understanding and expression.

A simple illustration of this is the story of creation and sin. Let us presuppose that the initial participatory knowledge of the meaning of creation and sin is drawn simply from an unreflective and fundamentalistic appreciation of the accounts in the Book of Genesis. A critical study of the origin of this symbol will radically change the form of one's appreciation of the story. As was said in the last chapter, it will appear not only as a symbol and not an explanation, but as a symbol that was generated in an antique and distant culture. But what is so obvious with regard to this mythic symbol is also true of the other symbols from our past. The closer historical research gets to the Jesus of history, the further away from us he seems. Jesus shared some eschatological beliefs of his day that are radically alien to today's world-view and mode of thinking. Jesus was not a present-day Christian, and one must be suspicious of every account that makes him appear as such. When one studies critically the genesis through long development of the doctrine of the Trinity, one cannot but be impressed by the historically conditioned quality of the thinking and the otherness of the kinds of presuppositions and arguments that generated the resultant doctrine. From a present-day perspective one simply cannot accept the arguments as presented, which means that one must question the symbol and supply new arguments to understand it. These examples could be multiplied; they simply point out the degree to which a critical historical knowledge of the meaning of the symbols of the past situates them in a culture distant from the present. History in its first moment produces an appreciation of the difference between symbols in their origins and the unquestioning appreciation of them that is current in the present experience of the church. And this must be the case, because the current experience of the church is precisely a present-day experience that consists in the strange mixture of past symbol received into the horizon of current consciousness.

This contrast between the past historical meaning of a particular symbol and present-day consciousness forces the theologian to transcend that historical meaning and ask the question of the point of the symbol.[14] The question of the point of a religious symbol always leads back to fundamental anthropological questions concerning salvation. The point of a religious symbol is to mediate and communicate transcendence. It does not consist in the particular historical meaning that is determined by its historical genesis and context. The question of the point of any given religious symbol, therefore, both breaks down its past historical meaning, transcends it or gets behind it, and breaks open its transcendent meaning as a mediation of encounter with God's Presence.

There is a certain simplicity to this mechanism or insight and it can be stated bluntly: the symbols of the past are not accepted on the basis of their historical or categorical meaning in the past; they are rather accepted insofar as they mediate transcendence, that is, a present experience of the salvation that is mediated through them. Thus one does not accept an historical story of a creation but the experience of being created it mediates.[15] One does not accept Jesus' belief in an imminent parousia, which did not occur, but Jesus' whole life as a mediation of God's salvation.[16] One does not accept a doctrine of three persons in one God in a naive tritheistic sense, but the experience of a real salvation from God in Jesus and God as Spirit which is protected and preserved by the formula.[17]

How does one arrive at the point of a particular Christian symbol? Several factors from the theology of faith, revelation, and the structure of symbols converge at this point. Religion itself emerges out of the negativities of human existence and the question for salvation. Faith in and revelation of transcendence are themselves joined at the juncture of this question for salvation. The transcendent power of salvation, which is mediated by religious symbols, consists in its most fundamental form in the reality of God's Presence. But arrival at this salvational point of any given doctrinal or theological symbol is not merely a matter of intuitive experience. More practically one can discover the point of a symbol by an analysis of the theological expression and reasoning that surrounds it. One of the clearest examples of this is found in the development of the trinitarian and christological doctrinal symbols. The presuppositions, the arguments, and the processes of reasoning all have soteriological underpinnings. The bottom line is always that Jesus is the bringer of God's salvation. This example shows that the theoretical view of the primacy of salvation through encounter with God's Presence is actually played out in theological reasoning and can be uncovered through analysis.

The distinction of a religious symbol in itself from its point of mediating an encounter with saving transcendence is crucial. Without an insight into this distinction, which is consistent with the theories of faith and revelation already proposed, there cannot be any explicit or conscious reinterpretation. We now move on to how this experience of the point of a religious symbol can be thematized.

Dimensions of an Adequate Anthropology

How can one thematize the point of religious symbols which is the salvation they mediate? How can one bring to the level of understanding that which, in a symbol from a past and distant culture, is the same as one experiences in one's life today? In the last chapter we said that, apart from the sameness of God and God's Presence, one must look for a sameness of experience in a common humanity. Thus the basis for historical communication with the past is a common anthropology. We communicate with and learn from the salvific meaning of past symbols across the differences on the basis of a principle of analogy which has its basis in common human experience. In terms of anthropological constants, the experience of negativities, questions, and salvation today is analogous to the experience which generated the foundational symbols.

But human existence is many-faceted; it unfolds on many levels and, as was already shown, these give rise to a variety of different kinds of negative experiences and questions. Thus salvation too is experienced as differentiated; it has a variety of dimensions and bears meaning for the whole of human life in the various aspects of existence. Therefore one can lay down this axiom for the comprehensiveness in thematizing the point of traditional symbols: the adequacy of its interpretation will depend on the adequacy of the anthropology that is used to articulate or express it. In other words, an interpretation that focuses on only one or other of the dimensions of human existence in thematizing salvation, in the same measure fails to do justice to the full impact and meaning of salvation. A comprehensive interpretation of the salvific point of religious symbols will respond to the full range of negativities and questions that are part of our common human existence.

The anthropological lever for interpreting the salvific meaning of past symbols and doctrines is easy enough to understand on the personal individual level of human existence. All human beings are threatened in their very being by finitude, sin, suffering, and final death. This common anthropological condition, its negativity, and the questions of the possibility of authentic existence, really creative freedom, and final being define a common matrix for understanding salvation. It underlies the language of the New Testament, the foundational doctrines of tradition, and the meaning of religious symbols experienced today.[18] Salvation is a personal encounter with God's Presence which responds to sin by forgiveness, suffering by the impulse of courage to resist it, death by the promise of resurrection. Salvation is an individual's personal encounter with God's Presence.

So prominent in both personal experience and theological mediation is the individual personal dimension of salvific meaning that the social historical dimension is often neglected. Current theology, however, has retrieved this dimension and shown that it is more concrete, existentially vital, and real for human beings than the question of merely individual salvation. Indeed, once one has an insight into the sociality of human existence, every idea of a merely individual concept of human existence and hence salvation simply vanishes. To appreciate this one must understand the social nature of human existence itself. One cannot describe human existence adequately by a series of qualities that charac-

terizes every individual. Such a degree of abstraction neglects the social-historical constitution of human existence. One of the central insights that feeds historical consciousness today is that one cannot bypass
social history if one wants to understand human existence. Human existence is its history. To understand human existence means to examine
what it has been and is historically and socially.

In this light, one can understand how the social sciences enter
intrinsically into the discipline of theology. They are not extrinsic to
theological understanding itself, not related merely consequentially by
proposing an analysis of society for the direction of Christian-motivated
individual action. Rather the social sciences are anthropological; they
help define a concrete or actual anthropology. Human existence is
political; human beings are economic; human existence is intrinsically
social and cultural and ecological. And all these real dimensions of
actual existence are confronted by negativities that do not exclude but
include and transcend the merely individual dimension of existence,
threaten human existence with meaninglessness, and raise the question
of salvation. A purely individual notion of the salvific point of religious
symbols is not adequate at all, because it exempts from the need of
salvific meaning all-encompassing spheres of human existence. Once
one realizes that human existence is socially constituted, one can also
recognize that a salvation that is exclusively individual in this world is no
salvation at all because it leaves concrete social life unredeemed. At best
it affords an unrealistic individual consolation and a motive for waiting
for an end-time. In short, since human existence itself is social and
historical, the salvific point of the religious symbols that mediate salvation must also be social-historical.[19]

The religious symbols of the past, moreover, do bear a social-historical meaning and relevance. Since they emerged in a political and social
environment, they cannot not have borne social relevance and significance, even when that dimension is not explicit or has been neglected.
The role of the theologian is to ask the social historical questions and
draw the analogous meanings forward for current historical, social and
political experience. For example, Jesus was a public religious figure in
an intensely religious and political social environment in which these
dimensions were not carefully differentiated as they are today. It is
historically impossible that the public, moral, and religious activity of
Jesus did not also bear a social and political meaning and impact in his
own mind and on his audience.[20] Therefore one can find, because his
life does display it, moral and religious meaning of a distinctly social and
political nature. But, like individual salvific meaning, this social salvific
meaning must be understood analogously and as responding to the deep

social negativities of human existence. It is not a question of literally imitating Jesus, but of finding salvific meaning in response to the negativities, the meaninglessness, and the death-dealing social structures that mark common social human existence.

An adequate anthropology must stretch toward universality and try to encompass all of humanity in its ken, that is, as a unity, as the human race. As impossible as this is historically and socially, still the imagination must try to grasp the human condition as such and the destiny toward which it is heading. This universal scope of questioning opens up the horizon of interpretation beyond individual and particular social-historical perspectives. It allows the radical pluralism that characterizes human existence to appear, and it thus provides a context for inter-religious dialogue. Within the Christian sphere this universal perspective provides a context for dialectics of different interpretations. It forces theology to look beneath or beyond cultural differences to find the real point of transcendent salvation. It allows the questions of eschatology and the final meaningfulness of human creativity in history to come to the fore. The expansion of the horizon of interpretation to include the whole race historically deepens one's appreciation of God's creation and salvific will for humanity as such. Without this stretching, theology will inevitably lapse into parochial and narrow interpretations of the salvific point of God's revelation which is intended for the whole world.

And, finally, an anthropology must take account of both the passive and the active dimension of human existence. Too often the stress in religious anthropology falls on human passivity. The apologetic structure of theology is reduced to underlining the negativities of human existence that are passively endured, so that God appears as the problem solver and fulfiller of human needs. But human freedom is also active. The human mind creates new meaning; human freedom is a center of responsibility, decision, and action; human freedom creates new reality and in so doing shapes human existence and the world into the future. The negativities of human existence, therefore, include the idols we create and the spurious goals we set for our activity. The salvific point of revelation, therefore, does not merely appeal to human passivity—in obedience, submission, acceptance of forgiveness, a promise of eternal life. The encounter with God through religious symbols also mediates God's will, goals, and challenge to human freedom. A merely passive interpretation of the salvific point of religious symbols radically short-circuits their full significance for human life.

In sum, the anthropology that implicitly or explicitly underlies any given theology is what enables it to communicate with and appropriate the salvific point that is mediated by the religious symbols of the tradition. A thematic analysis of human existence uncovers the deep and perennial religious questions that characterize human experience on a variety of different levels. All of these questions are the questions of salvation which contribute to uncovering its meaning. Thus the comprehensiveness and adequacy of the thematization of the point of religious symbols will depend on the comprehensiveness of the theologian's anthropology. This distinction of dimensions in the description of the anthropological constants of human existence also serves to differentiate among the variety of different theological methods used by theologians today and to draw them into an integrated framework. We now move to the issue of constructing theological positions on the basis of a thematized appreciation of the salvific point of religious symbols.

RECONSTRUCTION OF THE SALVIFIC POINT
OF RELIGIOUS SYMBOLS

What is the theologian doing when he or she constructs a theological position? How are theologians able to make affirmations about the world, human history, human existence, and God in the light of their encounter with transcendence? What is going on when theologians propose new understandings of the doctrine of sin, Jesus as the Christ, or the end-time? In giving a descriptive response to these questions I distinguish four elements or moments of this process. They are arranged in a certain logical order. But it would be a mistake to think that the theological mind moves along step by step. It is not a question of the proper order of things. Rather it would be better to see all of these processes going on at once and mixed up with each other. Neither should they be considered as separate from the logically defined moments that we have already discussed.

A first element in theological construction consists in the role of the imagination. Although imagination is difficult to define in itself, people know what it is by its function, by what it does. The imagination imagines: it seeks, produces, and then finds meaning; it projects new forms of unity on the data and construes it in this way or that. The imagination is active and creative. But the theological imagination at this point is not mere fancy. It is already laden with the experience of transcendence mediated by religious symbols, shaped by them, and in possession of the salvific point communicated through them. Moreover the imagination has many sources to work with: the data of traditional symbols themselves, the traditional language of the church, the history of theological portrayals, the spontaneous or strained beliefs of the community, other disciplines which provide insight and new leverage for understanding, the work of other theologians. The imagination can exercise itself also through a variety of genres in taking up the data and other sources of insight. It may express itself in concrete images or root metaphors; it may use abstract or rationally derived concepts and logic; it may construct models that sum things up or go to the heart of the matter. It may proceed laboriously by trial and error; it may discover what it seeks in a flash of insight. Its goal is to make things fit, to discover a unity in the plurality of data, to make preliminary sense out of it, to begin to understand it.

A second and perhaps distinct moment in theological construction consists in conceptualization or the reasoning faculty that uses logic and clear concepts. I do not propose a radical separation between understanding through images and through rationally grounded concepts that was prevalent during and after the Enlightenment. Conceptualization draws the work of the imagination up into itself, builds on it, preserves it. Nor should one think of a conceptual understanding as less symbolic than images. The subject matter of theology is transcendence, received by faith through revelation, and the only way to deal with it is symbolically. One should also always bear in mind the polysemy and multivalence of even conceptual symbols; one cannot tie transcendence down.

The goal of conceptualization is clarity, and it proceeds by critical, reflective reasoning.[21] This critical thinking defines, makes distinctions, clarifies its conceptions by opposition to others, uses logic, arrives at conclusions. Only very generally is this reflective reasoning homogeneous. It can borrow from a variety of different disciplines and use different logics. It can appeal to existential experience, social mechanisms or "laws," or philosophical conceptions of the cosmos. But it should always work from potentially shared premises and assumptions, and since it seeks communicative understanding should draw others into the process. Since the goal of conceptualization is clarity and coherence of understanding, it should integrate the variety of data and try to eliminate internal contradictions or contradictions of things which from other sources are known to be true. Conceptual reflective understanding brings the work of the imagination to another level of unity and intelligibility without, as was said, leaving it behind.

A third element of the theologian's construction of a position consists in what might be called horizontal dialogue. Up to this time we have been envisioning a dialogue between the interpreter and the religious symbols of the tradition, between the present and the past. But historical consciousness in a new way reinforces synchronic pluralism and simply demands the dialogue among theologians in a community of interchange. From beginning to end the theological process is historically conditioned, particular, limited, relative, and partial in the neutral sense of being biased in this way or that simply because of finitude. Thus even within the same community at any given time there will inevitably be a conflict of interpretations and theological affirmations.

The function of horizontal dialogue then consists in mutual criticism of positions. It consists in dialectical reasoning, in measuring one position against another or others, in an attempt to achieve a self-critical leverage on one's own thinking. The goal of this dialogue should not be thought of as an arrival at the single position that encompasses all the others. It is impossible to overcome pluralism in theology. Yet one can strive to establish some normative criteria that account for some unity in diversity, or a framework within which differences can be appreciated.[22] The goal of any given theological position is a relative adequacy that accounts for most of the data at any given time.[23]

Fourth, the goal of theological interpretation is in the end to empower human life. All knowledge, all understanding, all theological doctrines imply directions for the Christian life. If they did not, it would be difficult to assign their relevance. Thus the theologian should give explicit thought to the consequences of the interpretation of religious symbols. The symbols themselves mediate a transforming encounter that reaches down to freedom and action. This should be brought to the surface by drawing out the consequences for spirituality.

At this point one should be able to appreciate the extent to which the priorities of these elements of interpretation and theological method can be ordered differently. Action as a category points to a level of human existence that is prior to explicit conscious reflection, and practice is prior to second-order reflection. This is especially evident on the social historical level. Thus, in fact, the negativities of human existence are met first in life and practice, and they generate a spontaneous resistance. The meanings of theological positions and doctrines change first in and through the practice of the community. The *social* history of Christian theology and doctrine demonstrates this. Therefore theology begins with experience generated by the practice of the Christian community and can be defined as reflection upon Christian praxis. We have in the course of this essay focused on the logic of theological reflection. But one should not imagine that that begins in the mind only to lead consequentially to action. In fact theology always begins with the corporate experience of Christian praxis and is reflection on that praxis.[24]

Since faith is a form of praxis, theology can be said to begin and lead back to active spirituality. Especially here both the passive and the active dimensions of human freedom must be attended to. All Christian spiritualities are forms of action, even when they respond directly to God's Presence in prayer and worship. But today much more prominence should be given to the positive direction for the creativity of human freedom because it has been so consistently neglected as genuine spiritual activity. Christian theology should provide the deep values and goals for human freedom that correspond to the reign of God.

CRITERIA FOR CONSTRUCTIVE THEOLOGY

We can conclude these chapters on interpretation and method in theology by drawing out the criteria for theological interpretation that have emerged in the course of the discussion. Basically these are three: fidelity to the tradition, intelligibility, and empowerment of the Christian life.

Constructive theological interpretation must be faithful to the scriptures and to the history of the central Christian doctrines. There is no need to repeat the logic of an historical revelation that underlies this demand. The very point of interpreting past symbols is to keep their original meaning alive. This exigency for fidelity can be seen by reversing the dialogue of question and answer. The symbols of the past shape Christian consciousness, give form to it, and address questions to it. The scriptures do not go away upon interpretation; our past is always with us. Original revelation constantly asks new questions of theology. It confronts present-day consciousness and is decidedly counter-cultural. The tradition to which theology must be faithful is a living, dynamic, and ever-present source of new questions because of the changing times it addresses.[25]

This fidelity to scripture and classical doctrine, however, can only result in a sameness within difference. The only way theological affirmations today can be faithful to the past is analogously. This sameness and difference, however, is not to be left a mere vague and diffuse paradox; its structure can be further defined. Sameness does not and cannot lie in a mere comparison of present-day interpretation with the symbol of the past in itself. The symbols of the past in themselves are particular, historically conditioned forms of theology. They are human creations, but ones that point to something other than themselves. The criterion of "orthodoxy" therefore does not and cannot lie in a comparison of one theology with another theology. This is not where sameness but rather difference lies. Sameness consists in the mediation of transcendence, and interpretation is faithful to past symbols when it is faithful to the salvific point of encounter with transcendence that the symbols of the tradition mediate. The criterion of "orthodoxy," there-fore, lies in the experience of transcendence mediated by the symbols of the past, and any constructive theological interpretation that succeeds in coherently expressing that experience is "orthodox."[26]

This conclusion is really quite basic in the understanding of what is going on in theology. It can be illustrated very briefly with the example of interpretation of the Council of Nicaea. Interpretation of Nicaea does not consist in simply repeating it. Nicaea is itself a theological symbol that interprets something else, namely, the experience that Jesus is God's salvation bringer. In its interpretation of that foundational Christian experience it says that no less than God is at work in the appearance and life of Jesus. So too, theological interpretation of Nicaea must be faithful to what Nicaea itself was faithful to and mediates, namely, the experience that Jesus is God's salvation bringer. Any and every interpretation of Nicaea that explains or expresses how Jesus is salvation bringer from God is *eo ipso* "orthodox," for that is what is mediated by Nicaea and what theology must be faithful to. Repeating the words of Nicaea in a new context in no way ensures the faithfulness that is required. If this were the case, theology would begin to lapse back into a fundamentalism, revelational positivism, or creedalism which pre-cisely do not preserve the point of the doctrine of Nicaea. The impor-tance of this principle is that it exposes the degree to which this still prevails in a good deal of theology.

The second criterion for theology is intelligibility. If theological symbols are really to illumine reality, they must be interpreted in such a way that they are critically coherent among themselves and with other things about the world one knows to be true. Criticism, critical reflec-tion, questioning, argument, dialectical comparison and reasoning, are all part of integral theological construction. This principle then must be held together in tension with that of faithfulness. The principle of faith-fulness as it has been explained, however, really opens up to this princi-ple of intelligibility and invites it. But at the same time one must keep checking back to make sure that the salvific point of a past symbol is really preserved in new cultural interpretations. Surely one must also ask: Who decides intelligibility? What appears as coherent and intelligi-ble to some may be no more than fancy for others. This issue will always be the subject of debate. It is for this reason that critical reasoning should always be made explicit and the conflict of interpretations be turned into a dialogue of interpretations and interpreters.

The criterion of intelligibility takes on a new dimension when the horizon of interpretation includes the theme of apologetics. The goal of intelligibility is to show not just coherence in a particular culture, but universal relevance. Within this horizon of consciousness intelligibility must be mediated by anthropology. In other words, interpretation will appear intelligible when and in the measure that what is interpreted appears intelligible for human existence as such.[27] This anthropology, however, cannot be unidimensional in an individualist way; it cannot be mediated merely by a transcendental analysis that prescinds from the social constitution of human existence. It cannot bypass the actual concrete anthropological constants of social oppression and liberation. It cannot ignore other vital religious traditions. Interpretation must show the universal anthropological relevance of God's Presence within the context of an anthropology that is constituted by social history.

Finally, theological assertions must be empowering for Christian life, if they are faithfully to mediate the impact of an encounter with transcendence that is the point of religious symbols. This empowerment should extend to the whole of life, because theological symbols illumine a human relation not just to God but also to the world, human history, and the self. This criterion, then, is not merely a moral exhortation for theologians that they in turn add a moral lesson to their constructive theological positions. It is a critical principle. If one cannot find an intrinsic bearing on human life within theological understanding itself, there is no reason to take it seriously. It quite literally does not make any difference. But if theology really does mediate the meaning of an encounter with God, it is really hard to see how this could not make a difference.[28]

These three criteria should not be regarded as independent of each other; each one implies the other two in integral theological interpretation. The goal of theological interpretation is to render the salvific point of God's Presence which is mediated in original revelation in such a way that it appears universally relevant for the praxis of all human beings. Such is the nature of God's Presence that it is a universal Presence of personal and empowering love. It is to this that interpretation must be faithful. But to render this intelligible is at the same time to show its universal relevance, applicability, and credibility. For intelligibility cannot be conceived for human life without applicability, and applicability remains abstract until it passes into action. The final measure of intelligibility is credible action on the basis of God's Presence in the face of the negativities of human historical existence.[29]

CONCLUSION

Chapter Eleven

DYNAMICS OF THEOLOGY

_____

Theology is an ungainly discipline. Unlike many other pursuits of wisdom, even its most fundamental principles are disputed by those who practice it. This results in more than a mere pluralism of Christian theologies in the sense of different conceptions of the content of Christian faith. Beyond that it yields a pluralism in the very understanding of what theology is. In a sense there is no single discipline of theology. Christian theology consists in a loose collection of various analogous paradigms for going about the task of interpreting the Christian vision of reality.

Each of five main divisions of this book represents an approach toward an understanding of the discipline of theology. Although they are discrete or distinct essays, each perspective is fundamental or foundational, so that one could go on to give a comprehensive account of the discipline of theology from any one of these points of view. Every theology and every conception of theology involves in its very foundations an understanding of the nature of faith, the dynamics of revelation, the character and function of scripture, the structure of religious epistemology and language, a method for generating theological interpretations and positions. In this essay the treatment of these topics has been thematized by the same question: What is a theological statement or assertion? What is going on in the discipline of theology? Although all these chapters are consistent and together represent a single interpretation of the nature of theology, each distinct approach has uncovered different aspects and dimensions of theology as a whole. The variety of approaches has thus displayed the enormous complexity of this discipline.

The goal of this essay is not to overcome the pluralism that reigns in theology. Rather more modestly the effort here has been simply to offer a consistent view of the discipline that takes account of the many foundational issues upon which it is based. Because these issues are foundational, decisions on how they are to be understood determine the way

215

theology itself is understood and the way it is practiced. On that premise, the treatment of each one of these five topics yielded some hermeneutical principles for understanding the nature of theology, and, on that basis, for interpreting the meaning of any theological statement or position. One's conception of theology is governed by the tacit or reflective and acknowledged preconceptions of these foundational questions.

In this conclusion I now wish to try to draw together into a single statement the many principles that have emerged in the course of this book. I will do this by using these principles to fashion a description of theology. In other words, the description of the dynamics of theology that follows consists in a summary of the conclusions that have been arrived at in the preceding analyses. The point is not to repeat the analyses, but to weave the various conclusions into a single coherent understanding of the discipline of theology itself.

A DEFINITION OF THEOLOGY

We begin with a general definition of theology that may serve as the subject matter for further elaboration. Theology can be characterized by a great variety of formulas. Etymologically *theo-logia* is talk, thought, reasoning about God. Perhaps the most common designation for theology comes from Augustine and Anselm: theology is faith seeking understanding. The adequacy of these formulas of course really depends on the fuller explanation of their meaning. The understanding of theology that underlies this essay, however, is the following: theology is the construal of reality in the light of Christian symbols. More fully, theology is a discipline that interprets all reality—human existence, society, history, the world, and God—in terms of the symbols of Christian faith. This view of theology contains a number of distinctive traits that can be briefly noted preparatory to a fuller explanation.

The first regards the scope of the subject matter of theology. In this conception theology is not limited to dealing with God and the transcendent sphere. Theological interpretation extends to the whole of reality, indeed to everything that is. As in the sacred doctrine contained in the *Summa Theologiae* of Aquinas, nothing escapes the consideration of the theological imagination.[1] But that which formally determines the specifically theological interpretation of areas normally considered non-theological consists in revelation, or the vision of faith, or more concretely the symbols of the Christian tradition. These define the perspective and thematic lens that constitute the interpretation as properly theological.

This view of theology corresponds to actual theological literature. There is scarcely an area of human experience that is not the subject of theological interpretation.

Second, this expanded view of the scope of theology is significant because of the way in which the intentionality of the discipline is thematized. Theology is open to all reality because all reality is its subject matter. Theology is open to all data and to every historically new datum. It enters implicitly into dialogue with all human experience, with other disciplines of human knowledge, with other religions which also should be interpreted from a Christian perspective. This openness in turn underlies the apologetic character of theology; it must give an account of itself before the world even as it seeks to understand the world. Theology strives for universal relevance; the meaning of Christian symbols are brought to bear on every facet of the human experience of reality. No data are beyond its ken; all data influence theology by soliciting a Christian theological interpretation.

But, third, this outward extension of the discipline of theology does not mean that Christian symbols themselves are exempt from critical examination. On the one hand, the tradition of Christian symbols is a given; they define the circle of faith from within which the Christian theologian operates. But on the other hand, the very dialogue with the world forces theology to reflect critically on the meaning of these symbols themselves. Theology is also an essay at self-understanding and self-appropriation. For example, the central symbol of Christian faith and revelation is Jesus of Nazareth, and formal christology deals with the very meaning of Jesus' being the Christ of God. But there is always a danger in Christian theology that it become so turned in on itself in the quest for self-understanding that its relevance for the world and the world's impact on self-understanding become lost. Theology cannot be reduced thematically to a quest for self-definition with the normative and disciplinary connotations that this involves. Self-understanding and the explanation of Christian symbols themselves should always unfold in the wider context of universal relevance and responsibility.[2]

With this general characterization of the discipline as a background, let us now review its foundations which consist of faith and revelation.

THE FOUNDATIONS OF THEOLOGY

The foundations of Christian theology are faith and revelation; these are its sources; theology is based on and emerges out of a religious faith that is informed by revelation. These foundations will thus determine some of its fundamental qualities as a discipline.

Faith and revelation are distinguishable realities but they exist in reciprocally caused unity and are inseparable. Faith and revelation are not the same thing. Faith is human response and commitment; revelation is God's activity which has its ground in God's Presence to human subjectivity. But neither exists formally without the other. For revelation involves God's self-communication which is complete only when revelation is received and responded to. And although faith can exist on a variety of different levels, including a diffuse basic trust and openness to reality itself, it only becomes faith formally in response to a specific object. Faith and revelation, then, become one in actuality. They constitute each other in the existential relationship of God revealing and human beings responding. It is out of this actual engagement of human beings with divine transcendence that theology arises.

From these foundations one can formulate the principle that theology does not consist in knowledge or a body of knowledge in any ordinary sense of the term. The object of faith is transcendent and must be transcendent for religious faith to be authentic. That toward which religious faith tends and with which it becomes engaged is strictly speaking not the object of knowledge of this world, for which religious faith is neither needed nor appropriate. Theology therefore has its foundation in engagement with absolute mystery, with what is qualitatively transcendent, other, and incomprehensible. Faith, then, is not knowledge. This elementary principle becomes significant against the background of the natural social tendency of theological interpretation and belief to take on the qualities of accepted knowledge.

The same conclusion may be drawn from the nature of revelation. God's Presence and self-communication to human existence comes to fruition in the most fundamental form of an interpersonal encounter. This human experience of an encounter with God should be construed as a knowledge of God but not a knowledge about God. The analogy of interpersonal encounter is relevant precisely because it preserves the transcendent mystery of God's reality or "objectivity" within the very experience of God's subjective self-communicating Presence. What is communicated in this encounter, therefore, is not objective information about God. Revelation does not consist in objective knowledge about God, and there is no revealed theology in this sense.

The significance of this analysis of theology in relation to its very foundations in faith and revelation consists in an elementary evaluation of what is going on in this discipline. Theology itself should not be construed as a divinely communicated body of knowledge. It is a human discipline, a human effort to understand and express in human terms the nature of God and reality. Its source lies in the human response and commitment to God who is experienced in an encounter of Presence and self-communication. The interpretations of reality that spontaneously flow from this encounter and faith do not yield objective knowledge in the ordinary sense of knowledge of the world. But neither is the content of theology lacking in some correspondence with the real Presence of God to human existence. Nor is this body of interpretations stemming from faith and revelation some sort of esoteric human behavior. Faith and revelation are universal human phenomena, and all human life unfolds within a personal and social context of such interpretations of ultimate meaning, value, and reality. What is important here is that the status of this interpretation be brought to self-critical awareness. Because theology is not a matter of knowledge, when one is dealing with knowledge that can be verified on the basis of experience of this world, one is not dealing with theology. An internalization of this simple principle would go a long way in clarifying many disputes in areas where Christian theology attempts to interpret the world, history, and society.

THE SYMBOLIC NATURE OF THEOLOGY

Another way of determining the consciousness that underlies theology is found in the structure of symbolism. Theology is a symbolic discipline. The epistemology upon which it rests is symbolic. Its concepts, language, and affirmations are always symbolic. A symbol is any piece of finite reality, any thing, event, person, situation, concept, proposition, or story that mediates to human consciousness something distinct from and other than itself. In the case of theology, the only way its proper and specifying subject matter is available to human consciousness is through the mediation of finite symbols. Symbolism thus defines the way in which human consciousness comes in explicit contact with the transcendent order and comes to represent it in human language.

This symbolic nature or structure of theology flows from its foundations in faith and revelation. The object of religious faith in itself is transcendent and other than any finite object of this world, or the whole of finite reality. The only way it can be represented in or to the human mind is through images, concepts, and language drawn from ordinary experience of this world. Human freedom is enfleshed in physicality, and the human spirit is bound to the concreteness of this world in all its experience and knowledge. Thus the structure of revelation corresponds to that of faith experience. God's universal Presence to human subjectivity and God's self-communication to experience is always and necessarily mediated in and by history through the particularities and concreteness of the world. The world, then, is symbolic of God; and God is mediated to human consciousness through knowledge of the world. Although theology is not knowledge in the ordinary sense, for this refers properly to knowledge of this world, still knowledge of this world can mediate a religious experience of transcendence and an encounter with God. Such an experience of transcendence is not available to neutral and objective investigation of the world; no scientific inquiry can of itself produce it. Yet no experience of transcendence that bears any specific content can be separated or isolated off from a knowledge of the world that mediates it and supplies its thematic content.

Because the structure of theology is symbolic, because the only way to an experience of that which transcends the world is through the world, theological language is always and intrinsically dialectical. This dialectical quality means that from different points of view the symbol both "is not" and "is" that which it mediates, represents, and communicates. By definition the symbol is not that which it symbolizes; a symbol mediates something other than itself. The object of faith and revelation is transcendent and thus precisely not something of this world. Yet the symbol really participates in that transcendent other, and thus renders it present through itself as something other than itself. This dialectical quality of religious symbols is perhaps best represented in the central Christian symbol, Jesus of Nazareth, and it is reproduced exactly in the classical christological doctrine of the Council of Chalcedon: Jesus is truly human, that is, not divine but consubstantial with us; Jesus is truly divine. But all theological statements share this same dialectical quality. Indeed it is absolutely crucial because it alone preserves the ambiguity and tentative quality of all human attempts to understand and speak about the transcendent order. Any thematic attempt on the part of theology to bypass this dialectical tension, to neglect either the "is" or the "is not," will radically distort the nature of the discipline, its transcendent subject matter, and a foundational principle of interpretation.

The epistemology of symbols also helps to clarify how religious language and hence theology is meaningful and communicative. Religious faith arises out of a human subjectivity that is intrinsically and dynamically oriented toward transcendence. The anthropological basis for and impulse toward faith consists in an implicit quest and search for an absolute principle of being. Out of the negativity of a finitude that is characterized by suffering, sinfulness, and mortality, human freedom and action necessarily look for that which by its transcendence of finitude bestows comprehensive and final meaning, value, and permanence in being. What is at stake here is the being itself of human existence. When transcendence is disclosed to this quest of human faith, it comes as a response to an ultimate interest or concern and involves an encounter that is an engaged participatory experience. Religious knowledge of God is such a knowledge. It is not objective disinterested experience and knowledge. It must arise out of the question of salvation which in turn must involve transcendence. In like measure religious symbols are disclosive and meaningful only in response to this religious concern; their meaningfulness is a function of engaged participatory interest; they can only communicate religiously across the bridge of religious subjectivity, that is, a religious interest, questioning, concern, and experience.

This characterization of the epistemology of religious symbols also provides the clue for understanding the ultimate logic that underlies theological argumentation or explanation and which finally decides the truth of theological assertions. We shall have occasion to insist that critical reason is intrinsic to theological method. But insofar as the conclusion of any theological argument or explanation is itself theological, it cannot be decided on the basis of objective reason alone. Theology always unfolds within the context of religious or potentially religious experience; the affirmation of the truth of theological judgments is always a function of engaged participatory experience and knowledge. Theological explanation, therefore, like the religious language and experience upon which it is based, is always itself symbolic and disclosive. It always consists in appealing to, mediating, or eliciting the engaged participatory experience that alone can validate theological meaning and truth. In other words, theological conclusions are never the result of an argument from objective premises and ordinary knowledge of this world. Insofar as the subject matter is transcendent, it can only be appreciated symbolically through an engaged participatory experience. Theological argumentation and explanation, therefore, ultimately consist in coherently describing and mediating such an experience. In short, a valid theological argument or explanation or demonstration is really no more than a description of a symbolic religious experience that successfully mediates it to others. Theology in the end cannot transcend or escape the engaged participatory symbolic experience that grounds it in the first place.

This account of the symbolic character of religious consciousness should not be confused with subjectivism, immanentism, or the reduction of theology to anthropology. It is necessary to stress the subjectivity of religious knowledge because the realm of transcendence is not phenomenal; it does not as it were appear as such in this world. If it did, it would not be transcendent. God is not an object of this world or its history. One needs a religiously differentiated subjectivity, a consciousness that is open to and looking for transcendence, even to appreciate the religious sphere and the world of meaning that theology deals with. Yet what has been summarized here is a symbolic realism. The transcendent other, precisely as other, is intrinsic to and mixed up with the finite order of reality. God is intrinsically present to finite created reality constituting it in its existence. God is personally present to human subjectivity. Thus once again one must appreciate the dialectical quality of religious symbols and hence of the whole world of theological affirmation. What one says of God theologically may really and symbolically, but more or less adequately, represent and communicate the way God actually is in relation to human existence. But theology is never able to represent God objectively, or the way God's reality is in and of itself, in order to then measure the relative adequacy of its conceptions of God by comparison with this objectified concept of God. Ultimately, the only way to check the truth of any theological statement is in and through corporate human experience chastened by a dialogue of experiences.

THE HISTORICAL CHARACTER OF THEOLOGY

Along with the necessary turn to subjectivity and experience the other dominant characteristic that governs all modern theology is historical consciousness. All human experience is influenced by the culture and society in which it occurs. All human experience is individual and particular insofar as it is bound to this or that time and place in history. No texts, however classic they may be, no symbols, however transcultural they may appear, no reasoning, however logical its development, can escape their bond to the particularities of history and their relativity to context. The result of historicity is the sheer pluralism of ways of thinking and the discordant diversity of basic human values to which history bears too obvious a witness. The experience of this relativity is not restricted to those versed in critical thought. It has filtered down to a large segment of the general population. All educated people share in some measure or degree an historical consciousness. All human thought including theology is historically conditioned and hence relative to the conditions and experience that generate it.

The historicity of human existence reaches down below theology to the very structure of revelation. Although the internal and transcendental ground of revelation lies in God's universal and personal Presence to all human subjectivity, this can only come to consciousness through historical mediation. Revelation is necessarily mediated by the particular symbols of history. Christianity is not based upon some universal experience of God mediated by transcendental reasoning nor some imaginary general revelation. Christianity has its beginning in a point of time; it has its basis in an original historical revelation. The specifically Christian movement originated with the event of Jesus of Nazareth who was himself a concrete particular human being who operated in a particular culture and dealt with specific problems and spoke a distinct language embodying distinctive ideas and values learned from a particular tradition. This original revelation was codified into the New Testament, its classical expression. But it too is an historically conditioned work whose meaning is bound to a culture of the past.

The historicity of revelation and all theology, which has come to a heightened awareness in our time in historical consciousness, defines a problem which characterizes all Christian thought. This problem operates as a kind of deep structure that must always be faced in every case of substantial theological reasoning or explanation. On the one hand Christian revelation has been given in a point of history and it has found its classical form in a particular and relative document. And once given historical and public expression in history, it becomes subject to the vagrancy of history. In other words, it can be lost or, what amounts to the same thing, substantially altered by historical change. Christian sensibility always and from the beginning has resisted every threat to the preservation of historical revelation.[3] And yet, on the other hand, once released into history, revelation cannot fail to change; it has changed; it continues to change. This problem of sameness and difference, continuity and change, unity and diversity reaches down through all theology to touch Christian religious sensitivity itself. A Christian is one who shares in original revelation in a dependent way in unity with all other Christians.

This problem does not involve a logical antinomy; it does not lack a theoretical solution. For despite the radical pluralism of human existence, there is a foundational unity of the human race; despite the diversity of human experiences, there are deep anthropological constants; and despite the multitude of the historical mediations of revelation outside and inside Christianity, Christian revelation itself points to and mediates a universal personal Presence of God to all human beings. The symbolic structure of revelation, therefore, of its very nature posits a dialectical tension between unity and diversity, sameness and difference. Without some such dialectical tension between levels or dimensions within revelation itself, and consequently in the structure of theology, no solution to this issue is possible. With such a dialectical structure, the problem of the historicity of theology still remains an issue in every concrete case of constructing a theological position in every new historical situation. But at least a framework is available within which a process of interpretation can unfold.

THE AUTHORITY OF SCRIPTURE AND INTERPRETATION

Historical consciousness has a direct impact upon the notion of the authority of scripture and the traditional doctrines that served to support that authority. Indeed the implications of historical consciousness seem to call into question the very possibility of the authority of a document from a culture that is so distant and different from those of the present age. How is the authority of scripture to be understood? How is it reconcilable with theological reinterpretation, and how does it come to bear upon it?

First of all, it is easy to establish that scripture is authoritative in the church and that it is recognized as such.[4] The authority of scripture stems from the historical nature of revelation and the recognition of it as the classical formulation of original revelation. Scripture is the constitution of the church; it defines the faith and the beliefs of the Christian community. This status of scripture was decided by the church in a deliberate and reflective judgment after the scriptures were written in the historical process of determining the canon. And this judgment has been for the most part universally accepted by the Christian community and its theologians. In other words, the church itself recognizes the authority of scripture in its own life.

But what is the nature of this authority? It is a mistake to construe the authority of scripture in terms of a this-worldly authority. Ultimately religious authority is unlike any other historical authority; the authority of scripture is *sui generis*. This is so because scripture is symbolic and mediates an authority that comes from God's being experienced in and through it. As a religious authority it is authoritative insofar as it mediates God's authority in God's self-revelation. The authority of scripture, then, does not lie in this word, or that concept, or that story. The symbols, the fashioning of which are the work of human beings in history, are not authoritative of themselves. Rather their authority consists in their ability to mediate God's revealing Presence which alone is religiously authoritative. The authority of scripture, then, should not be understood statically in terms of this or that symbol in itself. Scriptural authority must be understood in terms of the dynamic process of dependent revelation. Scripture is authoritative in the very process of mediating God's Presence to the community.

The exercise of this authority of scripture in the Christian community is not mysterious. Scripture shapes the consciousness of the church and individuals in the church. Scripture is read, preached, and prayed. For the theologian, too, because scripture is constitutive of dependent revelation and the faith-life of the community, it is that to which theology appeals in fashioning a theological position. The theologian ordinarily works from inside the church. The symbols of scripture are authoritative for the theologian because they are the very data he or she brings to bear on theological issues. The theologian interprets reality through the data of the religious symbols of the tradition of the Christian community constituted by scripture.

But this process of interpreting reality through the symbols of scripture also involves a constant reinterpretation of the meaning of the symbols themselves. The symbols of scripture, insofar as they are the positive historical data of the past with which the theologian works, must also be explained in order to be brought to bear on theological issues today. The authority of scripture cannot be understood in a way that requires the recital or repetition of scriptural language. The mere repetition of scripture in a new situation and context both changes the original meaning of scripture and robs scriptural symbols of their religious symbolic authority. This fundamental insight which stems from historical consciousness is counter-intuitive; it is not obvious; but it is crucial for understanding the very possibility of theology today. One must reinterpret scriptural and traditional symbols to preserve their meaning. But this interpretation in no way undermines the authority of scripture. It reinforces it. In science the testimony of the data that must be interpreted and explained by a given hypothesis, theory, or conclusion has absolute authority for the conclusion itself. So too for the theologian. The symbols of scripture are the data of theology that bear witness to an understanding of reality. In bringing them to bear upon a theological issue they too must be accounted for and explained, and the very process of doing so is a recognition of their authority.

The possibility of reinterpreting the data of scripture while at the same time remaining faithful to their original meaning is itself explained by the symbolic structure of revelation and its scriptural expression. Scriptural language is symbolic; it is not a flat two-dimensional expression of knowledge of this world or information about God. Symbols embody a transcendent dimension and mediate to human consciousness God's Presence in a way that can be experienced today. This transcendent and universally relevant religious significance of religious symbols is one with their original meaning.

The symbolic structure of religious language also helps to explain the logic of reinterpretation in a way that is consistent with the authority of scripture. Reinterpretation follows the pattern of dependent revelation. It proceeds through disclosure and elaboration. Scriptural symbols open up human consciousness to the experience of God's Presence in the community and in the human lives of the members of the community. And this experience itself is what is elaborated by the theologian. Theology constructs its interpretations of reality not on the basis of a reception by dictation of the words and propositions of scripture or traditional doctrine. Indeed, insofar as they are products of a past culture the symbols of tradition may have no direct or unmediated bearing on theological positions taken today. Rather their authority and bearing are always indirect. The symbols of the past mediate the experience of God's Presence to Christian experience in this way or that way, and that present-day experience becomes the ground for fashioning a theological position for today. On the one hand, it is impossible in theological construal to escape a present-day horizon of consciousness. Interpretation is interpretation of reality as reality is manifested to current experience. But on the other hand, by a fusion of horizons, current Christian experience is shaped and formed by the classic and authoritative tradition that was initiated by original revelation.

Finally, the symbolic structure of revelation and the nature of religious authority also help to determine the inner criterion and norm for an "orthodox" or valid and authentic interpretation of Christian doctrine. That norm cannot lie in one theology as opposed to another theology. In a situation of historicity there will always be a pluralism of theologies. One historical theology, whether it be scriptural or conciliar, because of its historical relativity, cannot be the norm for another equally historically conditioned theology. Rather the norm for the authenticity of theology must be the interior and experiential norm of the encounter with God as mediated by the central Christian symbol, Jesus of Nazareth, for human salvation. This is what has to be explained, described, or accounted for in theological interpretation, for this is where the authority of scripture itself lies. Any theological position that successfully accounts for this experience is *ipso facto* orthodox.

THE METHOD OF THEOLOGY

The issue of method is crucial in theology because method determines how one understands theological assertions. If theology is to be more than gathering and cataloguing information, if it means the interpretation of reality through a critical understanding of Christian symbols, it would be difficult to over-emphasize the need for a thematic appropriation of the method involved in the discipline.[5] There are of course many different concrete procedures for generating theological positions. There are many methods in theology. But beneath them all, if they are not fundamentalistic or based on revelational positivism, one can discern a common structure that flows from the relation between original and dependent revelation, the symbolic structure of revelation and scripture, and the historicity of human existence and the church.

We have said that the interpretation of the symbols of tradition involves a process of disclosure and elaboration. This process itself can be elaborated more fully as a method of correlation. A method of correlation consists in a dialogue between theology or the theologian and the symbols of tradition. This dialogue generates a critical understanding of the symbols themselves and an interpretation of present-day reality through them or in their light. In this dialogue the theologian cannot escape the present situation and the horizon of his or her own consciousness. Current understanding can only begin and end within the context of present existence. This is the reason for the designation "correlation." The questions that generate inquiry and understanding necessarily arise out of the situation and consciousness of the world, church, and theologian at any given time. And thus interpretation and theological conclusion are necessarily correlated with a current situation.

A method of correlation involves dialogue with the past, and dialogue implies attending to the symbols of the past and the beliefs that are enshrined in them on their own terms. But this is a critical exercise, that is, it involves intellectual criticism. It was established in the theology of faith that, although faith does not consist in pure formal reasoning, for it is more than that, still faith is a form of reason. Faith is an act and attitude of human spiritual freedom involving consciousness and thought. Thus the critical or questioning dimension of reason is intrinsic to faith, and in theology it is explicitly brought to bear upon the symbols, beliefs, and theological positions of the past. This critical reasoning is not merely philosophical or logical reasoning. It involves philological and semantic analysis, historical reasoning, literary reason, critical-social reason, psychological analysis, and so on. The intentionality of this critical questioning is not to undermine the symbols of the past, although it will surely call into question naive and unreflective assumptions about them. Rather the goal of this critical questioning is to understand better the symbols of the past in their own terms, in their past context, which is the condition for the possibility of honest dialogue. The kind of questioning that is required for such an understanding of the past can be illustrated by an enumeration of some of the areas that need to be investigated.[6]

1. In order to understand a theological symbol or proposition from the past, one must appreciate its historical context. What was the historical situation of society and culture that produced the symbol? For example, was it a slave society? A patriarchal culture? This line of questioning will generate a distance between the symbols of the past and the present situation that is needed for critical appropriation.

2. Many of the doctrines of the past rest on suppositions no longer held today. What are the tacit presuppositions concerning cosmology, anthropology, faith, and revelation? For example, was faith considered as objective knowledge and revelation a matter of information? Conclusions that rest on suppositions or arguments no longer considered valid today need to be revised.

3. Religious symbols, the language of religion itself and of second-order theological reflection, must be understood in the terms of the system in which they are used. What did the terms used in the language of the past mean? What, for example, does "Son of God" mean in its various New Testament usages? The answers to these critical historical questions will often create a further distance between original symbols and current general appropriation of them.

4. What is the genre of the symbols of the past? What kind of concept or statement is it? This question applies most obviously to biblical systems, but also has relevance for the history of theology and doctrine. For example, theology today would think twice about basing its conclusions on the hymns sung in church without some nuanced appropriation. Song is often exaggerated in its enthusiasm. The same is true of biblical hymns.

5. Especially in doctrinal symbols but also with regard to biblical data one must ask about the genesis of the symbol. What was the issue or problem or historical question to which a religious statement is a response? In a situation of historicity, "wherever the state of the evidence on any question materially changes, you have a new question that cannot be fully answered by appealing to old authorities."[7] This principle alone virtually rules out all mere citations of texts as proof in theology.

6. Especially in doctrinal matters which are often decisions made in controversy, but also analogously in scriptural teaching, it is always very helpful to examine the meaning of a position by attending to what it excludes. To what exactly was this theological assertion opposed? What was the precise point affirmed as distinct from residual or attendant

understandings and arguments? This enables one to recognize what a theological symbol does not exclude, and also how the point of what is affirmed might be expressed in another way.

7. It is always necessary to see traditional symbols as parts of a whole. They do not exist in isolation, and relating them to other symbols of the same period gives a better idea of their deeper sense. How does this symbol relate to other theological statements? For example, what is the relation between the christology in the prologue of John's gospel and other New Testament christologies? This comparative question will help to uncover the pluralism of the biblical world and the history of theology and doctrine. It both relativizes any particular symbol and at the same time uncovers a deeper meaning shared analogously with other symbols. This analysis thus contributes to a recognition of the point of the particular symbol in question.

8. One must also attend to the personal and social behavior in the church in trying to understand its religious symbols. What social behavior is reflected in this or that doctrine? What were the implications of this theological symbol for the exercise of personal, social, and transcendent freedom? What kind of Christian life did it suppose and lead to? The practice of the church is often the ground of the real meaning of a religious symbol. Religious symbols arise out of behavior patterns and, in turn, invite and empower them. There must be a mutual critique of meaning and action.

9. Finally, in the course of a critical examination of the symbols of the past, one must move to a more universal perspective. On a transcendental level, did this religious symbol respond to a universal anthropological question concerning ultimate reality itself? What is being asserted or mediated by this theological symbol that has universal significance?

This last area of questioning is central for theological interpretation. It forms a kind of bridge in the dialogue between past and present. It enables the symbols of the past to be disclosive of meaning that is relevant to the present. It looks for the meaning of past theological assertions both within the situation of the past and on a level of transcendental or universal significance. It tries, in the very examination of the particularities and eccentricities of the past, to discover and crystallize the response of those symbols to universal religious questioning, and hence to questions that are shared today. This interpretative question allows the theologian to grasp the point of the religious symbols of tradition which always concerns salvation in response to some form of negativity characteristic of human existence itself. Disclosure is the disclosure of this point, which, because of its universal relevance, must also inform, illumine, and empower present-day experience, questioning, and consciousness of the world. It is this salvific point which then needs elaboration in constructive theological imagination, reflection, and symbol.

The second phase or aspect of a method of correlation consists in elaborating the answer to religious questioning provided by the symbols of tradition in terms that are intelligible and credible today. This should not be thought of as a "one-two" mechanical process. A preapprehension of the answer is always involved in the questioning that motivates a critical study of the tradition. And the data of tradition mediate content that questions present-day experience of reality. The poles of the dialogue are internal to each other in the consciousness of the theologian. But constructive theological interpretation and elaboration can only arise from within a current horizon of consciousness. This too should be critically reflective upon itself, and the following series of questions will help to illustrate the demands of this critical self-reflection.

1. Constructive theological interpretation always operates at least implicitly on the basis of a broad general conception of the nature of human existence itself. What are the anthropological suppositions of any given theological position? Does the anthropology account for the historicity of human existence? Does it take into account the concrete historical and social dimensions of the human? Too much of modern theology is abstract and privatistic and fails to deal with the actual conditions of the human race.

2. Theology must be in tune with the historical context and situation in and for which the interpretation is being made. What are the characteristics of intellectual culture? What are the deep values, ideas, and ideals that give substance to more general cultural life? Whether or not explicit analysis of a particular culture or the world situation becomes part of theological elaboration, there must be congruence here lest theological reasoning be simply unintelligible.

3. Theological interpretation must be internally coherent. There must be a certain unity, coherence, and integrity between the various doctrines and interpretations of reality. This requires some kind of center of gravity or holistic conception of the core of Christian truth.[8] What is the center of the Christian message? What is the view of the whole that underlies this and other particular interpretations? Such an imaginative construal is almost always operative in the interpretation of specific symbols, and interpretation will be more coherent when it is reflectively conscious of this often tacit supposition.

4. Theological interpretations and assertions are not disinterested and objective statements of a state of affairs. They respond to specific

existential questions and engage participatory experience and knowledge. What existential question is being responded to with this theological position? This question can operate on different levels. It could refer to the overall focus that is judged to be the centering issue for all theology today. Such would be, for example, the question of the meaningfulness of our common history as a human race given the degree of meaningless social suffering that marks so much of it. Or it could refer to the specific question or issue to which a particular Christian symbol provides a response. In both cases, however, the issue must be a common human issue lest the interpretation be so particular that it become eccentric. Much theological confusion could be eliminated if these questions were answered out in front of particular theological positions.

5. For whom is this theological interpretation made? Who is its audience? These questions are straightforward. Theological interpretation is always addressed to an implied audience and clarification of this makes the interpretation more explicit. But this line of critical reflection contains a twist. Does the interpretation contain a bias toward a certain group? Is it an advocacy position? And who will be the beneficiaries of this interpretation? This line of questioning uncovers the social ideological underpinnings of all theological understanding. A critical understanding of history and society shows that religion and theology always take sides despite the concern to be universally relevant. The issue, then, is not to remove social bias, but to direct it in a way that is consistent with the original and intrinsic intention of Christian symbols themselves. These symbols are authentic and universally relevant when they show bias for those who are most desperately in need.

6. How is the central salvific point of the symbols of tradition to be imagined, construed, and stated in a theological position today? This question sums up the performance of constructive theological elaboration. But this reinterpretation elicits further reflection on itself.

7. Theology as a pluralistic discipline must involve dialogue if it seeks to represent the community's faith. How does this theological interpretation compare with other current theological interpretations? Can valid elements of other positions be accommodated? Genuine dialogical interchange on this level helps to ensure a self-critical interpretation that is clearly situated in a community of different interpretations.

8. Since faith and belief are for life, since theology governs spirituality, one must ask the reflective question of how any given interpretation empowers human freedom. How does this assertion and explanation illumine, open up, and energize human freedom? This is not quite a question of objective consequences. Religious faith itself is loyalty to a cause, and existential participatory engagement includes the impulses of

action. The issue of opening up possibilities for action must be seen as a theme that is intrinsic to the meaning of theological assertions themselves.

9. A distinct reflective question concerns moral consequences. One must also ask about the moral implications of the life and action that is empowered by theological interpretation. Where does this theological position lead logically? What specific kind of praxis does it generate? This kind of moral reasoning is too often neglected in what is sometimes considered an isolated sphere of doctrinal theology. Theological interpretation is intrinsically moral and implies ethical reasoning.

This enumeration of areas of questioning illustrates the kind of critically reflective reason that is needed in a method of correlation. The questions also illustrate, because they embody, the criteria for an integral theological method that were summarized at the end of the last chapter. Theology must be faithful to scripture and the church's tradition of scriptural interpretation. This is the given past that constitutes what the Christian message is. Theology must be intelligible in terms of any given contemporary culture. Unless it takes on the language of the present, it cannot represent a meaningful witness to the Christian message. Theology must empower Christian life. Ultimately this is where credibility lies. Only in this way will theology open up the true impact of the Christian message on the future.

THE ETHICS OF THEOLOGY

Theology is critical witness to the truth that sets one free. It is a defense of that truth insofar as it renders it intelligible in contemporary terms and introduces people into the credibility of a way of life. Like all human endeavors the practice of the discipline of theology requires some fundamental moral attitudes. We might conclude this essay by drawing attention to three such moral dispositions. It should not be imagined however that these three completely encompass the ethics of theology.

A first moral attitude integral to the task of the theologian is responsibility. Theological interpretation must be responsible in the first place to tradition. Our past defines our present. We are what we are because of the past. We speak and understand the way we do as Christians because the tradition of scripture has provided us with a language. But responsibility to tradition requires a critical understanding of it. Responsibility means doing justice to the theology of the past, and that demands a critical examination of what was said in the context and terms of the past. By contrast, it is irresponsible to naively accept the words or symbols of tradition into our present historical context and situation without noting the distance that separates us. Such a procedure is irresponsible because in fact it misrepresents and distorts tradition.

The theologian must also be responsible to people in the world and in the churches today. Theology must be responsible to their present situation, to their culture, language, and experience. This responsibility can only be exercised once again by critical reasoning. The theologian must ask the questions that the people in the churches are asking, as well as the questions that were asked by people who are no longer in the churches because no one would answer them. This responsibility reaches beyond the church to the whole world. Such is the logic of a church which is founded as a mission. Here one sees that this responsibility is really a responsibility to the one God who has been revealed as the God of all. The apologetic dimension of theology simply responds to the universal relevance of God's Presence. Theology is not merely a discipline that satisfies personal inquiry. It is a public enterprise that must be responsible to the world situation, to other religious traditions, and to all people in the concrete intellectual cultures and social situations in which they exist. Responsibility to the situation implies that mere repetition of tradition, traditionalism, is irresponsible.

A second moral attitude that must underlie the task of theology is honesty. Honesty here is rarely opposed to outright dishonesty. Its opposite is equivocation or a failure to entertain a line of questioning. The lack of honesty may take the form of placing limits upon critical reason because of some fear of where it may lead. It does not respect the dynamics of open and honest inquiry in the search of truth. It may even be based on a lack of faith, a faith which reaches so far beyond the power of merely critical reason that it has nothing to fear about the truth that has set reason free.

The theologian must be honest about what critical reason uncovers concerning the tradition. Theology must be straightforward and unequivocal about the data of objective research. It should not hide behind what is taken to be the traditional faith of the church. People today know that the church is an historical institution, and they are more likely to be scandalized by the theological pretense that it is not. Nor should theologians assume the cowardly defense of protecting the faith of the "simple," "ordinary," or "unthinking" faithful. There are problems of pastoral sensitivity here, but they must be met by honest discussion and mediation and not dishonest reticence.

The theologian must also be honest about his or her own presuppositions of interpretation. This is required not only by the Christian message itself, but also by the current situation of pluralism. Intelligibility in one theological interpretation may appear as unintelligibility in another or be scandal to a third. This situation of pluralism thus requires inter-theological dialogue, a respect for the positions of others, and an honest, comparative, and self-critical evaluation of one's own position within the common ground for discussion.

A third moral disposition underlying the discipline of theology is a sense of freedom. Responsible and honest theological interpretation should be free, creative of meaning, and a stimulus to the freedom of others.

Responsibility to history and tradition creates freedom. Fidelity to history, to the reasons and causes of particular theological affirmations in the past, frees one to interpret for the present. Critical history enables one to recognize the contextuality of past theological affirmation, and yet one can identify with the deeper transcendent and transcultural intentionality or salvific point of past formulas. Nothing is more liberating for present understanding of the meaning of Christianity than a responsible and critical approach to the tradition. The more one is critically responsible to tradition, the more one is free to interpret the meaning of that tradition for contemporary understanding. Critical knowledge of the past liberates us from bondage to the past. "The present," Dulles writes, "helps us to liberate ourselves from the tyranny of the past, and the past, to escape the idolatry of the present."[9]

Responsibility to the present situation also engenders a creative freedom in the interpretation of Christian doctrines for the present situation. The doctrines of the past are not external law; theology is not the interpretation of extrinsic legal documents. The magisterium of the Roman Catholic Church and the creeds and confessions of other churches are not theological commands that appeal only to obedience, although in certain special non-theological respects they may function like law. They are rather the data for interpretation, the data for theology. The history of doctrine is the history of the expression of a history of religious experience and behavior. The point of interpretation is to reexpress the salvific point of that religious experience and action in a new language. Theology must consistently appeal to the experience of contemporary culture and ask: What can this symbol possibly mean today? What should it mean? How can it illumine and empower Christian life? Responding to these questions involves a free, imaginative, and creative enterprise, one that constantly tries to create a new language that moves from within contemporary culture and discloses the meaning of the tradition to it. Only a free and creative imagination can responsibly preserve the meaning of tradition in new situations.

And, finally, theology must always appeal to freedom. Religious truth is for freedom and can only be freely received. The very purpose of revelation, one must presume, is to enhance human freedom and life by its truth and power. The inner dynamism of revelation and faith lies in the direction of the release of human freedom from bondage. All theological interpretation, then, should be aimed by the theologian at the opening up of human freedom for creative salvific life as liberation in this world that in turn leads toward eternal liberation.

AFTERWORD

<hr>

These words are being written twelve years after *Dynamics of Theology*. I intended *Dynamics* as an introductory analysis of the structure of Christian theology and a working model for the investigation of the most fundamental areas that define Christian faith. Although the terms "structure" and "working model" seem to imply a mechanistic method, few disciplines are as fluid as theology. The nature and method of the discipline as it has been constructed here project a broad logic that admits many different applications in turn. But at the same time *Dynamics* does represent some distinct alternatives within the discipline, especially over against fundamentalism and revelational positivism in their various forms. Once *Dynamics* was in place, I intended to apply this method of theology to Jesus Christ in a sustained reflection on this centering focus of Christian faith in God. *Jesus Symbol of God*[1] was published in 1999. At present I am engaged in a work on the church. *Dynamics of Theology* thus represents the first part of a sustained reflection on the core elements of Christianity.

It is one thing to write on method and another to display a method in the analysis of a specific subject matter. Although *Dynamics* explicitly foreshadows its application to christology, it was well received with relatively little negative criticism. By contrast, *Jesus Symbol of God*, although it recapitulates in a condensed fashion the major axioms of *Dynamics*, elicited reactions that are both favorable and negatively critical. In itself and at its best this discussion has consisted in a critical conversation about fundamental christological issues: there can be little doubt that Christian theology has to confront some serious questions today, the answers to which are not yet apparent. Relative to the positions taken in *Jesus Symbol of God*, it appears that those who react positively to that essay have internalized foundational per-

237

spectives that are analogous to those formulated in *Dynamics*. By contrast, I find that the majority of those who have reacted in a generally negative fashion are either unwilling to engage or hostile to the kind of considerations that are offered in *Dynamics*.

I do not intend this Afterword as a response to critics of *Jesus Symbol of God*. But I do have critics in the corner of my eye as I propose a recapitulation of the argument of *Dynamics* in the broadest of terms and draw the bold lines of how it cashes out in the dynamic terms of interpretation and appropriation when applied to Jesus Christ and the church. More in simple, straightforward, descriptive language than in technical terms I want to sketch out the ligaments that hold this prospective trilogy together.

THE PRESENT

Dynamics of Theology, in addressing the present-day world, represents a contextual theology. I will indicate further on why the present plays an important role in the perception and judgment of truth. For the moment, however, I want to dwell on a characterization of our time and place. In *Dynamics* the term "modern" is used to describe our world; in *Jesus Symbol of God* the category of postmodernity has come to the fore. What is going on here?

Robert Schreiter describes a new cultural context for theology in terms of the process of globalization, that is, the many political, economic, technological, and cultural processes that are gradually making all the peoples of the world interdependent.[2] All are aware of these historical processes which have increased dramatically after the Second World War, and picked up more energy with the fall of the Soviet Union. This global process has set up sometimes dramatic examples of tensions between closed local cultures and outside worlds of meaning, perhaps an invading world culture, with its alien ways of thought and doing things, its foreign norms of standardization. As more and more people are moving faster and farther—in a world that is smaller and smaller—so too local ideas, local identities, and local ways of doing things become disrupted. Schreiter believes that globalization is responsible for the new intellectual culture which is being called postmodern.

Paul Lakeland describes this new culture on various levels.[3] It has its empirical symbols in architecture and life-style and popular culture. But it is accompanied by principles and axioms formulated by literary critics, philosophers, and theologians. David Tracy refers to this phenomenon as a period without a name, which can only name itself by its difference from modernity.[4] The terms "postmodern," "postmodernism," and "postmodernity" have become commonplace in the course of a decade, but the meaning attached to them is so different in both their reference and their value that the category risks becoming dysfunctional. One has to attend carefully to what each author intends with the terms.

Two qualities of the particular use that I make of this category of postmodernity will allow its continuity with *Dynamics* to appear. First, with the term postmodernity I wish to point to a culture and not a set of doctrines, or particular truths, or a distinctive closed worldview. By a culture I mean something deeper and more diffuse, a set of convictions and values that are internalized and often taken for granted, which define in a generalized porous fashion a group of people.[5] Many elements or characteristics of nineteenth- and early twentieth-century intellectual culture have almost come to overtly define the world as young people find it today at the beginning of the twenty-first century. This is a culture of war, disruption, and relativism. The whole has been torn into fragments; the universal is an assembly of disconnected parts.

Regarding postmodernity as a culture allows one to take a more neutral stance in addressing it. Educated people have by and large adopted a position of openness to other cultures that allows them to deal with them on their own terms, even when these cultures contain convictions and certain ideas or behaviors that appear to be profoundly wrong. Conservatives make their peace with postmodernity by drawing the circle of their particular identity tighter. Progressives feel more comfortable with seeking commonalities through open conversation. In both cases, the recognition of the inevitability of pluralism among the cultures of different groups allows the interlocutor to recognize something approaching a corporate identity. This identity stands above criticism in its *being* even though it may be riddled with faults, which rightly deserve critique. In other words, one extends to others what one expects from others relative to one's own culture.

Second, therefore, one can identify with a culture without fully accepting it, or without accepting all of its aspects and characteristics. Postmodernity as I see it has too many definitions and represents too many valuations to engender anything like a clear-cut allegiance. But one can find something common to all appreciations in a conviction that western culture is moving into a period that is new, that shares significant differences from what went before, and which consequently calls forth new value responses and new interpretations of traditional ideas. Thus one reason why the term "postmodern" may still perform a valuable function lies precisely in its appeal to a *novum*; it jars the imagination into attending to what is new and different in our current situation.

In the light of both of these aspects of this usage of the term, it becomes apparent that it serves no productive purpose to define oneself or another as "postmodern." To do so is to miss the point of how this category functions. It is meaningless to name a thinker postmodern without a clear meaning and referent for the designation. Moreover, the thinker in question may be very sympathetic to the culture of postmodernity, because he or she lives within it and is defined by it, while at the same time being critical of it from the perspective of specifically "modern" themes that continue to suffuse postmodernity. The debate on whether we live in a postmodern or a late modern period is interesting, but not because either side could possibly exclude the other.

In *Jesus Symbol of God* I point to four dimensions of present-day experience that help distinguish it from modernity. The first is the consciousness of being in history; the particularity and distinctiveness of historical phenomena undoes easy homologization between epochs, cultures, and groups—difference reigns. The second is a sense of relativity in human affairs that easily slides into a supposition of relativism, but need not. Even those dedicated to the unity of the race, those who search for common dimensions of human existence, understand that pluralism constitutes human community and the human condition itself. When pluralism is recognized as difference within some common frame of reference, or as some form of unity amid difference, one need not confuse it with relativism. Thirdly, a striking characteristic in late twentieth-century thought that distinguishes it from the modern period lies in the incredibility of turning to the transcendental ego as the subject of a phenomenology representative of the human as such. I argued earlier in this book that historical and social consciousness do not undermine transcendental analysis. But at the same time one must remain conscious of the formal character of such an effort. Because the human race is one, a fundamental anthropological character engenders all kinds of common dimensions in human existence as such, but always analogous in their concreteness. Thus one must immediately ask, whose subjectivity is being analyzed, from what standpoint, toward what end? The social constitution of the individual and the social construction of the interpretation of reality by each one put all essays at universal assertion in the parentheses of particularity. But in the end, this does not destroy the unity of the human race (Christianity, creation), nor the value of attempts to find a formal universal structure of knowing (Lonergan), nor a common drive toward transcendence (Augustine, Blondel, Rahner), nor the ability to establish within historical life anthropological constants (Nussbaum, Schillebeeckx). These efforts help establish the bonds of human communication. But they are not to be confused on the level of specific content with a totalizing human story that supercedes pluralism. Finally, the various physical sciences are rapidly opening up to human imagination new frameworks for the understanding of human origins and constitution. Whatever can and should be said of this picture, it is neither Aristotelian nor Newtonian, and Christian formulas of belief that inextricably entail these older views of the world are losing their plausibility.

When this increasingly common intellectual culture acquires a name, it will no longer be necessary to call it by the non-name, postmodernity. But whatever its name, as long as Christianity retains its mission to address the world's cultures, theology will hardly be able to avoid entering into dialogue with this one.

THE STRUCTURE AND METHOD OF THEOLOGY

The strategy of theology consists in addressing a given culture in order to render the tradition intelligible in its terms; when culture provides the form of Christianity, one may hope that Christianity will provide the substance of culture.[6] Because this is a common Christian task, I have not proposed denominational arguments in describing the method of theology, nor appealed to the Roman Catholic magisterium in applying it to christology. In this section I want briefly to recapitulate this inculturating method of theology with an eye to showing in what follows how it may be brought to bear on the subjects of christology and the Christian church. The point of this is not to review the content of this book, but to underline those factors which have an explicit bearing on the applicability of the method.[7] I will highlight four elements in the argument of the present book that are especially significant for the constructive efforts in christology and ecclesiology.

The Symbolic

The symbol and more generally the symbolic have long been present in Christian vocabulary. The sacramental refers to the symbolic structure of mediation into the sacred; sacraments are sacred symbols. But Christianity by no means has a monopoly on the category of symbol; symbolic mediation or practice extends to the whole range of human life, and symbolic knowledge plays a major role in many disciplines. The language of symbol, then, provides an apt means of communicating with postmodern culture. I will highlight two aspects of symbol that are traditional and yet keenly appropriate for a contemporary understanding of how we have commerce with transcendent reality and enter into relationship with God. These are the realist cognitional dimension of symbols and their dialectical ontological structure.

A postmodern context could be defined by its consciousness that transcendent religious knowledge does not lie on the surface of social life today. Life in western society has become overtly secularized, so that religion itself seems reduced to the realm of the private and interior. How is one to explain where and how the sacred is available in such a situation? An adequate response to this problem must find and appeal to the religious question that in various forms lies latent in the secular endeavor itself.[8] But to do so one has to appeal to the symbolic for access to this transcendent reality. For, given the human condition of material, historical existence that is bound to the world by bodily senses, the only way the human spirit can rise to the transcendent is sacramentally or symbolically. If the drive of human existence is adequately described, the very dynamism of human action and being themselves will be recognized as self-transcending. And that transcendent goal can only be appreciated through the mediation of this world, even as it is described by the neo-Platonic sixth-century Pseudo-Dionysius, who had so much influence on medieval Christianity. Symbols are images or realities, derived from the sphere of the perceptible, by which human beings are uplifted into the sphere of the divine.[9] Reality, the one reality of this world, thus has a double density, and one that can be led, once the religious question is raised, to a discovery of the transcendent by means of symbols. While this sounds, and is, medieval, the thesis here is that it is classic, and that even postmoderns can experience mystagogy, or a process of being drawn into transcendence by the symbolic. This symbolic structure of mediation can be experienced analogously in widely different human phenomena: in the question of what was going on in the building of Chartres, or in the negative experience of the social degradation of a whole group of people and the committed energies to resist and redress it. The dynamics of knowledge through the symbolic, therefore, consists in mediation, participation, and expanded cognitional reach. As for the realism of this cognitional anthropology, one cannot convince people who have been thus led into transcendence that their actual experience is mere projection.

The second aspect of the symbol, equally important in the application of this theological method to concrete topics, consists in its dialectical structure. This has been clearly laid out in this book with specific reference to christology in the sharp terms of "is" and "is not." This dialectical structure applies to symbols on the level of knowing and on the level of being. A symbol both is and is not that which it symbolizes. But one can also express this dialectical character in the terms of sameness and difference: the symbol is both one with or the same as that which it symbolizes and different from what it symbolizes. In this formulation of the dialectical tension that structures a symbol, its resemblance with analogy becomes more apparent, for the analogous refers to sameness in difference, to that which is both similar and different from its analogue. The place of analogical knowledge in Christian theology, whether analogy of being or of faith, is familiar and secure. And when one translates analogy into a theory of predication it retains its sharply dialectical character: is and is not. Thomas Aquinas offers a good example in his adaptation of a *triplex via* of affirmations about God: one affirms what one knows of God from the data of this world, and then one denies its applicability in precisely the symbolic terms by which God is known, only then to reaffirm this mediated knowledge with a mysterious higher meaning.[10] The dialectical quality of this structure often goes overlooked. The point of Thomas is to assert the ability to know God from creatures because of the continuity between creator creating and the creature, and at the same time the discontinuity involved in affirming a kind of being radically other than a creature, in this case, infinite being itself.[11] The deepest Christian tradition concerning knowledge of God remains deeply symbolic: realist, dialectical, and apophatic. Without some form of dialectical mediation such as this, one is left with a comic-book understanding of Christianity.

Hermeneutical

I shall not review the dynamics of hermeneutical retrieval presented earlier. But I have to underscore a fundamental principle that lies at the basis of this cognitional anthropology, but which sometimes vanishes in the discussion of details. Hermeneutical theory in the tradition of Schleiermacher to the present is formulated against relativism, against a radical historical consciousness that recognizes no claim of the past or the culturally other on the present. Its reflections are designed to show how the past in its otherness discloses possibilities of truth in and for the present. This occurs both despite and precisely through the distance that separates the present and the future from the past. The dynamics of this epistemological theory, therefore, directly respond to the historical consciousness of today's culture; it reflects an historicist anthropology that is not relativist but dialectical, open, and critical, pluralist but affirmative of norms, values, and truth.

Correlation

From one perspective, the description of correlation as the placing in conjunction of the data of tradition and the present situation, and placing in dialectical interaction the divine influence of revelation with the human cultural receptors of experience and language, are commonplace. More and more the idea of a mutually conditioning correlation as a structure within which theological interpretation takes place is taken for granted. But once again a primal axiom with far-reaching implications lies embedded in this dialectical structure of correlation that often enough does not enter into the reckoning. I refer to the distinction between meaning and truth, and more importantly to the principle developed earlier that one cannot escape the present in affirming truth as distinct from meanings which may or may not correspond with reality. Once this principle is recognized, the importance of trying to interpret the present situation, the forms of current experience, and the specific nature of the religious questions that are encoded in this mix becomes apparent. It is not the case that thorough analysis of the present diverts the meaning of the past into heterogeneous forms. It is rather precisely the case that in the exact measure that one fails to understand the cultural forms of present experience, one also loses control of the meaning of the past in its sheer repetition. Such repetition distorts and miscommunicates. The seemingly elaborate conceptual apparatus of hermeneutical theory has the single aim of preserving the truth of the past and making it relevant and operative in the present.

Critical Conversation

I call upon the metaphor of critical conversation as a vehicle for bringing to bear the norms of theology and making them operative. When one's hermeneutical method of correlation precisely fosters pluralism, how does one know whether or where one has engaged the truth? Does not ecumenical theology, not to mention interreligious dialogue, foster relativism? It is one thing to assert that fidelity to the tradition, intelligibility in the present, and hope-filled praxis or engagement with reality into the future are the norms for theology. It is another thing to envisage how these norms actually work, for more often than not they seem to fail. But one must inquire into the reason for this failure. To what extent is it due to the simple unwillingness to engage the other in conversation? To what extent are divisions over conceptions of transcendent realities created not on the basis of evidence but on simple assertion of one's own view of things or, analogously, a particular group's own particular position? Critical conversation does not create consensus automatically, but it opens up reality in many diverse ways, and thus allows consensus to happen on the basis of the reality that is mutually engaged. Critical conversation respects pluralism, and it does not break off relationships on the basis of sheer assertion. It engages. The structure of Christian theology that is envisioned here is one that allows for unity and diversity in the community; it preserves classical Christian literature, in scripture and doctrine; it encourages diversity of interpretation in correlation with different cultures and within the boundaries of the inner logic of faith itself. But how is that known? Not apart from critical conversation practiced with what might be called Christian civility, if not Christian charity.

AS APPLIED TO CHRISTOLOGY

What happens when one brings this method of theology to bear on the subject matter of Jesus Christ? Depending on one's prior conception of the discipline of christology, such an application could engender a good number of shifts relative to: perspective, point of departure, data to which one attends, appeals to evidence, modes of reasoning, and so on. Reactions to the use of such a method depend as well on the place and presuppositions of the reader. All of this cannot be adequately addressed in a couple of pages, but I want to signal in the broadest of structural terms how the application of the method of this book comes to bear in the work *Jesus Symbol of God*.

From Below

I begin with the broad characterization of the christology that would be generated out of the nature and method of theology of this book as a christology from below. One frequently reads how this phrase, "from below," has been overworked and become devalued; in fact the exact meaning of what is entailed by it differs in the use of different authors and thus remains unclear in itself. Despite these handicaps, the opposition between the two metaphors, "from above" and "from below," is arresting. The contrast with a method of christology "from above" thus remains telling, and if one defines what is meant by the phrase, a christology "from below" can be shown to delineate a real alternative. By a christology from below I mean two things: the first is a turn to experience in theology generally which has been amply represented in this book and which I shall not develop further. The second is a turn to Jesus of Nazareth as the point of departure for reflection in christology, as distinct from a christology from above where one presupposes or begins one's reflection with doctrines about Jesus.

The turn to Jesus as the starting point of one's christology carries significant adjustments in theological epistemology and method, as distinct from the content of christology. This first move opens christology to the significant developments in Jesus research over the past three decades. It is hard to imagine someone interested in Jesus Christ not becoming immersed in literature about Jesus of Nazareth. But such an immersion affects one's imagination, which always lies at the roots of one's personal christology and the church's public christologies. Among the data arising out of the consideration of Jesus one must list the historical consensus that neither Jesus nor those around him formulated to themselves his divinity in the pointed terms of Nicaea and Chalcedon centuries later and which have become our classic doctrines. This gives rise to the question of how these doctrines arose, and this can only be answered historically by a genetic method that traces the slow and patient genesis of these interpretive doctrines through the course of the New Testament period and the early Christians centuries.

I have just summed up in a few sentences a vast historical movement of life and thought, which can be called the genesis of christology. When one draws this historical development that began with the ministry of Jesus, not without his whole Jewish tradition as its background, into the phrase "christology from below," one can see that one has a major shift in the whole imaginative framework within which christology unfolds. By an imaginary framework, here, I mean the broad vision of reality within which we locate things and assign them relational intelligibility and value. Often these frameworks are taken for granted, not noticed because they are written into ordinary language. All operate with a whole set of assumptions that act as arbiters for objective truth and goodness, and even our aesthetic responses and basic feelings. Certain ideas are simply and unquestionably true or erroneous; certain actions are simply and unquestionably good or bad. An imaginative framework, therefore, cannot be reduced to a static warehouse of conceptions; it resembles more a potency or active agency of interpretation and a lens that shapes our perception. Its elements make up a framework for understanding, one that is partly individual and always socially constituted and shared by groups, so that we always choose, collect the elements for, and construct an imaginative framework along with our memberships. Imaginative frameworks define both our public presence and our private opinions. I call them imaginative because they are socially and historically constructed: behind them lies a narrative, and the narrative implies physical interaction with the world. All experience occurs in a present time that had an historical context established by prior events and that led into a future; no experience makes any sense without its before and after. Our most abstract ideas can thus always be led back to sensible experience and images. All this is what is implied by being rooted in history. In sum, the shift to a christology from below entails a shift in the imaginative framework within which christological understanding is generated. This shift can often occur only slowly and over a period of time, largely because of its imaginative roots and integrative scope. Often one who lives within a significantly different imaginative framework will find it difficult to appreciate the positions generated from within another.

Hermeneutical Method

I noted earlier that a premise of hermeneutical theory consists in its acceptance of human existence as historically constituted and its rejection of historical relativism. The result is a strong respect for the historical antecedents of communities of meaning and value. This translates into theology as a strong concern for tradition, the long, gradual, historical construction of any present, and the continuing normative bearing of the constitutive moments of a tradition. A christological understanding constructed with an hermeneutical imagination and method will inevitably engage at length the scriptural witness to Jesus and the various interpretations of him as the mediator of God's salvation. It will analyze the formation of the patristic tradition of christology, and provide an archeology of the basic doctrines as they arose in the course of Christian history. In an historicist framework, in order to be accepted by the community constituted by a specific tradition, a christology must be shown to grow out of and correlate with that tradition.

Symbolic

In the last section I underlined two aspects of symbol that make it an apt theological category, namely the manner in which symbol expands human cognitional reach, ultimately by mystagogy, into transcendence, and its strictly dialectical character. Both of these qualities give it a singular relevance for christology.

As for the first, the idea that Jesus Christ is sacrament of God is not a new idea. In fact this deeply traditional theme received a resurgence prior to the Second Vatican Council. When religious symbol is explicitly equated with sacrament as in both this book and *Jesus Symbol of God*, this move may be considered as part of a recent movement and a longer tradition.[12] Because the category of symbol is much more widespread and known across academic disciplines and ordinary life, it provides a means to explain what is going on in christology in broadly familiar terms. The breadth, depth, and epistemological reach of the category of symbol make it particularly apt for introducing the mediating function of Jesus Christ in history.

But its dialectical character provides symbol with even deeper resonance with the formal christological problem of conceiving how the humanity and divinity are united in Jesus without being confused. The appropriateness of the category of symbol is founded upon an insight into the formal, structural dimensions of the christological problem, and the recognition that the formula of Chalcedon of one person and two natures is not an explanation but a statement of the christological problem itself: tensive unity in difference, the one person constituted by real difference on the level of being. Karl Rahner realized this structural issue when he formulated his theology of symbol precisely in the terms of the structure of being: all being is plural; all beings express themselves; all beings are expressive of themselves in another. The clearest example of this ontology is found in the analysis of the body as the symbol of the human self.[13] It is the structure of symbol, as a structure of being that is intrinsically tensive and dialectical, that makes it such a strong category for christology. Hermeneutical theory helps one to grasp this through the category of "distance." Because of our distance from the philosophical world and debate that generated the christological formula of Chalcedon, one can step back from it and grasp what is going on there in structural terms that are released from the culturally determined language of the time. This in turn allows for a reappropriation of the point of the doctrine in terms structurally faithful to the past and more comprehensible to a postmodern culture.

Critical Correlation

Hermeneutical theory generates the principle that theology employs a method of critical correlation between the past and the present.[14] A phenomenology of understanding and affirmation reveals the role that present experience plays in construing meaning and affirming the truth of any proposition. It must fall within the range of ontological possibility as perceived by the knower. This means that the present situation in which people live, the worldview that structures present-day imagination, the conceptions of world, history, and ontological plausibility, all enter into and condition an understanding of Jesus Christ. This does not mean that kerygma and tradition themselves do not shape the way Jesus is to be understood today, often enough in counter-cultural ways. But correlation does mean that announcement of the kerygma with no concern for context will not only inevitably fail to communicate the Christian message but also distort it. Although such reflections seem self-evident, one has to marvel at the number of people who, with the best intentions, seek to preserve the tradition, but can only recite it by rote, and thus compromise both the tradition and those interested in comprehending it.

All this means that one cannot come to an understanding of Jesus Christ without addressing the problems and questions that typify the present-day period, which for many qualifies as a postmodern situation. Such questions as, "What does resurrection mean?" "What exactly is salvation and how did and does Jesus save?" "Can Jesus be savior of people who existed before him, or who today never heard of him?" "How does Jesus relate to other religious mediations of ultimate reality?" "What does it mean to say that Jesus the human being was divine?" These questions have been asked before, but they take on a distinctive meaning in a postmodern culture and thus have to be addressed with distinctive purpose. A method of critical correlation, therefore, really represents a loosely defined method of inculturation which, in the case of the essay *Jesus Symbol of God*, has been applied to a postmodern culture.

Critical Conversation

Critical conversation responds to a situation of pluralism. Most people in Europe and North America have a rather heightened sense of pluralism, and the phenomenon itself affects the churches. It is not the case that pluralism merely describes the situation obtaining among the churches, so that the differences can be restricted to Lutheran, Anglican, Orthodox, and Roman Catholic christologies. Pluralism describes the situation within the churches and even within the congregations. Every educated person knows that Christianity is one religion among many, but that knowledge has a new quality today. And that new sense of difference and pluralism also allows us to recognize that pluralism always characterized Christianity more radically than might have been previously imagined. The pluralism of New Testament christologies may be taken as normative in this regard.

Pluralism, which refers to diversity within a broader unity, cannot in itself be construed as something negative. In any case, it will not be overcome. Postmodernity in part corresponds with a recognition of how deeply pluralism can run and that it can be a value. Once one assumes an imaginative framework in which pluralism is a given, the role of critical conversation takes on a crucial importance in christology. One can delineate criteria for the relative adequacy of any given christology; what they are and how they function are extremely important questions. But that very consideration should not be understood as an effort to overcome pluralism within Christianity or within any given church. Rather, pluralism remains valuable in itself, and it provides a context within which one must define and apply the norms for an adequate christology. What makes pluralism valuable is precisely the engagement among the various parties. The role of critical dialogue and the value of critical conversation, then, appear most strikingly over against polemic and unthinking reassertion of past formulae, two genres which seem to be based on some kind of fear or insecurity and are, in today's world, particularly contrary to Christian valuation of the other.

AS APPLIED TO ECCLESIOLOGY

What consequences will an adaptation of the nature and method of theology as it is characterized in this book have on the discipline of ecclesiology? Once again, the far-reaching implications for ecclesiology, especially in terms of specific content, can hardly be indicated in a couple of pages. But I shall try to indicate the broad lines of a shift of perspective, something analogous to what was just described in christology.

From Below

I take the christology from below described in the last section as a prime analogate for an ecclesiology from below. It too would begin the study of the church with a consideration of the historical Jesus for he lies at the origin of the Christian church. But New Testament scholarship today does not support the idea that Jesus intentionally set up a Christian church. Jesus research does establish Jesus as an itinerant prophet, teacher, and healer who gathered a following of disciples, which even then had some rudimentary structure. In this sense he was at the center of a certain form of "community." But this same research turns up little or no evidence that Jesus intended to found a church in the sense that this term assumed. This quite diverse body of scholars is almost united in the premise that Jesus was a Jew whose horizons were contained within the Jewish world. As a Jewish reformer, Jesus did not set out to establish a new religion.[15]

An ecclesiology from below thus represents a new imaginative framework for understanding the church. That is to say, it replaces the set of assumptions embedded in the elementary idea that Jesus appointed the twelve, who were intended to be the pillars of a Christian church. That older imaginative framework can be described as organic: in the embryonic form established by Jesus a church was established, so that what developed was simply an expansion of an already programmed nuclear community. The model postulates growth within a preestablished permanent structure; the oak tree is genetically contained in the acorn. By contrast, the new imaginative framework would see Jesus as the foundation of the church, for at no time, neither during his earthly life nor during the time of the formation of the church was he not the center of the religious imagination of his followers. But the development of the church, first within Judaism as a movement or sect, and then as it gradually broke away from Jewish authority to assume its own autonomous authority structure, was historical. This means that development was spontaneous, contingent, and pragmatic as it faced new historical conditions and problems.

Historical analysis and reconstruction shape the point of departure of an ecclesiology from below and provide a first groundwork for understanding the church. This historical work can also be augmented by sociological reconstruction. The church is a human organization which follows the laws of human social behavior. The sociology of nascent religious movements, of organizations, of urban or rural life in any particular period of the church's existence, can all deepen the historical understanding of the church.[16]

Hermeneutical

Ecclesiology cannot be reduced to the historical and sociological study of the church. Ecclesiology is an explicitly theological discipline. If sociological analysis provides "depth" to historical data, theological analysis provides "height" in the sense of transcendence. Ultimately, behind external historical event and social structure, the subject matter being studied in ecclesiology consists in the religious faith of people, which in its corporate social form is religion. Ecclesiology reaches to the major defining element within the historical data, that is, transcendence, or perception of and response to God. This subject matter itself rules out reductionism, a name for various ways of canceling the defining religious character of this form of human response and organization. Ecclesiology can avoid reductionism by always bearing in mind that it depicts a religious organization. The subject matter of ecclesiology is people who confess that God acts in their lives, and who thus bond together as a church principally and centrally because of this faith in God.

But theological interpretation does not consist in superimposing the theological upon integral social-historical phenomena, or laying theological constructs on top of historical data. Theological understanding of the church is not something extrinsic, something that descends from outside and from above, or is added on in order to transform human structures otherwise secular. An analogy might be helpful here. In an evolutionary framework one can no longer imagine spirit as added to matter from the outside. Rather spirit is precisely that which arose out of matter and, from a perspective that allows us to look back in the light of the human phenomenon, lures it as a goal. Spirit is not less creature and from God because it emerged out of matter. Analogously, God as Spirit should be understood as present to and within the human developments that led to a Christian church.

These three levels of analysis, historical, sociological, and theological, thus form an integrated field for ecclesiological reflection from below. They have been described here one after the other for analytical clarity. But they should be understood to be mutually determinative in the historical genesis of the original church and the continued development of the church through history.

Symbol

The role of the church to be the symbol of God in history after the pattern of Jesus provides a fruitful way of understanding the mission or goal of the church. Moreover, the language of where and how God is found in the church will find friendly resources in the dynamics of symbols. Once one takes the church's mission to the world, to today's societies and cultures in their various actualities, and allows this to function as a dynamic framework for understanding the *raison d'être* of the church in history, the idea of the church as symbol or sacrament is transformed. The structural dimensions of symbol continue to apply, but the dynamic communicative aspects are brought to the fore. In a church whose mission lies in addressing the hopes and concerns of the world, actual communication and interaction with the actual world define its authenticity to itself.[17]

Critical Correlation

Critical correlation with present-day culture provides a formal description of how the present situation enters into theological interpretation in an intrinsic way. Present-day experience does not play the role of an external audience to which one should adapt one's language after having developed a coherent position prior to encountering them. Rather the situation gives rise to the issues that shape the very questions theological interpretation must address and provides the language for doing so.

Postmodernity provides several distinctive experiences and questions with which ecclesiology must deal. I will do no more than list a few of them here. First, the church today exists in a new way in a religious context larger than itself, the pluralistic world of many different religious faiths. And in a postmodern culture, this religious pluralism counts as a value and not as something to be overcome. This raises several questions for the church. What is the mission of the church in this context? What is the status of the church comparatively in relation to these other religions? Second, when it is studied historically, the church appears as a single, though highly differentiated, movement in history. This common identity as Christian becomes accentuated in a religiously pluralistic context, where the differences among Christians shrink in size and relevance by comparison with interreligious difference. Given a postmodern appreciation of pluralism, what role do denominations or separated churches play within the large Christian church? The divisions and separations of the churches from each other are beginning to appear archaic. A pluralistic sensitivity confirms the value of different traditions within the church, but postmodern common sense says these differences should not be divisive, and postmodern leadership would embrace pluralism within the boundaries of the church at the various levels of its existence. Third, postmodern culture, at least in the United States, does not appear to be less religious than before, and yet the mainline churches are losing their members who tend to be more educated, even as fundamentalist churches grow. Is the Christian church able to speak to educated people today, or is the church essentially oriented to a less than critical constituency? Can the truth of the tradition, what Christians are convinced represents a truth for humanity itself, be represented linguistically and institutionally in a way that can be appreciated by postmodern thinking people? Is it only the less educated who are not to be scandalized? These questions represent the kind of ecclesiological issues that arise out of the current situation and a postmodern culture.

Critical Conversation

In critical conversation lies the antidote to separation and division. Ecclesiology as a discipline has usually been contained by the denominations, each one providing the center of gravity for its own distinctive self-understanding. Postmodern culture demands an ecclesiology that transcends denominationalism while at the same time protecting the distinctive traditions within the whole church. This position is difficult to achieve, because no ecclesiologist is simply a member of the great church but always a member of it through a particular communion or church. But this means that critical conversation becomes required in the church today if the central message of Christianity, that love is the ontological basis and structure of the universe, is itself to be credible.

THE RELATIVE ADEQUACY OF SUCH A THEOLOGY

I raise the question of the relative adequacy of this conception of the nature and method of theology as a way of concluding this schematic account of where such a method might lead. This is not a systematic theology in the sense of a closed system. If it were so considered, it would not corner the market, but simply take a place on the shelf as one among many others in a discipline that is wildly pluralistic. But it strives for system in the sense of attempting to distinguish a set of principles that can be consistently applied. In part it may be considered as an attempt to gather together in an inclusive way elements that can contribute to an imaginative framework for theological understanding at this time and in this place. Such a "system" would be no more than formally so because it could always be employed from a different perspective or hermeneutical standpoint, would always be open to new data, in dialogue with other cultures, adjusting to new situations, and attending to other voices.

The relative adequacy and superiority of such a method only really appears over against various forms of fundamentalism and revelational positivism. I take fundamentalism to refer to imaginative frameworks that depend on certain "fundamentals," that is, a set of foundational truths, which are stable and even static, and whose content is secure and often held in a literal or unchanging propositional form over against a world of constant change. In some respects the term "revelational positivism" says the same thing. It lacks epistemological sophistication and depth, and tends to reduce God's self-communication to a form of knowledge of this world. At its worst it approaches creedalism or belief in propositions themselves, as distinct from symbolic understanding that leads into mystery. But fundamentalism also tends to transcend those groups that identify themselves as such. It implicitly lives within and inspires a more general proclivity to restrict or control religious imagination and freedom by overt unchanging bonds, and in so doing to quench the dynamic and creative Spirit of God at work in the human spirit. Over against such a fundamentalism, theology as it is depicted here tries to preserve the tradition and thus the grounds for hope, and render assent to its transcendent mystery intelligible and thus credible, so that as a theology it supports freedom and encourages creativity. This lofty goal for theology appears in three distinct tasks that flow from its hermeneutical character.

First, as an hermeneutical discipline theology intrinsically relies on tradition; historical tradition provides its principal source. Theology *is* tradition, borne by human subjects, reflecting on itself. Fundamentalism and revelational positivism pose as traditional, but in every case consist in raising up the understandings of some particular period of history as an a-historical norm for the historical existential truth of tradition.

Second, when it is understood as an hermeneutical discipline, theology defines itself as committed to render the tradition credible, that is, intelligible, relevant, and applicable to actual lives in the present time. Fundamentalism by contrast promises security, but in every case it buys this security at the cost of intelligibility, relevance, and applicability in and to a postmodern context. The strategy of embracing a radical postmodern stance, over against a pejorative construal of the modern and with a hankering for the premodern, often hides fundamentalistic tendencies. I refer to the isolation of traditions in the name of the superiority of one's own and an accentuation of radical difference. Such a retirement from critical conversation and the search for a field of commonality ultimately compromises the Christian doctrine of creation, the universal relevance of truth and salvation, and the mission of the church.

Third, as an hermeneutical discipline that addresses freedom in time, this notion of theology appeals to freedom, and to the basic trust in existence that lies beneath the secular project. Human existence alone, as far as we know, lives consciously into the future, and freedom is its distinctive mark. Theology provides a rationale for the creative exercise of freedom. By contrast, fundamentalism amounts to a destructive captivity of the human spirit, a prison that closes it off from dialogue with the world and other religious traditions.

The relative adequacy of any conception of theology and its method can only be judged by the results. One already knows the results of fundamentalism: a lifeless repetition of the past that falsifies the message itself and turns away contemporary listeners. By contrast, an hermeneutical method keeps the tradition alive, reasserts its truth, finds its existential meaning into the future, applies it to concrete cultures and problems, and thereby stimulates and nurtures life in Jesus Christ and his church.

NOTES

Introduction

1. I use the term confessional in the sense of H. Richard Niebuhr to mean that, because of historicity and our limited standpoint, we must proceed by "stating in simple, confessional form what has happened to us in our community. . . ." H. Richard Niebuhr, *The Meaning of Revelation* (New York: Macmillan, 1960), p. 41. Niebuhr, however, understands a confessional stance to rule out attempts at explanation and justification of the universal relevance of the Christian message (p. 42). Niebuhr, reacting against Christian imperialism and having internalized an historical consciousness, maintains that a particular and relativistic point of view does not undermine truth-claims. While this is true, still truth implies universal human relevance. Thus although Christian theology begins confessionally, and does not seek to impose its truth on others, it must seek to defend and justify its universal relevance. Universal or open and critical dialogue is the only way to prevent an easy security in the possession of one's own truth.

2. This principle in Chenu is explained by Christophe F. Potworowski, *The Incarnation in the Theology of Marie-Dominique Chenu*, Ph.D. Dissertation (Toronto: University of St. Michael's College, 1988), pp. 34–48.

3. Paul Tillich, *Systematic Theology* (Chicago: University of Chicago Press, 1967), pp. 3–8.

4. Johann Baptist Metz, in *Faith in History and Society: Toward a Practical Fundamental Theology*, trans. by David Smith (New York: The Seabury Press, 1980), shows that an apologetic approach, that is, an attempt to justify and defend Christian hope, "forms the basis of all genuine Christian theology" (p. 14). Today this demand for apologetics is not occasioned by other religions, but by reductionistic world-views that positively exclude religious faith. Moreover, the strategy for apologetic theology is not merely a theoretical task, but aims at describing and drawing forth a Christian praxis that will respond to the crises of world society. I am entirely sympathetic to Metz's project, and his perspective will be incorporated into the consideration of method in theology. For the most part, however, this essay engages issues that are prior to and presupposed by Metz's fundamental theology.

5. Ernst Troeltsch, *The Absoluteness of Christianity and the History of Religions*, trans. by David Reid, intro. by James Luther Adams (Richmond: John Knox Press, 1971), pp. 63–64.

6. H. Richard Niebuhr, *The Responsible Self: An Essay in Christian Moral Philosophy*, intro. by James M. Gustafson (New York: Harper and Row, 1963), pp. 55–68. The image of responsibility suggests that the human is an answerer, engaged in dialogue, always "acting in response to actions and forces on the person" (p. 56).

7. "[I]t is only through the ethical critique of the history of humankind's accumulated suffering that in a paradoxical yet real fashion contemplation and action can be intrinsically connected with a possible realization of meaning." Edward Schillebeeckx, *Jesus: An Experiment in Christology*, trans. by Hubert Hoskins (New York: The Seabury Press, 1979), p. 622.

8. It is not necessary at this point to subscribe to a substance philosophy of human nature which would correlate with transcendental analysis. Nor would it be necessary for one who worked from an historicist viewpoint to maintain a rigorous process philosophy that denied the notion of human "nature" or "substance." Change can be accounted for by substance philosophy and order by process philosophy; but each must "strain" to accommodate the other dimension.

9. Edward Schillebeeckx, in *Christ: The Experience of Jesus as Lord*, trans. by John Bowden (New York: Seabury Press, 1981), pp. 731–43, describes seven such anthropological constants.

10. This distinction is operative in virtually all of Rahner's philosophical and theological writing. "This experience is called *transcendental* experience because it belongs to the necessary and inalienable structures of the knowing subject itself, and because it consists precisely in the transcendence beyond any particular group of possible objects or of categories." Karl Rahner, *Foundations of Christian Faith: An Introduction to the Idea of Christianity*, trans. by William V. Dych (New York: The Seabury Press, 1978), p. 20. The specific transcendental element that Rahner usually focuses upon when speaking of the transcendental dimension of experience is an implicit "experience of absolute transcendence" which is constitutive of human existence itself. But this transcendental experience of transcendence is always mediated through the world. "What we are calling transcendental knowledge or experience of God is an *a posteriori* knowledge insofar as the transcendental experience of free subjectivity takes place only in one's encounter with the world and especially with other people" (pp. 51–52).

11. Roger Haight, *An Alternative Vision: An Interpretation of Liberation Theology* (Mahwah: Paulist Press, 1985), pp. 5–7.

12. Maurice Blondel, *Action (1893): Essay on a Critique of Life and a Science of Practice*, trans. by Oliva Blanchette (Notre Dame: University of Notre Dame Press, 1984).

13. Superficial and erroneous appreciations of North American pragmatism are conveyed in such a phrase as "sheer pragmatism" or "mere utilitarianism."

14. The notion of human existence as project is very pronounced in the

evolutionary anthropology and christology of Juan Luis Segundo. It is the main category that he brings to bear in his criticism of the christology implicit in the sixteenth century *Spiritual Exercises* of Ignatius of Loyola. See Juan Luis Segundo, *The Christ of the Ignatian Exercises*, trans. by John Drury (Maryknoll: Orbis Books, 1987), pp. 44–114.

15. One could draw out certain virtualities in Aquinas' dynamic understanding of human nature that would be analogous to this. For example, nature is not merely a static essence in Aquinas, but a source and principle of operation that is always in act, and a constant potency and virtuality for further actuality. This activity becomes channeled through the powers of intellect and will toward the ultimate goal of human existence which is reached through action.

16. For example, the importance of the symbol "liberation" for Christian theology today is presupposed in this work. Liberation points to the purpose of human action and the intentionality of God's grace. There is no need to repeat here this and other principles which have been developed in greater length in Haight, *The Experience and Language of Grace* (New York: Paulist Press, 1979) and *An Alternative Vision*.

17. For example, David Tracy's *Blessed Rage for Order: The New Pluralism in Theology* (New York: The Seabury Press, 1975) investigates the anthropological grounds for theological language as such, that is, as a discipline among other disciplines in the academy. He then proposes a nuanced method of correlation for theology that integrates and holds together faith in transcendence and knowledge and commitment to the human project. Johann Metz's *Faith in History and Society*, especially Chapter 4, lays the groundwork for a practical political fundamental theology. In it he shows that the social-political issues of our situation enter into the very foundations of all religious discourse, thus giving all theology a practical political cast involving strictly social praxis. Francis Schüssler Fiorenza, *Foundational Theology: Jesus and the Church* (New York: Crossroad, 1985), outlines the structure of traditional fundamental theology, sometimes called apologetics, and introduces a consistent hermeneutical approach that realigns the whole discipline. The essays in fundamental theology edited by René Latourelle and Gerald O'Collins entitled *Problems and Perspectives of Fundamental Theology*, trans. by Matthew J. O'Connell (New York: Paulist Press, 1982) are much closer to traditional Catholic fundamental theology in the division of the topics treated and the overall logic of their development. One senses only the beginnings of an historical consciousness characterizing the work as a whole. *Faithful Witness: Foundations of Theology for Today's Church*, ed. by Leo J. O'Donovan and T. Howland Sanks (New York: Crossroad, 1989), is a carefully structured collection that treats the major topics of fundamental theology in an historically conscious way.

CHAPTER ONE: *Faith as a Dimension of the Human*

1. See David Tracy, *Blessed Rage for Order: The New Pluralism in Theology* (New York: Seabury Press, 1975), p. 44, for an explanation of common human experience as critically examined and not naive experience.

2. It is at this juncture that Reinhold Niebuhr begins his analysis of sin. Cf. Reinhold Niebuhr, *An Interpretation of Christian Ethics* (New York: Meridian Books, 1956), pp. 74–75; *The Nature and Destiny of Man*, I, *Human Nature* (New York: Charles Scribner's Sons, 1964), pp. 179–86. Karl Rahner provides a remarkably similar characterization of the human person in "The Theological Concept of Concupiscentia," *Theological Investigations*, I, trans. by Cornelius Ernst (Baltimore: Helicon Press, 1961), pp. 347–82.

3. The following analysis of human action is inspired by Maurice Blondel, *Action (1893): Essay on a Critique of Life and Science of Practice*, trans. by Oliva Blanchette (Notre Dame: University of Notre Dame Press, 1984).

4. This understanding would view such self-destructive phenomena as a desire for death and suicide as anomalies that can be explained as a desire to escape a particular mode of being urged by an implicit desire for a new form of being.

5. See Augustine, *On Free Choice of the Will*, III, vii, 21, in *Earlier Writings*, ed. and trans. by John H. S. Burleigh (Philadelphia: Westminster Press, 1953), p. 183.

6. See H. Richard Niebuhr, *Radical Monotheism and Western Culture. With Supplementary Essays* (New York: Harper Torchbooks, 1970), pp. 78–98.

7. Blondel, *Action*, pp. 445–46. See also James Somerville, *Total Commitment: Blondel's L'Action* (Washington, D.C.: Corpus Books, 1968), pp. 362–65.

8. A negative contrast experience is one that recognizes with absolute certainty a situation or event that should not be. This can only appear in conjunction with a sense of what should be, and hence becomes a dramatic revelatory experience of positive value. Cf. Edward Schillebeeckx, *God, the Future of Man*, trans. by N. D. Smith (New York: Sheed and Ward, 1968), pp. 136, 153–54, 164. Gustavo Gutiérrez, in *On Job: God-Talk and the Suffering of the Innocent*, trans. by Matthew J. O'Connell (Maryknoll: Orbis Books, 1987), in commenting on Job's experience of negative contrast explicitly draws the analogy with the experience of the poor in history today.

9. "The aesthetic choice is either entirely immediate, or it loses itself in the multifarious." Søren Kierkegaard, *Either/Or*, II, trans. by Walter Lowrie (Princeton: Princeton University Press, 1946), p. 141.

10. Niebuhr, *Radical Monotheism*, pp. 24–31.

11. It is often pointed out that the word faith is not used as a verb in English. James W. Fowler, *Stages of Faith: The Psychology of Human Development and the Quest for Meaning* (San Francisco: Harper and Row, 1981), p. 16. In what follows I shall try consistently to distinguish but not separate the existential response of faith, "to have faith," from the act of believing. See *ibid.*, pp. 9–15, which relies on the work of Wilfred Cantwell Smith, *Faith and Belief* (Princeton: Princeton University Press, 1979).

12. Friedrich Schleiermacher, *On Christian Faith*, ed. by H. R. Mackintosh and J. S. Stewart, intro. by R. R. Niebuhr (New York: Harper Torchbooks, 1963), pp. 12–18.

13. Søren Kierkegaard, *Concluding Unscientific Postscript*, trans. by David F. Swenson and Walter Lowrie (Princeton: Princeton University Press, 1941), p. 182.

14. Paul Tillich, *Dynamics of Faith* (New York: Harper Torchbooks, 1958), pp. 1–4.

15. *Ibid.*, pp. 78–79.

16. A response to reality can be actual and operative even when it is not psychologically focused in one's consciousness. Examples abound of responses to values or to specific objects or persons which govern a whole range of activities without being immediately thematized in consciousness. One such example would be love for a parent that continuously influences a whole range or even all of a person's activity.

17. See Tillich, *Dynamics of Faith*, pp. 30–40. This conclusion is especially important for Roman Catholic theology which has had a theological tradition that practically reduced faith to an assent to truth, that is, essentially to an act of the intellect.

18. James Fowler, *Stages of Faith*, pp. 9–15.

19. *Ibid, passim.*

20. See Schubert M. Ogden, *On Theology* (San Francisco: Harper and Row, 1986), pp. 106–09, for a description of basic human trust as the anthropological groundwork out of which religious faith emerges.

21. H. Richard Niebuhr, "On the Nature of Faith," *Religious Experience and Truth*, ed. by Sidney Hook (New York: New York University Press, 1961), pp. 99–100. In another place Niebuhr writes: "Faith is an active thing, a committing of self to something, an anticipation." H. Richard Niebuhr, "Faith in Gods and in God," *Radical Monotheism*, p. 117.

22. See especially Jürgen Moltmann's transposition of faith into hope in *The Theology of Hope: On the Ground and the Implications of a Christian Eschatology*, trans. by James W. Leitch (New York: Harper and Row, 1967).

23. "The word 'hope' expresses this one, unifying self-abandonment into the mystery of God, and thus hope is this unifying center between faith-vision and imperfect-perfect love." "For hope is the center that lies prior to faith and love, and hence to knowledge and will also." Karl Rahner, "The Theology of Hope," *Theology Digest*, Sesquicentennial Issue (February 1968), pp. 82, 83.

24. That this fusion makes a difference epistemologically can be illustrated by an example: Karl Rahner said relative to universal salvation that "An orthodox theologian . . . is forbidden to teach that everybody will be saved. But we are allowed to *hope* that all will be saved." The quote is from an interview with Rahner by Eugene Kennedy, "Quiet Mover of the Catholic Church," *The New York Times Magazine* (September 23, 1979), p. 67, found in M. Carmel McEnroy, *A Rahnerian Contribution towards an Orthodox Theology of Apocatastasis*, Ph.D. Dissertation (Toronto: University of St. Michael's College, 1984), p. 276. For Rahner universal salvation can only be a function of hope, although this hope is founded on faith in the event of Christ. But one must ask: What is the difference? Upon reflection, what appears to be an immediate difference mediated by words begins to evaporate; faith provides no more certitude than hope. There is surely a difference in the usage of the terms faith and hope, between faith directed toward the past and hope in the future. But in the actual present and in the face of the future, the human response of faith in the past is really a

dimension of a single human act and attitude of sheer openness to God. Faith is hope in the past; hope is faith in the future; and beliefs can be read as a function of hope.

25. Tillich, *Dynamics of Faith*, pp. 96–97.

26. Needless to say, this is not an adequate characterization of human knowing. The point here goes no further than to show the qualitative difference between knowledge of this world, including human existence, and faith in transcendent reality. This does not mean that in many of the myriad forms or kinds of knowledge of this world one may not find implicit appeals to or experiences of transcendence. But the radical distinction between faith and knowledge in the ordinary sense helps to clarify how these two different dimensions of human awareness interact and interpenetrate each other.

27. See William James, *The Varieties of Religious Experience* (New York: Collier Books, 1961), pp. 299–301.

28. See James Collins, *The Existentialists: A Critical Study* (Chicago: Henry Regnery Company, 1952), pp. 146–55, on this distinction of Gabriel Marcel. I am transposing Marcel's distinction between scientific and participatory philosophical knowledge of being to the sphere of religious experience.

29. This logic warrants a much fuller treatment than is provided at this point, and I shall return to it in greater length and precision in the discussion of religious symbols. The point here has already been stated, namely, that faith is not an isolated phenomenon that is self-contained, but it bends back and influences the processes and conclusions of ordinary human knowing. It thus incorporates knowing into itself.

30. Gordon Kaufman, *The Theological Imagination: Constructing the Concept of God* (Philadelphia: The Westminster Press, 1981), pp. 21–30.

31. This formulation, and the neutral or positive use of the term ideology, is borrowed from Juan Luis Segundo, *Faith and Ideologies*, trans. by John Drury (Maryknoll: Orbis Books, 1984), pp. 3–116. One does not have to accept this usage of the term ideology to appreciate the point being made. Ideology in Segundo is roughly consistent with what has been called up to this point simply knowledge in an ordinary sense. The term ideology, however, calls attention to the relativity of human knowledge, the multiple ways in which everything in our world can be construed.

32. In his book, *The Nature of Doctrine: Religion and Theology in a Postliberal Age* (Philadelphia: Westminster Press, 1984), George Lindbeck describes the understanding of belief represented here as resting on an "experiential-expressivist" view. He himself rejects this in favor of what he calls a "cultural-linguistic" theory for understanding theology, belief, and doctrine. I accept much of what Lindbeck says concerning a "cultural-linguistic" method of appreciating the function of beliefs, and his point of view will find its way into the treatment of revelation, scripture, and religious symbol. But the polemical theme of Lindbeck's work, I believe, is simply wrong. These two models need not be considered as exclusive of each other. Moreover Lindbeck's understanding of belief according to the cultural-linguistic model as far as I can see fails theoretically to account for the genesis of doctrines. This too will be dealt with under the topics

of revelation and religious symbol in the pattern of experience-faith-expression. Finally, two other major problems have been brought forward to challenge the two central theses of Lindbeck's book. The first concerns doctrine and the possibility of limiting doctrines or dogmas to their function as rules for regulating the community. Doctrines also function outside the church as a public communicative witness of what the church believes. See Charles M. Wood, "Review of *The Nature of Doctrine*," *Religious Studies Review*, 2 (July 1985), p. 240. The second concerns theology and, on the one hand, the adequacy of his description of the experiential-expressivist approach to theology. On the other hand, his own method's ability to discuss and adjudicate claims of truth has been questioned. See David Tracy, "Lindbeck's New Program for Theology: A Reflection," *The Thomist*, 49 (July 1985), pp. 460–72, on both of these issues, and Timothy P. Jackson, "Against Grammar," *Religious Studies Review*, 2 (July 1985), pp. 240–45, on the latter.

33. In the treatment of revelation it will be said that experienced encounter with the object of faith also determines this meaning and its validity.

34. All of this should be understood within the context of degrees of knowledge. As I walk along the road, I know there is something up ahead. As I get nearer, I realize it is a human person. Then it becomes apparent it is a woman. Then I know who she is. But do I know her, or merely some facts about her? And so on.

35. More analysis will have to be given to the differences of levels within faith structured by beliefs in order to make this "sameness" of faith more apparent.

36. See Edward Schillebeeckx, *Jesus: An Experiment in Christology*, trans. by Hubert Hoskins (New York: The Seabury Press, 1979), pp. 401–515, for an analysis of the development of New Testament christologies.

37. By creedalism I mean a faith that attaches itself to the propositions of doctrine, dogma, or creed instead of the reality to which they point. In other words, propositions, as opposed to the transcendent reality to which they point, have become the object of faith. The discussion of religious symbols will further clarify this distortion.

CHAPTER TWO: *Faith and the Community of Beliefs*

1. The public character of faith is analyzed with clarity and acumen by Langdon Gilkey, *Message and Existence: An Introduction to Christian Theology* (New York: The Seabury Press, 1979), pp. 23–38. In all of this discussion we are speaking of a social and historical necessity. It seems clear that any individual could consciously conceal in a privatistic way his or her deepest personal faith.

2. The public social character of faith dominates George Lindbeck's account of doctrine and theology according to a "cultural-linguistic" theory. See George Lindbeck, *The Nature of Doctrine: Religion and Theology in a Postliberal Age* (Philadelphia: Westminster Press, 1984). This social character is so clear that it could become the starting point for an analysis of faith. In the order of

DYNAMICS OF THEOLOGY

everyday life in history the faith of the community is prior to the faith of any individual. This social perspective will be emphasized more strongly in the sections on revelation and scripture where the sources and media of the specific faith of the Christian community become the focus of the discussion.

3. Not only liturgists ascribe to the principle that the law of prayer and worship is the law and normative standard of belief. Historians of doctrine constantly show how doctrines are generated and continually emerge out of the devotional practices of the Christian community.

4. In the view of Juan Luis Segundo faith is communicated by significant witnesses, and the medium of the communication he calls "iconic" as opposed to "digital" language. Juan Luis Segundo, *Faith and Ideologies,* trans. by John Drury (Maryknoll: Orbis Books, 1984), pp. 134–36, 145–74. I understand iconic language in two related senses. In the first sense it refers to a disclosive way of life. Witnesses bear witness by the way they live lives that give testimony to a viable and meaning-giving ultimate concern. In a derivative secondary sense "iconic" language may be the written language of texts that narrate or depict in concrete images the logic of faith as a coherent way of life lived under the impact of transcendent data. The gospels would be a primary example of this latter form of "iconic" language.

5. Along with Segundo, see William James' analysis of the value of the saints in the world. He writes that the human charity of the saints is "a genuinely creative social force, tending to make real a degree of virtue which it alone is ready to assume as possible." *The Varieties of Religious Experience: A Study in Human Nature* (New York: Collier Books, 1961), p. 283.

6. H. Richard Niebuhr, *The Social Sources of Denominationalism* (New York: World Publishing, A Meridian Book, 1957). This early work of Niebuhr was written during a period when his own community was engaged in an ecumenical discussion geared toward union with another church. The historicist perspective reflects the influence of Ernst Troeltsch on whom he had just completed an extended study.

7. Reason is always historical and by definition a subjective human action. The term "objective" is thematic; it describes an intention and goal of laying things bare "as they are." If one could determine a formal universal structure of human understanding and knowing by transcendental analysis, objectivity would be approached by being deliberately attentive to the criteria of the various levels of evidence, that is, by a disciplined subjectivity. But reason still cannot transcend its historicity. See the principal works of Bernard Lonergan, *Insight: A Study of Human Understanding* (New York: Longmans, Green and Co., 1958) and *Method in Theology* (New York: Herder and Herder, 1972).

8. See Peter Gay, *The Enlightenment: An Interpretation* (New York: Alfred A. Knopf, 1966).

9. John Henry Newman, *Newman's University Sermons: Fifteen Sermons Preached before the University of Oxford, 1826–43,* intro. by D. M. Mackinnon and J. D. Holmes (London: SPCK, 1970), pp. 202–08. Cf. also pp. 251–77 on implicit and explicit reasoning. These matters were taken up again more extensively by Newman later in his life in *An Essay in Aid of a Grammar of Assent,* intro.

by Etienne Gilson (New York: Doubleday, 1955). An excellent analysis of Newman's epistemology of faith is provided by A. J. Boekraad, *The Personal Conquest
of Truth according to J. H. Newman* (Louvain: Editions Nauvelaerts, 1955).

10. Paul Tillich, *Systematic Theology*, I (Chicago: The University of Chicago
Press, 1967), pp. 79–81, 111–15. "Ecstasy unites the experience of the abyss to
which reason in all its functions is driven with the experience of the ground in
which reason is grasped by the mystery of its own depth and the depth of being
generally" (p. 113).

11. Newman, *University Sermons*, p. 276.

12. Of course one should ask the question of whose or which critical reason
is being employed in any given theology. For critical reasoning too is historical,
subjective, biased, premised by presuppositions, class interests, and so on. But
when critical reasoning is authentic, it is also self-critical and open to discussion
and debate.

13. This is no more than a first general principle regarding a complex issue
that will be taken up again from different points of view. Sameness and difference, unity and diversity, are themes that run through this whole work.

14. Any given theological interpretation may appear to be a reduction of
belief to ordinary knowledge by one segment of the community and at the same
time be considered uncritical and fideistic by another segment. These terms are
always relative, and the community is always marked by a pluralism of beliefs.
For this reason all theological interpretation is always the subject of critical
discussion within the community.

15. There are criteria for judging fidelity to the object of faith as it is given
in the tradition and these will emerge in the course of this work. The issue will be
discussed directly in terms of method in theology.

16. Boniface VIII, *"Unam Sanctam,"* in *The Christian Faith: In the Doctrinal
Documents of the Catholic Church*, ed. by J. Neuner and J. Dupuis (Westminster:
Christian Classics, 1975), p. 211. This doctrine was reaffirmed by the Council of
Florence. It has been contradicted in the Roman Catholic Church by the Second
Vatican Council. It is interesting that the rejection of this doctrine was not based
on critical reason, but on the strictly theological proposition of the universality
of God's saving grace. However critical reason was at work stimulating the
recognition of this transcendent data.

17. Maurice Blondel considered doctrines and beliefs as "teachings for
thought only in view of becoming principles of action." Maurice Blondel, *Action
(1893): Essay on a Critique of Life and a Science of Practice*, trans. by Oliva Blanchette (Notre Dame: University of Notre Dame Press, 1984), p. 380. See the
whole discussion, pp. 363–88. For a general introduction to the thought-world
of Blondel and its relevance for theology, see Gregory Baum, *Man Becoming: God
in Secular Language* (New York: Herder and Herder, 1970), pp. 1–36.

18. Edouard Le Roy, an early twentieth century religious thinker in
France, developed a comprehensive theory of the meaning of dogmatic propositions based on the idea that doctrine expresses a faith which is constituted by
what he called "thought-action." Thus the meaning of doctrinal propositions

can be understood in terms of the logic of "thought-action." Cf. Edouard Le
Roy, *Dogme et Critique* (Paris: Bloud, 1907). For a synthetic interpretation of his
theory see R. Haight, "Edouard Le Roy's Theory of the Nature and Meaning of
Dogmatic Propositions," *Science et Esprit*, 35 (1983), pp. 171–90, 353–77.

19. The idea of the moral substance of Christian doctrine is borrowed from
Lucien Laberthonnière, a colleague of Blondel. See his *Le Réalisme Chrétien
précédé d'Essais de Philosophie Religieuse* (Paris: Editions du Seuil, 1966), esp. pp.
39–134. For a clear interpretation of Laberthonnière's moral dogmatism, especially relative to hermeneutics, see Gabriel Daly, *Immanence and Transcendence: A
Study of Catholic Modernism and Integralism* (Oxford: Clarendon Press, 1980), pp.
91–116.

20. From an anthropological point of view, one moral response that all
theologians might accept as relevant to theological language about God would
be doxological, the moral response of reverence, love, and service of God. Many
theologians might isolate this as the primary moral response. From the point of
view of revelation and the portrayal of Jesus in the gospels, however, it is not
clear that this is the most basic moral response attached to the Christian
notion of God. One should think rather that love of neighbor as the response to
God's cause, the kingdom of God that Jesus preached, is first in the order of
action.

21. It has also impeded the development of a consistent Christian theological ethics, as distinct from but not excluding a natural law ethics, in the Roman
Catholic Church. This deficiency is beginning to be addressed today.

22. Peter Berger, "The Perspective of Sociology, Relativizing the Relati-
vizers," *A Rumor of Angels: Modern Society and the Rediscovery of the Supernatural*
(Garden City: Doubleday, 1969), pp. 35–60.

23. The question of how critical reason in the form of the social sciences
enters into strictly theological method will be discussed in chapter ten.

24. We have at this point arrived at conclusions that are analogous to the
practical fundamental theology of Johann Baptist Metz. His conception of fundamental theology, it seems to me, combines among many others these four
principal ideas: (1) The Christian message is for the whole world, that is, it is true
and relevant for the whole human race in its concrete social history. This is an
absolutely crucial premise. (2) Therefore Christian theology must be apologetic;
it must explain, justify, and defend itself against interpretations of human history and society that contradict its truth. (3) Historical consciousness implies
that all human thinking is socially conditioned and part of a social web of
meaning. Thus even the very idea of God is political in its meaning and relevance. This social-political relevance must enter explicitly into theological construal. (4) But, finally, the really final "apology" can come only through Christian praxis. Thus theology must reflect and engender a social church praxis that
is consistent with the object of its faith. To these Metz adds other principles that
flow from the content of Christian faith. See J. B. Metz, *Faith in History and
Society: Toward a Practical Fundamental Theology*, trans. by David Smith (New
York: The Seabury Press, 1980), esp. pp. 3–13, 49–83.

CHAPTER THREE: *The Structure of Revelation*

1. The idea that the object of faith is known has the special sense of religious knowledge which will be explained in the course of the discussion.

2. See the opening methodological discussion of Avery Dulles, *Models of Revelation* (Garden City, NY: Doubleday, 1983), pp. 3–18.

3. Immanuel Kant, *Religion within the Limits of Reason Alone*, trans. and intro. by Theodore M. Greene, Hoyt H. Hudson, and John R. Silver (New York: Harper Torchbooks, 1960).

4. For example, Ernst Troeltsch defined the normativity of Christian revelation on the basis of comparison of it with that of other religions along axes which he considered intrinsic to all religious experience. See his *The Absoluteness of Christianity and the History of Religions*, trans. by David Reid, intro. by James Luther Adams (Richmond: John Knox Press, 1971). But twenty years later he surrendered this idea and accepted the historical and cultural relativity of all revelation. Ernst Troeltsch, "The Place of Christianity among the World Religions," *Christianity and Other Religions*, ed. by John Hick and Brian Hebblethwaite (Glasgow: Collins, Fount Paperbacks, 1980), pp. 11–31.

5. See Paul Knitter, ed., *The Myth of the Uniqueness of Jesus* (Maryknoll, NY: Orbis Books, 1988).

6. Another form of an objectivist theory of revelation ties it to a particular set of events in history. For example, this objectivism would view certain key events in Jewish history as God's acts in history and the final objective revelation in history the event of Jesus of Nazareth and his teaching. Cf. Dulles, *Models of Revelation*, pp. 53–67. Dulles' strategy in *Models of Revelation* is to characterize various types of theories of revelation but to reject none of them. All have some value to contribute to a general theory of revelation, but not indiscriminately. Rather Dulles establishes certain criteria for criticism of all the various models. I agree with the ecumenical openness of Dulles' approach and the implied criticism of fundamentalism. Fundamentalism is unacceptable as a comprehensive theory, but this does not mean that it completely lacks some implied values.

7. One can trace this movement beginning with Friedrich Schleiermacher, with Kant behind him, through the line of liberal Protestant theology, in the abortive modernist movement in Roman Catholicism, and in Roman Catholic theology prior to and after the Second Vatican Council. Even the strong Protestant reaction against liberal theology in the early twentieth century still held on to a subjective view of revelation. Revelation is not reducible to objective propositions or forms in scripture but consists in a faith encounter with God's Word that illumines by operating through them.

8. H. Richard Niebuhr, "Religious Realism and the Twentieth Century," *Religious Realism*, ed. by D. C. Mackintosh (New York: Macmillan, 1931), pp. 413–28; *The Meaning of Revelation* (New York: Macmillan, 1960), pp. 22–38. As a general criticism that has some significance for understanding the differences between liberal and neo-orthodox theology, this critique can stand. But the charge applies unevenly to nineteenth century theologians and should be vali-

dated in each case. Moreover one must distinguish between the structure of various liberal theologies in principle and the actual performance of any given liberal theologian. Quite frequently the criticisms of liberal theology are too facile and over-stated; they do not take account of the distinctions and nuances of its authors and the many variables at stake. For a sound critical account of the transition from liberal to neo-orthodox theology see Langdon Gilkey, *Naming the Whirlwind: The Renewal of God-Language* (New York: The Bobbs-Merrill Co., 1969), pp. 73–106.

9. The theory of universal subjective revelation presented here is heavily indebted to Thomas Franklin O'Meara, "Toward a Subjective Theology of Revelation," *Theological Studies*, 36 (1975), pp. 401–27. As I read it, this essay by O'Meara represents a convincing transposition of Karl Rahner's theology of grace and a bringing of it to bear on the subject matter of revelation. This view of it will allow me to reach back into Rahner's theology of grace to further clarify the theory of revelation in question.

10. James M. Gustafson, for example, argues from within the Christian tradition that God should not be construed as personal. His argument not only is based on the mediation of the data of science, but also rests on a sensibility that is characteristic of his own religious experience and piety as that is described in his work. Cf. James M. Gustafson, *Ethics from a Theocentric Perspective, I Theology and Ethics* (Chicago: University of Chicago Press, 1981), pp. 251–79. This example shows that even belief in the personality of God cannot be taken for granted within the Christian tradition; certainly it cannot be proved to Gustafson's satisfaction. The point then is the confessional stance of all theology when measured against sciences based on ordinary knowledge. We shall presuppose and not argue to the personality and loving character of God.

11. Rahner frequently cites New Testament texts such as 1 Tim 2:1–6 at this point. See, for example, Karl Rahner, "Universal Salvific Will," *Sacramentum Mundi: An Encyclopedia of Theology*, V, ed. by Karl Rahner, with Cornelius Ernst and Kevin Smyth (New York: Herder and Herder, 1968), p. 406. But such a citation of texts is not probative here, even for Christian theology. This will be discussed further in the chapters on scripture. But even at this point it becomes clear that these texts carry a significantly different and new meaning for him than they had in past Christian experience. The real source of Rahner's argument is a construal of God in our present situation that is mediated by the whole "Christ-event" in history.

12. Karl Rahner, "Concerning the Relationship of Nature and Grace," *Theological Investigations*, I, trans. by Cornelius Ernst (Baltimore: Helicon Press, 1961), pp. 302–03.

13. John L. McKenzie, "Aspects of Old Testament Thought," *Jerome Biblical Commentary*, ed. by R. Brown, J. Fitzmyer, and R. Murphy (Englewood Cliffs, NJ: Prentice-Hall, 1968), p. 742.

14. This is the term favored by O'Meara in his essay "Toward a Subjective Theory of Revelation," *passim.*

15. Thus the standard formulation of Karl Rahner for the reality of grace is God's self-communication, the gift of God's own personal self from out of God's

own inner life of freedom. See, for example, Karl Rahner, *Foundations of Christian Faith: An Introduction to the Idea of Christianity*, trans. by William V. Dych (New York: The Seabury Press, 1978), pp. 116–33.

16. Juan Luis Segundo, *Grace and the Human Condition*, trans. by John Drury (Maryknoll, NY: Orbis Books, 1973), pp. 66–69. In the next chapter we shall speak of an explicitly mediated experience of revelation in which God can be encountered "distinctly" as transcendent God in contrast to the medium of revelation.

17. O'Meara, "Toward a Subject Theology of Revelation," pp. 413–16.

18. Avery Dulles, "Theology of Revelation," in *Revelation and the Quest for Unity* (Washington, DC: Corpus Books, 1968), pp. 58f., as cited by O'Meara, *ibid.*, p. 404.

19. The following considerations have been influenced by John E. Smith, "The Disclosure of God and Positive Religion," *Experience and God* (New York: Oxford University Press, 1968), pp. 68–98. Smith's views, however, are congruous with the philosophy of religion and theology of Karl Rahner, and the two sources are often merged together in this account.

20. The notion of a worldly or historical medium is identical with the concept of a symbol which will be introduced in later chapters.

21. This construal of the dynamics of mystical experience does not deny or undermine the phenomenon itself. It simply explains it as in the end mediated experience. This mediation is seen at least in the social conditioning of the mystic. One cannot escape being in the world. Nor does this imply any limitation of how God can deal with human beings. It merely postulates that God operates through the very structures of human existence that God created.

22. Rudolf Otto, *The Idea of the Holy*, trans. by John W. Harvey (New York: Oxford University Press, 1958), pp. 1–40.

23. Smith, *Experience and God*, pp. 75–76.

24. This dual approach to revelation and the tensive differentiated view of revelation that is yielded by it can be seen, on the level of revelation, to overcome the opposition that Lindbeck sets up between an experiential-expressive and a cultural-linguistic model of faith experience. Cf. George Lindbeck, *The Nature of Doctrine: Religion and Theology in a Postliberal Age* (Philadelphia: Westminster Press, 1984), pp. 30–41.

25. These two dimensions of revelation correspond to what Karl Rahner calls transcendental and categorical experience. Cf. *Foundations*, pp. 14–23.

26. Karl Rahner, "Christianity and Non-Christian Religions," *Theological Investigations*, V, trans. by Karl-H. Kruger (Baltimore: Helicon Press, 1966), pp. 125–31.

CHAPTER FOUR: *Revelation and Theology*

1. This task will not be completed here. The distinctions established in this chapter will be complemented by a fuller discussion under the heading of religious symbols in chapters seven and eight.

2. Hans Küng, "Toward a New Consensus in Catholic (and Ecumenical) Theology," *Consensus in Theology?* ed. by Leonard Swidler (Philadelphia: Westminster Press, 1980), p. 5.

3. Such an analysis should be and is possible. It would look at Jesus' view of God as Father. It would analyze Jesus' depiction of God in the parables, and his presentation of God's will and reign. It would see in Jesus' prayer a personal relationship to a personal Presence. It would find in what was called Jesus' obedience to God a faith commitment to God's cause. None of this would suppose that one could analyze the consciousness of Jesus. Rather these historical data about Jesus would open up our own Christian consciousness to the God Jesus called Father.

4. See Emil Brunner, *Truth as Encounter* (Philadelphia: Westminster Press, 1964); *Revelation and Reason: The Christian Doctrine of Faith and Knowledge,* trans. by Olive Wyon (Philadelphia: Westminster Press, 1946). Cf. also Joseph Smith, *Emil Brunner's Theology of Revelation* (Manila: Ateneo de Manila Press, 1967). Brunner's theological analysis of revelation rings true; it corresponds to experience. I am also impressed by its ability to be appropriated into a different overall theological framework than Brunner's own, as in the case of its use by H. Richard Niebuhr. See *The Meaning of Revelation* (New York: Macmillan, 1960). In my reading of Niebuhr, he never really abandoned his historicist and anthropological starting point for theology learned from the liberal tradition. But he severely modified the liberal approach by finding within faith experience itself a theocentrism and realism in which God's initiative of self-disclosure is the primary element.

5. Right away this mode of proceeding runs contrary to Brunner's stated intentions. In his theology the primary analogue for interpersonal communication would be God's revelation of God's self to human beings. Our strategy will be to use a description of interpersonal communication as a framework for a phenomenology of the Christian experience of revelation. Brunner's analysis of revelation does not appear as a phenomenology of the human experience of revelation. Rather he piles up its characteristics by citing scriptural sources and texts. But one could ask the critical question about what is really going on in Brunner's theology at this point.

6. The difference, at least as it is explained here, seems to be challenged by Fergus Kerr, *Theology After Wittgenstein* (Oxford: Basil Blackwell, 1986), *passim.* Kerr polemicizes against the idea that the human person is an integral subject inside a body, so to speak, that can be imagined as separable from its external manifestations in action. I accept most of Kerr's analysis, but he leaves some phenomena unexplained. Cf. *infra.* I would want to argue that there is an element of transcendence of spirit beyond matter, of freedom over physicality, of experience beyond language. This transcendence however is not to be conceived apart from freedom's immersion in and dependence upon matter, physicality, and language.

7. As far as I can see Kerr either does not take this phenomenon fully into account or does not adequately explain it. Nor does he adequately explain what

the Christian hope for eternal life can mean when the whole empirical person is dead and laid in the grave. On this latter point, see *ibid.*, pp. 177–80.

8. This distinction does not require separation or separability. On the one hand I agree that there has been a history of minimizing the concrete reality of bodily life in a doctrine of the primacy of the spiritual dimension of human life. But a distinction between spirit and matter need not entail the kind of "dichotomizing" that is often involved here. In the discussion of religious symbols I will appeal to Karl Rahner's view of the inseparable unity of spirit and matter.

9. These distinctions have been developed in dialogue with George Tyrrell, a Roman Catholic modernist theologian who had to face the question of the distinction and relationship between revelation and theology. The issue forced him to analyze the dynamics of revelational experience. See George Tyrrell, "The Rights and Limits of Theology" and "Revelation," in *Through Scylla and Charybdis: Or the New Theology and the Old* (London: Longman, Green, and Co., 1907), pp. 200–41, 264–307; " 'Revelation as Experience': An Unpublished Lecture of George Tyrrell," ed. and notes by Thomas Michael Loome, *Heythrop Journal*, 12 (1971), pp. 117–49. Cf. also Francis M. O'Connor, "Tyrrell: The Nature of Revelation," *Continuum*, 3 (1965), pp. 168–77. The intention is not to reproduce Tyrrell's theology here. For example, the idea of an historical medium, while it is implicitly present in Tyrrell's theology, is not carefully developed.

10. Tyrrell, *Through Scylla and Charybdis*, pp. 278ff.

11. Edward Schillebeeckx, *Jesus: An Experiment in Christology*, trans. by Hubert Hoskins (New York: Seabury Press, 1979), pp. 545–50. Schillebeeckx makes a distinction between "first order" assertions which are more closely related to the experience of salvation, and "second order" assertions which are more reflective and systematic. *Ibid.* Strictly speaking, however, first order assertions are also properly "theological."

12. The subjective and experiential character of revelation, and hence the source of theology, does not imply that there is no objective referent which may serve as a criterion for theology. Theology is not the expression of purely immanent and subjective experience. On the one hand, as has been insisted upon all along in this development, there must be an external and objective medium to provide thematic content to revelational experience of God's Presence. On the other hand, this whole account represents a revelational realism. The encounter of God's Presence is a *real* encounter of God's *real* Presence.

13. Often in the actual exercise of the theological imagination this constant appeal to Christian encounter is implicit and presupposed. Theologians do not at every stage of the game make this connection explicit. But it may be tested. For example, when one asks at any stage of a theological argument how its author "knows" what he or she says to be true, the answer will always be led back reductively to an experience of encounter with transcendence.

14. The distinction is made by Paul Tillich, *Systematic Theology* I (Chicago: University of Chicago Press, 1967), pp. 126–28.

15. Schillebeeckx's hypothetical reconstruction of the Easter experience of the earliest disciples seems to me to be getting close to what is referred to here as

original Christian revelation. Cf. Schillebeeckx, *Jesus*, pp. 379–97. It is important, however, to think of this not merely in terms of the experience of single persons, but in terms of a corporate experience that may have needed time to come to some distinctive and discernible shape, especially vis-à-vis Jewish tradition.

16. This solution to the problem of the development of revelation and theology is similar to Tyrrell's but differs at one point. Tyrrell finally held that it is theology that develops while revelation does not. This non-paradoxical view virtually pushes the distinction between revelation and theology to a separation. It fails to recognize the historical, interpretative, and theological dimension of revelation itself as it comes to expression, and the close connection of theology with revelational experience. Cf. Tyrrell, *Through Scylla and Charybdis*, pp. 292–97. In contrast to Tyrrell, then, the position here is that revelation both does and does not develop. This paradoxical assertion is based on distinct levels of the phenomenon of revelation that allow it to be regarded from different points of view.

17. This is not reductionist because, first, this center of gravity never exists historically without the fullness of an historical experience of revelation described at the outset. It is never isolatable. Second, therefore, this inner center of gravity could easily be expanded to include other transcendent data concerning God and human existence that are implicit in this simple experience and the statement of it.

18. This shows again the paradox involved in the notion of transcendental revelation. On the one hand, it is supposed to refer to a dimension that is universal in all revelation. But to assign it any content, as is the case here, involves historical categorical revelation. It should be recalled that the general theory of revelation proposed in chapter three was a Christian theory.

19. I do not use such expressions as kernel, core, essence, or even identity of Christianity because of the freight carried by them. Often such expressions were understood in an abstract and exclusive way. See the discussion of the essence of Christianity debate by Stephen Sykes, *The Identity of Christianity: Theologians and the Essence of Christianity from Schleiermacher to Barth* (London: SPCK, 1984).

20. This is not the last word on this subject. We shall return to this question when we deal with the role of scripture in theology where it functions as the first expression of Christian revelation. There we shall try to understand and defend the necessity of being faithful to the first expression of revelation and, by extension, the landmark interpretations of it that have arisen in the course of Christian history. The issue will also be discussed in the chapters on method in theology.

CHAPTER FIVE: *The Status of Scripture in the Church*

1. Hans Küng, *The Church*, trans. by Ray and Rosaleen Ockenden (New York: Sheed and Ward, 1967), p. 292.

2. See James Barr, *The Bible in the Modern World* (London: SCM Press, 1973), pp. 1–34 for his survey of the difficulties that surround the received notions about the Bible.

3. Karl Rahner, *Inspiration in the Bible*, trans. by Charles H. Henkey (New York: Herder and Herder, 1961), p. 12.

4. This is something of a rhetorical overstatement because there are many different uses of scripture, not the least of which is devotional. But it makes a point relative to the theological use of scripture.

5. Stephen Sykes, *The Identity of Christianity: Theologians and the Essence of Christianity from Schleiermacher to Barth* (London: SPCK, 1984), pp. 11–34.

6. See Gabriel Moran, *Theology of Revelation* (New York: Herder and Herder, 1966), p. 28.

7. I am indebted to James Barr for this descriptive account of the formation of the scriptures and for the logic of the view presented here. But at the same time Barr's position has been combined with a theory of revelation and complemented by other sources. See *The Bible in the Modern World*, pp. 114–18.

8. See Paul Ricoeur, *Interpretation Theory: Discourse and the Surplus of Meaning* (Fort Worth, TX: Texas Christian University Press, 1976), pp. 25–44 for a close analysis of the many changes that occur with the shift from speaking to writing.

9. Paul Ricoeur, "Toward a Hermeneutic of the Idea of Revelation," *Harvard Theological Review*, 70 (1977), pp. 1–37.

10. Barr, *The Bible in the Modern World*, pp. 114–18.

11. Emil Brunner, *Revelation and Reason: The Christian Doctrine of Faith and Knowledge*, trans. by Olive Wyon (Philadelphia: Westminster Press, 1946), pp. 8–10.

12. Barr, *The Bible in the Modern World*, p. 118.

13. The idea that the scriptures are the constitution of the church is suggested indirectly by Karl Rahner, *Inspiration in the Bible*, pp. 47–50.

14. From this normativity flows the qualitative difference between a theological and a socio-historical approach to Christianity. In the variety of historical or social-scientific methods for studying the church, what you see is what you get. The church is what it is. A good example of this is found in Wilfred Cantwell Smith, *Towards a World Theology: Faith and the Comparative History of Religion* (Philadelphia: Westminster Press, 1981), pp. 21–44. For the theologian the church is always measured against an ideal norm, and Christianity is always more than its actuality. This qualitative distinction of theology as a discipline from other forms of the study of Christianity is really quite crucial, and failure to recognize it is often a source of confusion in what is going on in theology.

15. See David Edward Aune, *The New Testament in Its Literary Environment* (Philadelphia: Westminster Press, 1987).

16. This view is stated on a priori grounds despite the fact that it is notoriously difficult methodologically to determine any exact contours of Jesus' experience. However some broad and important generalizations can be made on the basis of limited historical data.

17. Efforts at this are possible, for example, in terms of trying to determine what the first kerygma was. Cf. C. H. Dodd, *The Apostolic Preaching and Its Developments* (London: Hodder and Stoughton, 1963), and Schubert M. Ogden, *The Point of Christology* (San Francisco: Harper and Row, 1982), pp. 106–26. See also Edward Schillebeeckx's and Hans Küng's hypothetical reconstructions of the revelatory Easter experience: Edward Schillebeeckx, *Jesus: An Experiment in Christology*, trans. by John Bowden (New York: Seabury Press, 1979), pp. 379–97; Hans Küng, *On Being a Christian*, trans. by Edward Quinn (Garden City, NY: Doubleday, 1976), pp. 370–81. Certain expressions in the New Testament such as "Come, Lord!" might also be looked upon as first expressions of revelatory experience because of their primitive emotive quality. Reconstructions of Jesus' parables or prayer forms could be regarded as attempts to distinguish first expressions of revelation because of their being part of the medium of revelation itself.

18. This second "place" of revelation in relation to scripture, even though the question is discussed in terms of faith, is what receives most of the constructive attention in George Lindbeck's *The Nature of Doctrine: Religion and Theology in a Postliberal Age* (Philadelphia: Westminster Press, 1984). The cultural-linguistic form of faith, both in scripture and doctrine, is the stable form of faith in the church that is continually opening up new forms of faith response in different times, places, and cultures.

19. How Jesus is to be understood as God's initiative in history is of course the problem of christology. As such, this issue falls well beyond the confines of this work, for the response to it requires a whole christology. But a Spirit christology, as is found in the New Testament, that sees the human person Jesus as a freedom filled with God's Presence as Spirit would correspond neatly to this theology of revelation.

20. Speaking of mysticism William James writes: "Mystical states, when well developed, usually are, and have the right to be, absolutely authoritative over the individuals to whom they come." William James, *The Varieties of Religious Experience: A Study of Human Nature* (New York: Collier Books, 1961), p. 331. The same can be said analogously and more generally of religious experience.

21. It is out of this internal logic of the historical identity of a community that is set by language that Lindbeck develops his rule or grammar theory of doctrine. In this view what matters is not so much whether a doctrine is true or false, but how it determines a community's language and hence view of reality. See George Lindbeck, in *The Infallibility Debate*, ed. by John J. Kirvan (New York: Paulist Press, 1971), pp. 107–52; *The Nature of Doctrine*, pp. 79–90.

22. This logic can be seen at work implicitly in Irenaeus' appeal to apostolicity in *Against Heresies*, III, 1–5. See *Early Christian Fathers*, trans. and ed. by Cyril C. Richardson et al. (New York: Macmillan, 1970), pp. 369–77.

23. See Karl Rahner, "The Death of Jesus and the Closure of Revelation," *Theological Investigations*, 18, trans. by Edward Quinn (New York: Crossroad, 1983), pp. 132–35.

24. These implicit claims are merely stated here as the point of this doc-

trine that seems at first sight to be about scripture. The development of these themes would extend well beyond this work into the dynamics of christology.

CHAPTER SIX: *Scripture and Theology*

1. It should be clear from the outset that scripture can function in the church in many ways and not simply theologically. It can be read for personal devotion or publicly at liturgy and so on. The issue here is the narrow one of how scripture can be used in the critical discipline of theology.

2. David H. Kelsey, *The Uses of Scripture in Recent Theology* (Philadelphia: Fortress Press, 1975).

3. *Ibid.*, p. 207.

4. *Ibid.*, pp. 97–100.

5. Friedrich Schleiermacher held that "Dogmatic Theology is the science which systematizes the doctrine prevalent in the Christian Church at any given time." *The Christian Faith*, I, ed. by H. R. Mackintosh and J. S. Stewart (New York: Harper Torchbooks, 1963), p. 88. This is a reflection of Schleiermacher's historical consciousness; it does not mean that theology is mere opinion. It is a critical, purifying, and perfecting discipline with normative intent which relies on scripture. *Ibid.*, pp. 92, 112–17.

6. Karl Barth, *Church Dogmatics* I, 1, *The Doctrine of the Word of God*, trans. by G. T. Thompson (New York: Charles Scribner's Sons, 1936), pp. 1–2. Note that in a pluralistic situation the normativity of theology is a theme or intention of the discipline. This theme leads it into critical dialogue with other theologies. It cannot however yield a single uniform and normative theology.

7. For the most part Kelsey wishes to abstract the logic or functioning of this judgment from particular theologies of revelation. He wants in the end to establish the authority of scripture as independently as possible from theologies of revelation: it is a question of ecclesiology and can be understood functionally as part of the dynamics of the church. But at the same time the different a priori judgments are closely aligned with views of revelation. It would be interesting to chart the correspondences between the various uses of scripture in present theology and the models of revelation schematized by Avery Dulles in *Models of Revelation* (Garden City, NY: Doubleday, 1983).

8. Kelsey calls this a priori imaginative judgment a *discrimen*. This recourse to a Latin word enables him to avoid a narrow prejudgment of its character and at the same time open up by description its multiple functions. This foundational conception accounts for the differences or distinctions between various uses of scripture by theologians. It is the positive turning point defining the dynamics of how scripture is brought to bear on theology by each theologian.

9. "Experience is not the source from which the contents of systematic theology are taken but the medium through which they are existentially received." The event of revelation "is given to experience and not derived from it. Therefore experience receives and does not produce." Paul Tillich, *Systematic Theology*, I (Chicago: University of Chicago Press, 1967), pp. 42, 46. Our expla-

nation of revelation corresponds to the positive dimension of what Tillich is saying here.

10. See David Tracy, *Blessed Rage for Order: The New Pluralism in Theology* (New York: Seabury Press, 1975), pp. 43–46.

11. Kelsey, *The Uses of Scripture*, pp. 192–93, 205–07.

12. There will always be a tension between newness and fidelity with scripture in every Christian theological position or statement. With this conclusion we are encroaching upon the issue of method in theology and principles for interpreting scripture which will be discussed in later chapters. The point here has been to establish a logic for the use of scripture as a genuine authority in theology in the face of the problems that seem to render this idea impossible. This conclusion then is a limited one but a really significant one. Scripture does have a real authority in theology which cannot be bypassed even though it is not an absolutely determining external authority and not the only authority.

13. I use the phrase "religious medium" as synonymous with the idea of a "religious symbol." But as yet the idea of religious symbols has not been explored. This will be the topic of chapters seven and eight. There we shall discuss the epistemology of religious media or symbols, a topic which is intimately related to the use of scripture in theology.

14. See Kelsey, *The Uses of Scripture*, *passim*, for his analyses of different logics in current uses of scripture.

15. Paul S. Minear, *Images of the Church in the New Testament* (London: Lutterworth Press, 1961).

16. The non-possibility of a group of texts to decide a theological issue is illustrated by the debate that surrounded the first ecumenically decisive decision at Nicaea. Neither the series of texts piled up on the Arian side nor those on the Athanasian side could settle the matter. Indeed, from certain points of view the Arian texts appear more directly to the point. Therefore neither on their premises for the use of scripture nor on ours today, which will include more nuanced views of symbolic epistemology and method in theology, can mere citation of various texts be decisive in theological assertions.

17. For many theologians today an object-reference to Jesus in the gospels especially provides the grounds for a minimal but substantial reconstruction of the Jesus of history. In *An Alternative Vision: An Interpretation of Liberation Theology* (Mahwah, NJ: Paulist, 1985), pp. 314–15, n. 15, I misrepresented the position of Schubert Ogden by characterizing his distinction of the "existential-historical" Jesus as a kind of self-enclosed experience which sundered the subject-object connection. The opposite is the case. The fundamental kerygma is precisely an existential experience and reaction to Jesus. Cf. Schubert M. Ogden, *The Point of Christology* (San Francisco: Harper and Row, 1982), pp. 57–60.

18. This fundamental and all encompassing conception of Christianity finds its inspiration in Karl Rahner. In *A World Grace: An Introduction to the Themes and Foundations of Karl Rahner's Theology*, ed. by Leo J. O'Donovan (New York: Seabury Press, 1980) the authors seek to give a title to their interpretations of Rahner's theology that typifies the whole of it in a phrase.

19. See Karl Rahner, *The Shape of the Church to Come*, trans. by Edward Quinn (London: SPCK, 1974), pp. 57–8.

20. Kelsey, *The Uses of Scripture*, pp. 195–96. The reflections which follow are written in close dialogue with Kelsey. But at significant points his theory is altered here by the strong emphasis on revelation. For example, the insertion of the word "disclosure" shifts the meaning of the text cited and his own proposal for theology today as an analogous elaboration of scriptural models of understanding.

21. It should be clear that the idea of the ordered unity and wholeness of scripture represents a theological interpretative judgment. It does not describe the literary composition of the work.

22. William C. Spohn, *What Are They Saying About Scripture and Ethics?* (New York: Paulist Press, 1984), pp. 106–28.

23. Thomas Aquinas, *Summa Theologiae*, I, q.1, *passim*, esp. a. 8, ad 2. But Aquinas was not a fundamentalist because arguments from reason had the role of clarifying, that is, interpreting, authority.

24. Cf. *supra*, n. 16.

25. In the Roman Catholic Church a fundamental theology often also considers questions such as the authority of the magisterium and the meaning of infallibility. Some light may be thrown on these issues by analogy with the authority of scripture. But the narrow focus of this book on the nature of Christian theology prevents this further discussion here. Such questions might be discussed more fittingly within ecclesiology.

CHAPTER SEVEN: *The Symbolic Structure of Religion*

1. Maurice Blondel, "The Letter on Apologetics," in *The Letter on Apologetics and History and Dogma*, trans. and ed. by Alexander Dru and Illtyd Trethowan (New York: Holt, Rinehart and Winston, 1964), pp. 158–59; Karl Rahner, *Foundations of Christian Faith: An Introduction to the Idea of Christianity*, trans. by William V. Dych (New York: Seabury Press, 1978), pp. 31–35.

2. This account of the nature of the religious symbol follows closely the theology of symbol of Paul Tillich. See the following works which are somewhat repetitive in their account of the fundamental elements that make up his view. Paul Tillich, *Systematic Theology*, I (Chicago: University of Chicago Press, 1967), pp. 238–41; *Dynamics of Faith* (New York: Harper Torchbooks, 1957), pp. 41–54; "The Meaning and Justification of Religious Symbols" and "The Religious Symbol," in *Religious Experience and Truth*, ed. by Sidney Hook (New York: New York University Press, 1961), pp. 3–12, 301–21; "The Nature of Religious Language," *Theology of Culture*, ed. by Robert C. Kimball (New York: Oxford University Press, 1964), pp. 53–67; "Existential Analyses and Religious Symbols," *Four Existentialist Theologians*, ed. by Will Herberg (Garden City, N.Y.: Doubleday Anchor Books, 1958), pp. 277–91; "Theology and Symbolism," *Religious Symbolism*, ed. by F. Ernest Johnson (New York: Harper and Brothers, 1955), pp. 107–16; "The Problem of Theological Method," *Journal of Religion,*

27 (January 1947) reprinted in *Four Existentialist Theologians,* pp. 238–55. See also David H. Kelsey, *The Fabric of Paul Tillich's Theology* (New Haven: Yale University Press, 1969), pp. 19–50.

3. This correspondence is not complete, neither in principle nor in fact in the case of Christianity. A religious tradition can begin by a new understanding of transcendence, a new constellation of conscious symbols, and the dependent revelation of religious traditions usually include concrete symbols such as rituals and sacraments.

4. This is not the order of presentation used by Rahner in his familiar and important article, "The Theology of Symbol," *Theological Investigations,* 4, trans. by Kevin Smyth (Baltimore: Helicon Press, 1966), pp. 221–52. In this article Rahner begins with a symbolic theology of the Trinity and descends through a theory of incarnation to further considerations of "the body as symbol of man" (p. 245). But this is not what is really going on epistemologically. It is difficult to imagine how one could argue from an unknown inner life of absolute mystery to the dynamics of the human person. In fact, then, the article represents the fairly tight coherence of Rahner's metaphysics of the human person and the projection of this onto God in his trinitarian theology. For my part I wish to try to interpret Rahner's theology of symbol by bypassing his trinitarian theology. It should thus be noted that this is an interpretation and not simply a laying out of Rahner's views.

5. It is common today to complain about dualisms, especially in matters pertaining to body and spirit in anthropology. No dualism should be read into this account; it is an essay at understanding the one whole person in a differentiated way. This description of a groundwork for reciprocal causality should be seen as a conception that militates against and overcomes dualism.

6. The explanation of God's being present in all of creation, so that all things are manifestations of God's creative power within, would employ a concept of God's quasi-efficient causality. The cause is present and known in some measure in the effect. It is "a sort of" efficient causality because predicated of God, and thus also unlike any efficient causality we know.

7. Thomas Aquinas, *Summa Theologiae,* I–II, q. 113, a. 3.

8. The explanation of God's Presence to human beings in a personal way is provided by Rahner in his theology of grace in terms of quasi-formal causality. It is "a sort of" formal causality because it is predicated of God, and thus also unlike any formal causality we know. Specifically, it is analogous to the formal causality already analyzed, where the human person, in its potentiality for a transcendent communication, receives God's personal Presence in a manner analogous to matter's receptivity to form. Karl Rahner, "Some Implications of the Scholastic Concept of Uncreated Grace," *Theological Investigations,* I, trans. by Cornelius Ernst (Baltimore: Helicon Press, 1961), pp. 326–37. In this analogy, the impersonal categories of Thomistic metaphysics are strained considerably. But the whole conception of Rahner really constitutes a breaking open of these categories to a truly interpersonal understanding of grace which we have exploited in earlier chapters in terms of encounter.

9. Such a christology is of course not Rahner's who, consistent with his

trinitarian theology, develops a thoroughgoing Logos christology. The Logos, who is the symbol and image of the Father, is incarnate uniquely in the person of Jesus, making Jesus the symbol of God. Rahner's christology, however, includes at least one inherent difficulty. Rahner desires to establish the continuity between Jesus and other human beings. But his Logos christology makes this conceptually impossible, since God communicates God's self uniquely to Jesus as Logos and to other human beings analogously as Spirit. See Karl Rahner, "Divine Trinity," *Sacramentum Mundi: An Encyclopedia of Theology*, ed. by Karl Rahner with Cornelius Ernst and Kevin Smyth et al. (New York: Herder and Herder, 1968), p. 298. It is difficult to see how one can hold the qualitative uniqueness of Jesus and still affirm the doctrine of Chalcedon that Jesus is consubstantial with us.

10. The central christological doctrine of Christianity is that of the Council of Chalcedon whose formula states that Jesus is a single person with two natures, human and divine. It is rather crucial that this doctrine not be read as an explanation of the status of Jesus. It is rather an assertion of the dimensions of Jesus' person and life that are purely dialectical. As in symbols generally, this dialectical tension cannot be resolved. The main problem with most christologies after Chalcedon is that they did and still do resolve this dialectical tension in favor of Jesus' divinity, and thus compromise his status as a human being as expressed by this classical conciliar doctrine.

11. Paul Ricoeur, *Interpretation Theory: Discourse and the Surplus of Meaning* (Fort Worth, TX: Texas Christian University Press, 1976), pp. 19–22.

12. The easy answer to this question, "because of the resurrection of Jesus," is not really an answer to the question of objective historical mediation. It is an expression of the answer *post factum*, after it has been received. The question deals with historical mediation.

13. Paul Tillich, *Systematic Theology*, II (Chicago: University of Chicago Press, 1967), pp. 9–10.

14. David Tracy, *Blessed Rage for Order: The New Pluralism in Theology* (New York: Seabury Press, 1975), pp. 64–87.

15. Consider this reflective comment of Gregory of Nyssa, a near equivalent of the symbolic structure that has been put forward here: "We, . . . following the suggestions of Scripture, have learnt that that [the divine] nature is unnameable and unspeakable, and we say that every term either invented by the custom of men, or handed down to us by the Scriptures, is indeed explanatory of our conceptions of the Divine Nature, but does not include the significance of that nature itself." "[A]s we perceive the varied operations of the power above us, we fashion our appellations [of God] from the several operations that are known to us. . . ." Gregory of Nyssa, "On Not Three Gods," in *Nicene and Post-Nicene Fathers*, 2nd Series, Vol. V, *Select Writings and Letters of Gregory, Bishop of Nyssa*, trans. by William Moore and Henry Austin Wilson (Grand Rapids, MI: Wm. B. Eerdmans, orig. 1892), pp. 332b, 333a.

16. This dialectical structure is also reflected in classical theology, even within the context of an analogical imagination, in the form of the threefold logic of knowledge of God. The first moment of knowing God is affirmation on

the basis of creation as revelatory; the second moment is negation because of God's transcendence to all earthly reality and conception; the third moment is reaffirmation in a higher transcendent sense. See for example Thomas Aquinas, *Summa Theologiae*, I, q. 13, a. 2. Everything here depends on what is going on in the third moment. But as far as I can see it cannot mean simply overcoming the dialectic of the first two moments. This would render the whole insight and logic pointless. It must therefore mean an acceptance of that dialectical tension into the affirmation itself.

17. In this chapter I have brought together in what may appear to be a too smooth and easy way elements from the theology of symbol of Paul Tillich and Karl Rahner. There is no doubt that there are a good number of significant differences between these two theologians and their theologies of symbol. See James J. Buckley, "On Being a Symbol: An Appraisal of Karl Rahner," *Theological Studies*, 40 (1979), pp. 453–73. For example, despite his turn to the subject, Rahner's theology of symbol is considerably more objective in character than Tillich's. Moreover, as a Lutheran Protestant, Tillich's theology of symbol illustrates well the dialectical imagination, while Rahner, the Roman Catholic theologian, manifests the analogical imagination identified by David Tracy. See Tracy, *The Analogical Imagination: Christian Theology and the Culture of Pluralism* (New York: Crossroad, 1981), pp. 408–21. Yet despite these differences, I see no fundamental antithesis between these two theologies of symbol. Rather I see Rahner much more willing to emphasize the "is" side of the dialectic between symbol and symbolized, especially in the case of the concrete symbol Jesus. This is not the place to develop a full critique of Rahner's or Tillich's theology of symbol or their christology. But this can be said: the dialectical structure is still present in Rahner's christology, despite his tendency to emphasize Jesus' being the actuality of God in the world. Moreover, this must be the case if his christology is to be judged consistent with Chalcedon which, as was said, is a strictly dialectical confession.

18. See Rahner's concept of mystagogy, which will be taken up again in the next chapter, as this is developed by James J. Bacik, *Apologetics and the Eclipse of Mystery: Mystagogy According to Karl Rahner* (Notre Dame, IN: University of Notre Dame Press, 1980), esp. pp. 12–19, for its definition as initiating, introducing, and leading into mystery.

CHAPTER EIGHT: *Symbolic Religious Communication*

1. Avery Dulles, "The Symbolic Structure of Revelation," *Theological Studies*, 41 (1980), pp. 60–61.

2. H. Richard Niebuhr, *The Meaning of Revelation* (New York: Macmillan, 1960), pp. 59–73.

3. Schubert M. Ogden, *On Theology* (San Francisco: Harper and Row, 1986), pp. 17–19, and *passim*.

4. Therefore I agree with the point Ogden is making about the objective nature and critical function of theology. And his position that theology does not

require faith is actually very nuanced. For faith is a richly differentiated and analogous term, and Ogden brings out how faith at one level can be considered an anthropological constant. Understanding too exists on a variety of levels. One can understand vaguely and obscurely and then move to a level of more clarity and exactness. What theology requires is engagement in the religious question. If the sheer interest in and quest for religious meaning, which has its anthropological ground in basic trust, were considered a preliminary form of faith, then the very meaningfulness of theological assertions would require such a prior experience of participatory engagement.

5. This dimension of religious symbols is highlighted by George A. Lindbeck, *The Nature of Doctrine: Religion and Theology in a Postliberal Age* (Philadelphia: Westminster Press, 1984), *passim.*

6. Avery Dulles, *Models of Revelation* (Garden City, NY: Doubleday, 1983), p. 203.

7. This question will be taken up again in terms of hermeneutical theory and method in theology in the following chapters.

8. Paul Tillich, *Dynamics of Faith* (New York: Harper Torchbooks, 1957), pp. 42–43; Dulles, *Models of Revelation*, p. 137.

9. Gregory Baum, *Religion and Alienation: A Theological Reading of Sociology* (New York: Paulist Press, 1975), p. 240.

10. Paul Tillich, *Systematic Theology*, I (Chicago: University of Chicago Press, 1967), pp. 111–15.

11. H. Richard Niebuhr, *The Kingdom of God in America* (New York: Harper and Row, 1959), p. 51.

12. This statement may appear to conflict with many characterizations of Jesus that are current in theology today, good examples of which are found in liberation theology. In the chapters on method it will be shown that these portrayals of Jesus are the function, not of a purely or narrowly historical-exegetical imagination, but of a hermeneutical imagination whose explicit intention is to draw the past into the present-day range or horizon of consciousness. For a more resolutely historical approach to Jesus see E. P. Sanders, *Jesus and Judaism* (Philadelphia: Fortress Press, 1985), or Ben Meyer, *The Aims of Jesus* (London: SCM Press, 1979).

13. It should be recalled here that we are dealing with doctrines within the general framework of theological statements which intend to communicate religious content. When doctrines are considered from the narrow perspective of their limited function as meta-theological rules, analogous to grammatical rules that govern or norm Christian speech, they need not be reexpressed to perform this function. They remain in their past form and function as a constitution in a more juridical sense. See Lindbeck, *The Nature of Doctrine*, pp. 79–84.

14. Tillich, *Dynamics of Faith*, pp. 42–43.

15. Tillich, *Systematic Theology*, I, pp. 75–79.

16. William F. Lynch, "Faith and the Imagination," in *Images and Faith: An Exploration of the Ironic Imagination* (Notre Dame, IN: University of Notre Dame Press, 1973), pp. 3–33.

17. Baum, *Religion and Alienation*, pp. 242–43.

18. Reinhold Niebuhr, *The Nature and Destiny of Man*, II, *Human Destiny* (New York: Charles Scribner's Sons, 1964), pp. 298, 307.

19. See H. Richard Niebuhr, *The Meaning of Revelation*, pp. 109–32 where he discusses revelation providing intelligibility to the past, present, and future.

20. Dulles, *Models of Revelation*, pp. 136–37.

21. *Ibid.*, p. 137.

22. See Ignatius of Loyola, *The Spiritual Exercises of St. Ignatius*, trans. by Louis J. Puhl (Westminster, MD: Newman Press, 1954), pp. 101–13.

23. Niebuhr, *The Meaning of Revelation*, pp. 165–75.

24. H. Richard Niebuhr, *The Responsible Self: An Essay in Christian Moral Philosophy*, intro. by James M. Gustafson (San Francisco: Harper and Row, 1978), pp. 125–26.

25. Thus for H. Richard Niebuhr Jesus, who identified himself with the symbol of the kingdom of God, becomes the Christ who is the transformer of culture. This theme, which becomes explicit in *Christ and Culture* (New York: Harper Torchbooks, 1956), pp. 190–229, has roots in his earlier work.

26. See Karl Rahner, "The Concept of Mystery in Catholic Theology," *Theological Investigations*, 4, trans. by Kevin Smyth (Baltimore: Helicon Press, 1966), pp. 36–73, and James J. Bacik, *Apologetics and the Eclipse of Mystery: Mystagogy According to Karl Rahner* (Notre Dame, IN: University of Notre Dame Press, 1980).

27. Tillich, *Systematic Theology*, I, p. 239; *Dynamics of Faith*, pp. 48–54.

28. Karl Barth, *The Word of God and the Word of Man*, trans. by Douglas Horton (New York: Harper Torchbooks, 1957), pp. 33, 37.

29. Dietrich Bonhoeffer, *Letters and Papers from Prison*, ed. by Eberhard Bethge, trans. by Reginald H. Fuller (New York: Macmillan, 1962), pp. 165–66.

30. See Rudolf Otto, *The Idea of the Holy*, trans. by John W. Harvey (New York: Oxford University Press, 1958).

31. For a description of a negative experience of contrast, see Edward Schillebeeckx, *God the Future of Man*, trans. by N. D. Smith (New York: Sheed and Ward, 1968), pp. 136, 153–54, 164.

32. Dulles, *Models of Revelation*, pp. 141–45.

33. Paul Tillich, "Theology and Symbolism," *Religious Symbolism*, ed. by F. Ernest Johnson (New York: Harper and Brothers, 1955), pp. 111ff.

34. This seems to be the position of Rudolf Bultmann in *Jesus Christ and Mythology* (New York: Charles Scribner's Sons, 1958), pp. 66–70. As far as I can see everything that Bultmann says here about the experiential basis for theological statements is accurate. But these reasons do not justify his conclusion. It may be that behind his reasoning lies an excessively individualist and isolated concept of the person or self.

35. Karl Rahner, *Spirit in the World*, trans. by William Dych (New York: Herder and Herder, 1968), pp. 68–71.

36. It is for this reason that richness of meaning and value does not imply a poverty of clarity and precision. Mystagogy does not necessarily entail mystification. The openness of symbols to many meanings and values should never be used to promote theological carelessness. Rather it puts higher demands on

conceptual distinction, criticism, and clarity in theological argument and interpretation.

37. H. Richard Niebuhr, *The Kingdom of God in America, passim.*

38. Since one of the functions of theological doctrine is also the regulation
of church life, this disciplinary function also has a bearing on how church
teaching is put forward by the leaders of the church. This is a distinct issue, but
one that obviously should be closely related to theology and theologically informed. This issue falls beyond the scope of this work which focuses on the
internal logic of theology.

39. See chapter one, n. 28.

40. This does not entail any recourse to prelinguistic experience as though
such experience could be isolated from language; it does not presuppose any
"pure" experience apart or separated from its media. By definition all focused
experience is mediated experience. But at the same time experience is differentiated, and it would not make sense to ignore the different kinds and levels of
human experience. It may be stated categorically that experience transcends its
linguistic mediation. Experience both comes from regions that common language can never adequately penetrate and goes beyond what language can
encompass. The variety of the regions in which symbols operate bears testimony
to this. See Paul Ricoeur, *Interpretation Theory: Discourse and the Surplus of Meaning* (Fort Worth, TX: Texas Christian University, 1976), pp. 57ff.

41. This is neatly summed up by Gregory Baum in the following way: "The
objectivist approach regards revelation as primarily cognitive and the Christian
religion as a system of truths, while the symbolic approach understands revelation in symbolic terms . . . and the Christian religion as a set of symbols, which
people assimilate and celebrate, and out of which they define their lives and
create their world." "Doctrines are not cognitive statements offering information about another world but religious language that mediates access to the
divine ground and the divine orientation of human existence. What is being
discovered is that Christian truth is salvational: doctrines communicate salvation
only if they are understood as derived from symbols and leading back to symbols." Baum, *Religion and Alienation*, p. 252.

42. At the same time this historical work cannot be bypassed in theological
method. This will be the subject of the next two chapters.

43. Lindbeck, *The Nature of Doctrine*, p. 83.

CHAPTER NINE: *The Structure of Interpretation*

1. Even these most general characterizations are always made from some
position on a spectrum. For example, from the position of the neo-orthodoxy of
the middle years of this century, which leaned to the right, it was common to
judge the liberal (Protestant) and modernist (Roman Catholic) theologies of the
nineteenth and early twentieth centuries respectively as radically liberal. In my
view that judgment is suspect; as a generalization it needs to be tested in its
application to this or that theology or theologian, and the premises for the

judgment have to be examined. The problem of pluralism reaches even the characterizations of method in theology; because everywhere is always to the left or right of somewhere else, it is difficult to define a center.

2. Paul Ricoeur, *The Symbolism of Evil*, trans. by Emerson Buchanan (Boston: Beacon Press, 1969), p. 22.

3. See Stephen Sykes, *The Identity of Christianity: Theologians and the Essence of Christianity from Schleiermacher to Barth* (London: SPCK, 1984), pp. 11–34.

4. Rudolf Bultmann, "New Testament and Mythology," *Kerygma and Myth*, ed. by H. W. Bartsch, trans. by Reginald H. Fuller (London: SPCK, 1953), p. 10. Bultmann's definition of myth implicitly includes the idea that the "terms of this world" are construed in an objective, literal, and non-symbolic way.

5. Paul Ricoeur, *Interpretation Theory: Discourse and the Surplus of Meaning* (Fort Worth, TX: Texas Christian University Press, 1976), pp. 25–37.

6. Rudolf Bultmann, "The Problem of Hermeneutics," *New Testament and Mythology and Other Basic Writings*, ed. and trans. by Schubert M. Ogden (Philadelphia: Fortress Press, 1984), pp. 75–76.

7. *Ibid.*, pp. 72–74.

8. Hans-Georg Gadamer, *Truth and Method* (New York: Seabury Press, 1975), p. 262.

9. Paul Tillich, *Systematic Theology*, I (Chicago: University of Chicago Press, 1967), p. 64.

10. But how does one know it is the same experience if it is expressed differently? Does this not presuppose what cannot be held today, namely, that experience can somehow be separated from the language that mediates it? Not at all. One cannot *separate* the meaning of experience from the symbol that expresses it. Experience depends on the historical or linguistic form of the symbol that mediates it. Nor can it be maintained that this sameness exists without difference. The encounter with transcendence can only be considered the same within difference. But one can *distinguish* between finite symbols and the transcendence that is mediated by them. The very reference to transcendence implies this distinction. Of course continuity and sameness will always be open for discussion. But in the end sameness or fidelity to past symbols cannot be measured simply by the comparison of one symbol with another symbol. It must lie in the end within the experience of encounter with a transcendent object. There are also other indicators besides language to measure the fidelity of such an encounter, such as construal of other reality, behavior patterns, worship, and so on.

11. David Tracy, *The Analogical Imagination: Christian Theology and the Culture of Pluralism* (New York: Crossroad, 1981), pp. 101–02; Gadamer, *Truth and Method*, pp. 330–31. In this discussion of interpretation we focus on the dialogue between the interpreter and the data. In the chapter on method in theology we shall see that there should also be a dialogue between interpreters and between interpretations.

12. Gadamer, *Truth and Method*, pp. 335–36, 341. See also Ricoeur, *Interpretation Theory*, pp. 19–22 for his distinction between sense or meaning and reference, that is, between what is said and what it is said about. Language is

referential; it refers to an outer extra-linguistic world. "Language is not a world of its own" (p. 20). "It is because there is first something to say, because we have an experience to bring to language, that conversely, language is not only directed towards ideal meanings but also refers to what is" (p. 21).

13. The role of the question will be developed further in the following chapter on method but something should be said about it here because of its fundamental role in the structure of the hermeneutical process.

14. Gadamer, *Truth and Method,* pp. 329–30.

15. "Hence the sense of the question is the direction in which alone the answer can be given if it is to be meaningful. A question places that which is questioned in a particular perspective. The emergence of the question opens up, as it were, the being of the object. Hence the logos that sets out this opened-up being is already an answer. Its sense lies in the sense of the question" (*ibid.,* p. 326). See also Bultmann, *New Testament and Mythology and Other Basic Writings,* pp. 72–73.

16. Gadamer, *Truth and Method,* pp. 336–37.

17. *Ibid.,* p. 270.

18. *Ibid.,* pp. 300–02.

19. *Ibid.,* p. 270. See David H. Kelsey, *The Uses of Scripture in Recent Theology* (Philadelphia: Fortress Press, 1975), pp. 197–201 for a nuanced view of how exegesis enters into the theological task.

20. Ricoeur, *The Symbolism of Evil,* p. 350.

21. Gadamer defines the situation of human consciousness as "a standpoint that limits the possibility of vision." One's horizon of consciousness "is the range of vision that includes everything that can be seen from a particular vantage point." "A person who has no horizon is one who does not see far enough and hence overvalues what is nearest to him or her. Contrariwise, to have an horizon means not to be limited to what is nearest, but to be able to see beyond it. A person who has an horizon knows the relative significance of everything within this horizon, as near or far, as great or small." *Truth and Method,* p. 269. A fusion of horizons, within which interpretation takes place, means that the horizon of the past is drawn up into the present horizon of consciousness which is also constituted by the past. But this means that even in distinguishing the past as past, one cannot escape one's own present horizon; even the appropriation of the past as past is an appropriation from the standpoint of the present. See pp. 271–74.

22. Ricoeur, *The Symbolism of Evil,* pp. 347–57.

23. See Gadamer, *Truth and Method,* pp. 274–305.

24. "The meaning of application that is involved in all forms of understanding is now clear. It is not the subsequent applying to a concrete case of a given universal that we understand first by itself, but it is the actual understanding of the universal itself that the given text constitutes for us." *Ibid.,* p. 305.

25. David Tracy, *Blessed Rage for Order: The New Pluralism in Theology* (New York: Seabury Press, 1975), pp. 77–78; *The Analogical Imagination,* pp. 122–23. See also the discussion on revelation behind and in front of scripture in chapter four.

26. One cannot recreate within oneself in the present time the psychological experience of people in a past time because there is always a fusion of
horizons, and one cannot as it were escape one's own concrete standpoint,
experience, and horizon. Yet precisely on the basis of the analogy of human
experience, and the self-transcending ability to understand the objective expressions of another culture as distant and different than one's own, one can
communicate with and appreciate the experience of the past.

27. Faithful corresponds to Schubert Ogden's "appropriateness" and
David Kelsey's "aptness." See Kelsey, *The Uses of Scripture*, pp. 192–97, and
Schubert M. Ogden, *On Theology* (San Francisco: Harper and Row, 1986), pp.
4–5, and pp. 45–68 where the criterion of appropriateness to scripture is further nuanced.

28. Intelligible corresponds to Ogden's "credibility" and Tracy's "adequacy," that is, coherence and correspondence with common human experience. Ogden, *On Theology*, pp. 4–6 and *passim;* Tracy, *Blessed Rage for Order*,
pp. 64–87.

29. Empowering corresponds to Metz's criterion of praxis: the ultimate
apology for Christian truth is praxis. See Johann Baptist Metz, *Faith in History
and Society: Toward a Practical Fundamental Theology*, trans. by David Smith (New
York: Seabury Press, 1980), p. 7 and *passim.*

CHAPTER TEN: *Method in Theology*

1. One should always be curious about why some theologians resist the idea
that revelation is experiential or a form of human experience. How could it be
anything else? Yet the fact that the idea is sometimes rejected shows that the
significance of this assertion is not merely tautological. Although the position is
elementary, it carries critical value.

2. It is not necessary at this point to discuss the complex phenomenon of
Christian sectarianism. But the emphasis here upon the general condition of
Christians in the world should not be interpreted as a minimizing of the
counter-cultural values that are intrinsic to the Christian message and which
sustain sectarian communities. But at the same time this recognition of an
apologetic dimension to theology is a dividing line between methods in theology
because it helps determine a criterion of truth that extends beyond *mere* reliance
on the tradition to dialogue with human experience outside the tradition.

3. Paul Tillich, *Systematic Theology*, I (Chicago: University of Chicago Press,
1967), p. 64. On the role of the question in interpretation see Hans-Georg
Gadamer, *Truth and Method* (New York: Seabury Press, 1975), pp. 325–41.

4. In the words of Reinhold Niebuhr: "It is necessary therefore to apply
the Biblical doctrine to the facts of experience in order to establish its relevance." Reinhold Niebuhr, *The Nature and Destiny of Man*, II, *Human Destiny*
(New York: Charles Scribner's Sons, 1964), p. 107. In a way this formula characterizes this whole work of Niebuhr. It is a presentation of present-day human

experience in the shape or form of Christian language. See *ibid.*, pp. 108, 119, and I, p. 188.

5. As was noted earlier, Tillich, *Systematic Theology*, I, p. 42, denied that experience is a source for theology. His reason for doing so was sound insofar as he wished to prevent theology from being reduced to anthropology and a psychology of current experience. But the insistence on the dialogic structure of a method of correlation accomplishes the same thing.

6. See Paulo Freire, "Education as the Practice of Freedom," trans. and ed. by Myra Bergman Ramos, in *Education for Critical Consciousness* (New York: Seabury Press, 1973).

7. Tillich, *Systematic Theology*, I, p. 65.

8. No theologian on the North American scene has undertaken this task in a more deliberate and successful way than David Tracy.

9. Cf. Gadamer, *Truth and Method*, pp. 329–30.

10. Cf. Edward Schillebeeckx, *God the Future of Man*, trans. by N. D. Smith (New York: Sheed and Ward, 1968), pp. 136, 153–54, 164.

11. See Reinhold Niebuhr's analysis of how the experience of sinfulness can be the anthropological medium for revelation in *The Nature and Destiny of Man*, I, *Human Nature* (New York: Charles Scribner's Sons, 1964), pp. 123–49. See also John Henry Newman, *An Essay in Aid of a Grammar of Assent* (New York: Christian Press Association, nd), pp. 60–61, 97ff. where he argues that conscience is the medium for contact with God.

12. Alfred North Whitehead, *Science and the Modern World* (New York: The Free Press, 1967), p. 188.

13. This phenomenological point of view is in contrast, for example, with that of Bernard Lonergan who provides in an objective way the various tasks that together make up the enterprise of theological interpretation. *Method in Theology* (New York: Herder and Herder, 1972).

14. The notion of the point of a traditional doctrine or symbol is drawn from Schubert M. Ogden, "The Point of Christology," *Journal of Religion*, 55 (1975), pp. 375–95.

15. See, for example, Friedrich Schleiermacher, *The Christian Faith*, ed. by H. R. Mackintosh and J. S. Stewart (New York: Harper Torchbooks, 1963), pp. 131–52.

16. In Ogden's statement of the case, the point of christological belief is not primarily to believe something *about* Jesus; "it is quite simply to believe *in* him, in the word that he himself both speaks and is as God's own word of unconditional acceptance which sets us free." Ogden, "The Point of Christology," pp. 394–95.

17. Roger Haight, "The Point of Trinitarian Theology," *The Toronto Journal of Theology* 4 (1988), pp. 191–204.

18. This is the hermeneutical basis underlying Bultmann's program which he called demythologization. Its intention is not to abolish or do away with myth but to interpret it. Cf. Rudolf Bultmann, "New Testament and Mythology," *Kerygma and Myth*, ed. by H. W. Bartsch, trans. by Reginald H. Fuller (London: SPCK, 1953), pp. 1–44. An analogous hermeneutical method is at work in much

of the theology of Karl Rahner, although it is applied most forcefully to the traditional doctrines of the church rather than the texts of scripture. See Rahner, "Theology and Anthropology," *Theological Investigations*, 9, trans. by Graham Harrison (New York: Herder and Herder, 1972), pp. 28–45.

19. Cf. Dorothee Soelle, *Political Theology*, trans. by John Shelley (Philadelphia: Fortress Press, 1974), pp. 41–69. Soelle's contribution in this work is significant. Written in dialogue with Bultmann, she does not negate his program of demythologization, but expands it by overcoming the implied individualism in its anthropology. By insisting on the social constitution of human existence she implicitly shows how social analysis enters intrinsically into theological method through an expanded notion of human existence as such.

20. See Juan Luis Segundo, *The Historical Jesus of the Synoptics*, trans. by John Drury (Maryknoll, NY: Orbis Books, 1985) for a hermeneutical study of Jesus that focuses on the political dimension of his appearance.

21. It is common enough in theological literature to read attacks on an over-concern for clear and distinct ideas. This should not be taken, I think, as a recommendation of unclear and confused thinking. It is rather a certain reductionism and narrowness of thought that is being rejected. Clarity in theological writing is not a vice and one should applaud when a theologian can distinctly say what he or she means as opposed to something else.

22. A premier example of this dialogue in an ecumenical framework is found in Avery Dulles' *Models of Revelation* (Garden City, NY: Doubleday, 1983). Dulles' position in this book allows for a pluralism of understandings of revelation because more can be accounted for by the many positions than by any single one. Different paradigms for understanding held together in tension display most fully the nature of revelation. Yet at the same time Dulles establishes a critical norm for understanding revelation that adjudicates the strengths and weaknesses of each position. Cf. Joseph Hartzler, *The Function of Symbol in the Theology of Revelation of Avery Dulles*, ThM Dissertation, Regis College, Toronto (1989).

23. Cf. David Tracy, *Plurality and Ambiguity: Hermeneutics, Religion, Hope* (San Francisco: Harper and Row, 1987), *passim*.

24. This is another major contribution of liberation theology to Christian theology as a whole. See Gustavo Gutiérrez, "Liberation Praxis and Christian Faith," *Frontiers of Theology in Latin America*, ed. by Rosino Gibellini (Maryknoll, NY: Orbis Books, 1979), pp. 1–33.

25. In the view of H. Richard Niebuhr, development of theology and doctrine is always initiated by revelation. "Revelation is not a development of our religious ideas but their continuous conversion. God's self-disclosure is that permanent revolution in our religious life by which all religious truths are painfully transformed and all religious behavior transfigured by repentance and new faith." H. Richard Niebuhr, *The Meaning of Revelation* (New York: Macmillan, 1960), p. 182.

26. Cf. Karl Rahner, "The Two Basic Types of Christology," *Theological Investigations*, 13, trans. by David Bourke (London: Darton, Longman and Todd, 1975), pp. 215–16, 222–23.

27. Schubert M. Ogden, *On Theology* (San Francisco: Harper and Row, 1986), p. 5.

28. See Roger Haight, "Critical Witness: The Question of Method," in *Faithful Witness: Foundations of Theology for Today's Church, Essays in Honor of Avery Dulles*, ed. by Leo J. O'Donovan and T. Howland Sanks (New York: Crossroad, 1989), pp. 202–05, for an account of how practical spirituality is an internal criterion for the authenticity of theological positions.

29. "The fact that the Christian religion cannot be defended by purely theoretical arguments, but that an apologetical praxis has to be applied in its defense is fully in accordance with the biblical datum of apology." Johann Baptist Metz, *Faith in History and Society: Toward a Practical Fundamental Theology*, trans. by David Smith (New York: Seabury Press, 1980), p. 8. See also pp. 76–77.

CHAPTER ELEVEN: *Dynamics of Theology*

1. Thomas Aquinas, *Summa Theologiae*, I, q. 1, *passim.*

2. Hans Küng, *On Being a Christian*, trans. by Kevin Quinn (Garden City, NY: Doubleday, 1974) is a good example of a christology that does not deal exclusively with the formal christological problem but opens up the symbol of Jesus to an understanding of the world, other religions, and the Christian life.

3. This issue is one of the reasons why the Council of Nicaea and especially Athanasius' defense of it is so important for Christian thought. Athanasius knew that he was meddling with original revelation when he defended the insertion of the Greek concept and word, "consubstantial" with the Father, into the Christian Creed. He met fierce resistance and thus had to argue the necessity of adding to and changing Christian self-understanding in order to preserve its integrity. See Athanasius of Alexandria, *De Decretis or Defense of the Nicene Creed*, in *Nicene and Post Nicene Fathers*, Second Series, Vol. 4 (New York: The Christian Literature Company, 1892), I, 1; V, 18–21. This position became "orthodox"; it is accepted by most mainline Christians today; many simply read it back into the New Testament and original revelation where it certainly does not exist in that form. Nicaea is thus a classical case of a significant change in the theological interpretation of original revelation that was resisted because of inherent Christian sensibilities and yet came to be completely accepted after long and serious theological controversy. See John C. Murray, *The Problem of God: Yesterday and Today* (New Haven: Yale University Press, 1964) for a highly hermeneutical presentation of this development. I do not accept Murray's version of a Lonerganian position on that development, but his presentation of the issue is lucid and engaging.

4. In this discussion of the authority of scripture I include by extension the authority of the major doctrinal decisions of the church. There is no need to discuss here the relation between scripture and tradition for it is a non-problem. I understand tradition as the whole existential, historical life of the Christian church. See Maurice Blondel, "History and Dogma," in *The Letter on Apologetics*

and History and Dogma, ed. and trans. by Alexander Dru and Illtyd Trethowan (New York: Holt, Rinehart and Winston, 1964), pp. 264–87. Tradition preceded and accounted for the writing of scripture. The meaning of scripture is always carried by tradition. The two are inseparable; scripture is part of the historical tradition of the church. The document which is scripture, however, has a primacy of place in the tradition of the church, and all church doctrine should be related back to it. But at the same time church doctrines and the history of theology constitute the past and therefore the present church. One cannot bypass the history of doctrine. What applies to the interpretation of scripture, therefore, applies analogously to the authority and interpretation of church doctrine.

5. It is practically a cliché in the literature concerning theological education that there be a certain emphasis on the method itself of theology. But this is difficult to accomplish programmatically and rarely happens. Theology thus frequently becomes a learning of information on the practical level of learning about church doctrine. And the result is a kind of theological fundamentalism. With the passage of time clergy and educated ministers are unable to absorb new data ("That's not what we were taught"), because they lack the methodological tools to appreciate new developments and the requisite attitudes of inquiry and openness. See Edward Farley, *Theologia: The Fragmentation and Unity of Theological Education* (Philadelphia: Fortress Press, 1983), and Charles M. Wood, *Vision and Discernment: An Orientation in Theological Study* (Decatur, GA: Scholars Press, 1985).

6. The questions that follow are free adaptations and amplifications of hermeneutical issues proposed by Avery Dulles in "The Hermeneutics of Dogmatic Statements," *The Survival of Dogma* (Garden City, NY: Doubleday, 1972), pp. 171–84, 223–24.

7. Dulles, *The Survival of Dogma*, p. 180.

8. I am amplifying here what David Kelsey has called a *discrimen* that underlies the use of scripture in theology. See his *The Uses of Scripture in Recent Theology* (Philadelphia: Fortress Press, 1975), pp. 160–63. Cf. also *supra*, chapter six. This important concept, as Kelsey says, extends beyond this particular function. It also refers to a holistic imaginative conception that encompasses the whole Christian message. One can usually discover by analysis such a conception at work in every major theological interpretation. This is not an essence of Christianity on the basis of which one can then declare other aspects unessential; it is not a substance that renders all other elements of the whole Christian movement accidental. It is an inclusive insight which operates more like a center of gravity. In Luther it appears as justification by grace through faith. In Karl Rahner it appears as God's absolute self-communication to human existence in such a way that the human becomes the very expression of God. Even when particular theologians do not dwell on such a controlling insight, in the measure in which their interpretations are coherent some such conception is present and operative below the surface.

9. Dulles, *The Survival of Dogma*, p. 183.

AFTERWORD

1. Roger Haight, *Jesus Symbol of God* (Maryknoll, NY: Orbis Books, 1999).
2. Robert Schreiter, *The New Catholicity* (Maryknoll, N.Y.: Orbis Books, 1997).
3. Paul Lakeland, *Postmodernity* (Minneapolis: Fortress Press, 1996).
4. "We live in an age that cannot name itself." David Tracy, *On Naming the Present: God, Hermeneutics, and Church* (Maryknoll, NY: Orbis Books, 1994), 3.
5. The notion of culture itself, as it appears to the social and cultural anthropologists who study it, appears in a postmodern context to be a far less stable concept than previously described. Cultures are less tight, consistent, and monolithic than they appear, less stable, more pluralistic, less self-contained, less determinative of a given individual because more fluid and perhaps multiple. Those who share a postmodern culture, for example, may be divided as to its meaning and valance. See Kathryn Tanner, *Theories of Culture: A New Agenda for Theology* (Minneapolis: Fortress Press, 1997), 38-58.
6. Paul Tillich, *Theology of Culture* (New York: Oxford University Press, 1964), 40-51.
7. None of the critics of *Jesus Symbol of God* directly quarrel with the method of the work head on. Some do not understand it, others simply stand outside it, and others implicitly reject it on the basis of other commitments. Those sympathetic to the method of theology proposed here are by and large sympathetic to the constructive argument of *Jesus Symbol of God*, but not necessarily any given position.
8. Edward Schillebeeckx, "Secularization and Christian Belief in God," *God the Future of Man* (New York: Sheed and Ward, 1968), 74. In a classic apologetic move involving a kind of transcendental analysis of social existence, Schillebeeckx finds in the modern engagement with the human project, the autonomy and creativity of human freedom, and the hope for a better existence an implicit raising of the religious question. The agenda of secularization itself postulates the possibility of transcendent reality that alone can guarantee these truly worthy secular commitments.
9. Pseudo-Dionysius, "The Ecclesiastical Hierarchy," par. 1 and 5, *Pseudo-Dionysius: The Complete Works* (New York: Paulist Press, 1987), 198, 234.
10. Thomas Aquinas, *Summa Theologiae*, I, q. 13, aa. 2-3, *Basic Writings of Saint Thomas Aquinas*, ed. Anton C. Pegis (New York: Random House, 1945), 114-17.
11. Thus Aquinas can say "that a statue is like a man, but not conversely; so also a creature can be spoken of as in some way like God, but not that God is like a creature." ST I, q. 4, a. 3, ad 4 in *Basic Writings*, 41. Thomas reflects the influence of Pseudo-Dionysius whose dialectical understanding of knowledge of God, the tensive unity of affirmation through negation, based on the continuity and discontinuity between creator and creature, runs all through his works: "God is known to all from all things and God is known to no one from anything." "The Divine Names," 7.3, *The Complete Works*, p. 109. See also more pointedly his "The

Celestial Hierarchy," 2.3, his short assent to God through negation in "The Mystical Theology" and "The Divine Names," passim.

12. A number of polemical reviewers of *Jesus Symbol of God* erroneously use the language of "merely" a symbol to characterize the position represented there, despite explicit statements that something merely a symbol is no symbol at all, but merely a sign, and the explicit identification of religious symbol with sacrament.

13. Karl Rahner, "The Theology of Symbol," *Theological Investigations*, 4 (Baltimore: Helicon Press, 1966), 221-52.

14. The relation between hermeneutical theory and method in theology has been drawn with persuasive clarity by David Tracy, "Part Two," in Robert M. Grant, *A Short History of the Interpretation of the Bible*, 2nd ed. (Philadelphia: Fortress Press, 1984), 151-87.

15. John P. Meier, "Are There Historical Links between the Historical Jesus and the Christian Ministry?" *Theology Digest* 47 (2000), 303-15.

16. John A. Coleman, "The Bible and Sociology," *Sociology of Religion* 60 (1999), 125-48, surveys what amounts to the emergence of a new subdiscipline at this point.

17. Roger Haight, "Mission: The Symbol for Understanding the Church Today," *Theological Studies* 37 (1976), 620-49; "The 'Established Church' as Mission: The Relation of the Church to the Modern World," *The Jurist* 39 (1979), 4-39; J. Michael Byron, *The Poor When They See It Will Be Glad: An Ecclesiology of Symbol as Integral to a Socially Relevant Postmodern North American Church* (S.T.D. Thesis: Cambridge, MA: Weston Jesuit School of Theology, 2001).

INDEX OF NAMES

SUBJECT INDEX

Action: in relation to fundamental theology, 7–9; in relation to freedom, 16; as praxis, 47–48, 209–10; symbols as transformation of, 156

Analogy, principle of, 172

Beliefs: "believing" and faith, 26–29, 42–44; social function of, 34–35, 42–43, 47–48, 131; and theological statements, 35–37; as historically conditioned, 37–39, 41–42; and reason, 39–44; as principle of action, 44–46; as symbolic, 131

Christology, 245–50

Correlation: as method in theology, 191–212, 227–32, 244, 249, 253

Critical conversation, 244–45, 249

Critical social reason, 46–47

Demythologization, 172–73; *see also* Bultmann, R.

Disclosure, 119–20

Ecclesiology, 250–54

Elaboration, 120–22

Faith: as defined by author, 10, 15–16; as universal human phenomena, 16–19, 130–31; nature of, 19–21; object of, 21–22, 33; and knowing, 22–26; and imagination, 24–25; and interpretation, 25; and beliefs, 26–29, 39–46; as praxis, 29–30; as public act, 32–34, 47–48, 263–64; and theological statements, 35–37, 44; as described by J. H. Newman, 40–42; and revelation, 51–52; and symbolic, 130–31

Freedom: and human existence, 16, 20, 72–73; and revelation, 72–73

Fundamental option, 30

Fundamentalism: biblical, 55, 110, 122, 129; dogmatic, 55, 129, 169, 255, 267

Grace: postulate of, 57–58, 247–48; as God's love, 58–61, 150–52, 158, 268–69

Hermeneutics: explained, 12, 170; in relation to theological method, 12, 170, 176–77, 180,

Also by Roger Haight, S.J.

Jesus Symbol of God
ISBN 1-57075-311-3

First Place in Theology, Catholic Book Award Winner!

"This is a wonderful, mind-clearing, landmark book. It is the book I have been waiting for, the one that clears away much of the intellectual fog that has prevented any coherent, sensible preaching about the Holy Trinity for the last several centuries. Hooray!"   —*David Toolan, S.J., Associate Editor of* America

"A flagship in a fleet of late twentieth–century works that show American Catholic theology has indeed come of age. Deeply thoughtful in its exposition, lucid in its method, and by turns challenging and inspiring in its conclusions, this christology gives a new articulation of the saving 'point' of it all. . . . Highly recommended for all who think about and study theology."
—*Elizabeth Johnson, C.S.J., Fordham University*

"A major achievement that will become a very useful, if not standard, text in courses on Jesus and christology."
—*Francis Schüssler Fiorenza, Harvard Divinity School*

Please support your local bookstore, or call 1-800-258-5838.
For a free catalog, please write us at
Orbis Books, Box 308
Maryknoll, NY 10545-0308

Or visit our website at www.orbisbooks.com

Thank you for reading *Dynamics of Theology.*
We hope you enjoyed it.